T0283630

The Exiled

Lucy Fulford is an Australian-British journalist, historian and next-generation Ugandan Asian. Growing up between cultures has led to an interest in exploring belonging, and her work centres around migration and conflict. She has reported for the national press in London, covered the war in east Ukraine and written for NGOs including Save the Children. Lucy is also a Penguin WriteNow alumni of 2020.

The Exiled

*Empire, immigration and
the Ugandan Asian exodus*

LUCY FULFORD

CORONET

First published in Great Britain in 2023 by Coronet
An imprint of Hodder & Stoughton
An Hachette UK company

1

Copyright © Lucy Fulford 2023
Map copyright © Barking Dog Art 2023

A CIP catalogue record for this title is available from the British Library

Hardback ISBN 9781399711173
ebook ISBN 9781399711197

Typeset in Sabon MT by Hewer Text UK Ltd, Edinburgh
Printed and bound in Great Britain by Clays Ltd, Elcograf S.p.A.

Hodder & Stoughton policy is to use papers that are natural, renewable and recyclable products and made from wood grown in sustainable forests. The logging and manufacturing processes are expected to conform to the environmental regulations of the country of origin.

Hodder & Stoughton Ltd
Carmelite House
50 Victoria Embankment
London EC4Y 0DZ

www.hodder.co.uk

To adventurers and everyone searching for home.

In the end, stories are about one person saying to another:
This is the way it feels to me. Can you understand
what I'm saying? Does it also feel this way to you?

Kazuo Ishiguro[1]

Contents

Contents

Timeline

1600 – The East India Company starts establishing trading posts in India

1661 – The first permanent British settlement in Africa is made at James Island in the Gambia River

1843 – Slavery is abolished in all British colonies

1858 – Beginning of the British Raj – direct British rule on the Indian subcontinent

1880s – The 'scramble for Africa' – colonising the continent

1888 – British East Africa Company is established

1894 – Colonisation of Buganda and the declaration of a protectorate of British empire – extended years later forming the Uganda Protectorate

1896 – Construction of the East African Railway begins in Mombasa, Kenya, using Indians as construction workers

14 August 1947 – End of the Raj – the Partition of India

9 October 1962 – Uganda gains independence, Milton Obote is inaugural president

1962 & 1968 – Commonwealth Immigrants Acts introduced in the UK, reducing Commonwealth citizens' rights to migrate

25 January 1971 – Coup in Uganda, General Idi Amin seizes power

4 August 1972 – Amin announces Ugandan Asians must leave the country

5 August 1972 – Confirmation and ultimatum – UK passport holders must leave Uganda within ninety days

10 September 1972 – British Prime Minister Edward Heath publicly confirms that UK passport holders will be allowed in

18 September 1972 – First flight of Ugandan Asians lands in the UK

8 November 1972 – Amin's ninety-day deadline for all Ugandan Asians to leave

January 1974 – The Uganda Resettlement Board ends, having served over 28,000 people

4 July 1976 – Raid at Uganda's Entebbe Airport, hostage crisis

April 1979 – Amin flees Uganda after losing a war he started with Tanzania

May 1980 – Milton Obote returns as Uganda's President for a second time

January 1986 – Yoweri Museveni takes power and invites South Asians to return to Uganda

August 2022 – Fifty years since the expulsion

Prologue

Walking out of Entebbe International Airport, Kampala, I breathed in the prospect of discovery along with the warm night air. Nineteen and travelling independently for the first time, I'd arrived in the place I'd wanted to go more than anywhere else – a country I'd heard snatches of throughout my childhood and that filled my imagination with dreams.

Uganda was somewhere I had always longed for. Perhaps when you come from many places, your past is as much a tapestry of the lands of your forefathers as the people that came before you, a puzzle you can spend your whole life finding the pieces for. Spending weekends eating biriyani and appams with my beloved Indian grandparents, I had come to know some of that part of my background. Uganda remained both within touching distance and somehow mysteriously out of reach.

Soon I was wheeling down the Kampala–Entebbe Road to the city, thrown straight into the heart of a country and feeling intoxicated on the novelty, drunk on dopamine as I took in the colourful matatus (minibuses), the hot, sweet smell of roadside sellers' scorched corn and the tooting of motorcycle horns. Face pressed to the window, I soaked in the shapes and sounds we sped past. On quieter stretches of the road the nighttime bustle faded into shadows, from which I could make out small lights and fires, accompanied by the burning of hot coals and the frying of meat.

Then the sounds got louder, until the vehicles behind us started pulling over and my taxi driver followed suit, steering into the dusty kerb, kicking up a fine sheet of orange powder. One, two, three, four – more – cars peeled past, flanked by dozens of motorbikes. 'That's the president,' said my driver knowingly, and then, even more knowingly, took off again immediately behind them, tacked onto the back of the motorcade.

As introductions to a place of high expectations go, it wasn't bad.

Thirty-six years earlier, my grandparents had made the reverse journey under soberingly different circumstances.

Without the decision of a different Ugandan president to the one aiding my speedy journey into Kampala, they doubtless would have remained. Instead, they became some of the thousands of people exiled from Uganda who took refuge in the UK. Without whom I would not have ended up a next-generation Ugandan Asian in Britain.

Introduction – A General's Dream

They were either born in India or have retained close con-nection with India. They have no connection with Britain either by blood or residence.

Ronald Bell, Conservative MP for
South Buckinghamshire, UK, 1972[1]

[Ugandan Asians are] one of the most successful groups of immigrants anywhere in the history of the world.

Conservative prime minister of
the UK David Cameron, 2012[2]

D r Martin Luther King is not the only person to have had a dream of consequence. Nine years after his rousing speech, across the Atlantic Ocean, the president of Uganda was stirring from a dream of his own. Speaking to a some-what smaller audience of his trusted generals, General Idi Amin declared that Allah had instructed him to expel South Asian people from his country. Most likely a work of fiction, part of the folklore that fortified Amin, the actions that followed the dream tale were anything but. On 4 August 1972, Ugandan Asians retaining British citizenship were told their time was up. The president would later confirm that all South Asians had ninety days to leave the country and that their homes and businesses would be confiscated by the state. Along with accusing them of sabotaging the economy and encouraging corruption, in barely veiled threats Amin

1

warned that those who remained after the cut-off date would 'find themselves sitting on the fire'.[3]

Amin hadn't come to this conclusion overnight. In the decade since Uganda's independence, tensions had been simmering between the local population and the predominately affluent South Asian community, who made up the backbone of the country's economy, with politicians fanning the flames. All those who could trace their lineage to India, Pakistan or Bangladesh were told to pack their bags – more than 50,000 people.[*][4] A large number of these were British passport holders, many having been recruited from India to work for the then British protectorate, or their descendants, and Amin called for Britain to repatriate their citizens. Anti-immigration sentiment was already high in the UK, just four years after Conservative MP Enoch Powell's infamous 'Rivers of Blood' speech, and numerous voices spoke out against the arrival of foreigners. So alarmed at the prospect were councillors in one city that they took out a large advert in the *Uganda Argus* newspaper to forewarn would-be émigrés:

> The City Council of Leicester, England, believe that many families in Uganda are considering moving to Leicester. If YOU are thinking of doing so it is very important you should know that PRESENT CONDITIONS IN THE CITY ARE VERY DIFFERENT FROM THOSE MET BY EARLIER SETTLERS . . . In your own interests and those of your family you should accept the advice of the Uganda Resettlement Board and not come to Leicester.[5]

* The estimated size of the Ugandan Asian population varies, but an often-cited figure of 80,000 was a number given by Amin, and is seen as a significant overestimation by a magnitude of tens of thousands, based on outdated census data.

The release of classified papers has revealed the attempted permutations of Edward Heath's government, which included floating the idea of relocating the unwanted exiles to a remote island in the Pacific and encouraging the acceptance of a £2,000 payment in exchange for giving up the right to live in Britain.[6] A diplomatic offensive saw thousands of Ugandan Asians redirected to other countries, including Canada, India and America. In the end, the British government largely shouldered its responsibility and more than 28,000 people arrived to the UK from Uganda in late 1972 – the majority with just the clothes on their backs and the small suitcases they had been allowed to take. Everything else – homes, jobs, pets, friends and dreams – were left behind.

Having travelled from India in 1953 to take up teaching jobs in the British protectorate, my grandparents had spent close to two decades in Uganda before they left the country for good. Rachel and Philip Mathen – as their Anglicised names came to be – were born in Thiruvananthapuram, in the southern state of Kerala, India. In their first year of marriage they set sail to Mombasa, Kenya, and then went on by rail to Kampala, Uganda. Photo albums are filled with the hallmarks of a happy life, with black-and-white and sepia images marking birthdays in the capital, holidays by the Kenyan sea in Malindi and road trips driving through East Africa's national parks, filled with giraffes, lions, cheetahs and monkeys and tracking past the mighty Mount Kenya.

In the years in which I knew them, my grandparents didn't speak of Uganda often. It's perhaps unsurprising, given the way their lives there were upended. Their memories spoke more strongly of people, not places. I heard tales of aunties and uncles, of family trees woven of both friends and relatives, from the Ugandan and Indian days alike. When they left, it was a harried affair. Flights were booked, bags were packed and arrangements were made to sell or pass on what they could. They sold their Peugeot 403 and the new owner also took on their sheepdog Jack. The family wept as two German women took away their beloved Alsatian called Simba. Their cat had earlier been shot dead by a neighbour who thought it was a nuisance. Soon, new lives were being made. After the family's reunion in Cambridge on 13 December 1972, my grandmother wrote in her diary that, 'the Ugandan business, good or bad, was over.' But, of course, it wasn't over for them, or the ones that would follow. The exodus had set in motion a global migration, creating a diaspora that spanned continents, along with questions for the generations to come.

Fifty years on, Britain is an undoubtedly multicultural society that includes a South Asian community of around 4.5 million people. According to the census in 2021, Indians made up three per cent of the population of England and Wales, with a further 0.8 per cent identifying as mixed white and Asian.[7] There are some visible signs of traditional success for British Asians, from the highest echelons of the prime minister's office through to the Conservative MPs who have held high-profile ministries, from the chancellor of the exchequer to the home secretary. There's British-Pakistani actor Riz Ahmed's appearance in the *Star Wars* universe or the Hollywood success of Dev Patel, whose Gujarati parents were born in Kenya. These rare individuals are sometimes lauded as being demonstrative of inclusivity. Yet not only are they in the minority, but these examples perpetuate what author Nikesh Shukla refers to as the cult of the 'good immigrant', where migrants, and thereby migration, are hailed as a positive force only when they have achieved great success or broken into a mainstream white arena.[8] This particularly resonates when it comes to Ugandan Asians, who are often framed as successes for having proved their worth to the country that offered them refuge.

As I've spent more time reflecting on race and identity over the years, I've realised that my family came to Britain, and later Australia, as archetypal good migrants, and that the degree of colour blindness I was raised with was perhaps a natural part of fitting into predominately white environments. And yet as a person of colour in the UK, skin colour still matters viscerally. You feel it in second glances. You feel it in the weight in the air after racism hits the national stage, when missing a penalty in the World Cup final merits your mural being defaced, or being a cricketer means soaking up racial slurs as banter. And not least in the racial inequities in society. These feelings go hand in hand with narratives around immigration becoming increasingly charged. I've noticed parallels between my mother's generation and mine, seeing the same thorny themes that were visible to the Ugandan Asian arrivals of the 1970s moving out of the shadows into the public discourse. Behind all of this lies another shadow, that of the British empire, which continues to stand proudly in buildings, institutions and attitudes, as well as within the personal histories of people like myself. We need to breathe life into the stories that aren't told about these times, preserving the less celebratory moments along with the good. Modern Britain is a nation indelibly shaped by its empire, but one in which history lessons still stay silent on the lived experiences of people of colour of the past. Like the Ugandan Asian one.

It can be hard to place me. I've been variously identified as Iranian, Malaysian, Turkish and Italian. When I was younger,

I would complicate the subject and only answer that I was Australian or English when asked where I was from. It didn't occur to me then that some people were simply interested in finding out more about me – questions about my origins felt hostile, invasive and garnered a defensive and provocative response. For years I have been trying to work out a concise way of summarising my family history. Where you are from, when you come from many places, can't be answered in a word, or even a sentence. When I would try and give a word – Australia, where I was born, and where I ultimately feel I am from – it was dismissed as the wrong answer. You don't look Australian, or sound Australian now, so there must be something more. And of course, there is something more. There's lots more. There's my forefathers farming on the hills of Kerala, and my mother playing in the hot Equatorial sun in Kampala. There's my father growing up in suburban Surrey and my years along Sydney's shores. And at the heart of it, something broken, something unspoken, something – to most – unknown. A splinter, a crack in the tectonic plates of the past – Uganda, 1972.

Throughout my life I have been telling people the short-ened version of what happened to Uganda's South Asian people that year. How a dictator called Idi Amin decided to expel them and that led to my family's movements across the globe, and that's why I come from so many places. When I am speaking to the generation above me, there will sometimes be a flicker of recognition. Perhaps they recall the news reports from the time, or the day that some lost-looking children joined their class in school. But for people my age, I am almost always met with blank faces. Outside of South Asian communities, this recent past has been lost from public memory. It's not taught in schools, and, like so much minority history, is often only shared by those with a personal link to it. The only break-through reference came in the Hollywood film *The Last King of Scotland*, based on Giles Foden's book, where Idi Amin's erstwhile best friend, James McAvoy's Dr Garrigan, turns on the television at one point to see the president announcing the expulsion.

When Ugandan Asian history has been told, it often verges into stereotypes, telling singular, simplistic stories about victimhood and wealth, in which a madcap, archetypal African dictator threw thousands of people out of the country on a whim. In this U-shaped narrative arc, successful people lost everything in the expulsion and then, through hard work and perseverance, regained it again in Britain and beyond, a shining example of a model minority. Starting with nothing, twice, and making good every time, this can become a history of moneyed businessmen and self-congratulation, invariably focusing on certain higher classes and castes. While there's truth in the uniquely successful paths of some of this community, Ugandan Asians aren't a homogenous group, and history shouldn't only belong to those with the loudest voices. We need a diversity of stories to show the wide range of immigrant journeys and to challenge the politicisation of the past.

Too often in this version of the narrative, the British government is the hero, when you'll in fact see they did everything they could to avoid welcoming their own citizens. People's memories of Uganda often contain familiar themes, bathed in a rose-tinted glow. The weather was perfect, not too hot, not too wet. The ground was so fertile anything would grow. Lush fruits abounded, with a freshness unrivalled elsewhere. Mango, papaya, matoke – all bursting with the flavours of the sun-drenched soil they grew from. Going beyond this picture-perfect tropical lifestyle means looking at less comfortable truths. If something sounds too good to be true, it usually is. There were the inequalities within society, the advantages the South Asians had over the local population and to what degree they had agency within the colonial system. The presumption of authority, the subjugation and the racism. Viewing Ugandan Asians as simple victims of Uganda, and more specifically, Idi Amin's wrath, overlooks the complexities of decolonisation, racism and systems of divide and rule, in which they were at times active participants, and where Black* Ugandans suffered innumerable indignities and ultimately, far greater losses of life. We need to see the dualities in this story to view the reality of it. *The Exiled* seeks to add some nuance, offering a critical examination of this period, exploring the true fate of minorities at the end of empire, and representing just some of the immense diversity of Ugandan Asian experiences.

In the lead up to the fiftieth anniversary of this landmark migration, I began thinking of ways to tell this story in a bigger way, focusing on the human side. I wanted to showcase a snapshot of this time, weaving together first- and

* When referring to Black and Brown people, these words will be capitalised, while 'white' remains lower case. How to approach these three terms remains a live debate, with differing views across written media. Here, capitalising groups that have historically been marginalised is done to confer a degree of respect and acknowledge the impact of these self-claimed identities. There are convincing arguments for also capitalising 'white'. Not doing so arguably reinforces white as the norm and can also be said to allow white people to remain outside of vital conversations about race. However, capitalising 'white' also invariably centres whiteness in a way that doesn't feel appropriate in a book with such strong racial dynamics. See Nancy Coleman, 'Why We're Capitalizing Black', *New York Times*, 5 July 2020, https://www.nytimes. com/2020/07/05/insider/capitalized-black.html and 'White, white', The Diversity Style Guide, https://www.diversitystyleguide.com/glossary/white-white/.

second-generation stories to illuminate the recent past and demonstrate its enduring relevance today. Bringing it beyond 1972, this book shows how migrants settle and build new lives in challenging circumstances, taking in everything from race relations and immigration policies to identity and belonging. My grandmother wrote a diary of her life together with her husband after he passed away, reflecting on five decades of marriage. I've been fortunate to lean on this incredibly valuable resource for some of her reflections of her life's journey and vital factual detail, supplemented with lengthy conversations with my family. To further explore these living histories, I've spoken to a range of people who lived through the expulsion, and the children of that genera-tion, uncovering untold stories of resilience, painting a rich picture of exodus and assimilation and illuminating an essential chapter in British history, in which immigrants reshaped society. What did it feel like to build a new life in 1970s Britain, and what is it like living as a person of colour in the 2020s? How did the diasporic experience vary across some of the dozens of countries Ugandan Asians settled in, and what of those who returned to Uganda? In telling these stories I have tried to reflect the depth of feeling with which they were told to me, attempting to give words to the sights, sounds and smells that were experienced, and to bring these moments to life.

This story follows people's footsteps as they walk across continents, with three families providing touchstones throughout. This includes my own family, seen through the eyes of my grandparents Rachel and Philip, my mother Betty and myself. My grandparents started this whole journey as newlyweds by taking a step into the unknown and boarding a ship from Kerala, South India, to East Africa in 1953, bound to work as teachers for the colonial government. My mother, born in Kampala, and going on to live in England and Australia, is in her late sixties and reflecting on fifty years away from Africa. Secondly there's Kausar Chaudary, who meets us in Uganda and takes us on a journey through two more countries. After a childhood in Kampala, where she was the second generation of her family born in Uganda, she is a twenty-two-year-old teacher in Gulu, in the north of the country when her life splinters in a new direction in 1972. Thirdly, Hamida Sumar and her siblings Rashid Kassam Majothi and Abdul Gani Ismail share the shopkeeper experience across two continents. Their father Kassam Majothi was a leading businessman in the west of Uganda, and after leaving Iganga, took his business nous with him to Britain, along with his family of eight children.

Many more people appear to share parts of their journeys, from childhood memories of Uganda from friends of my family, to people who met in British resettlement camps and those who are part of the modern East African Asian diaspora around the world today. I've also heard from people who helped in the logistics of the expatriation, worked in resettlement and who have moved back to Uganda in the years and generations since the exile. Added to this are many experts, including historians, lawyers and analysts. Wherever possible across interviews and other source material, I've sought to give space to women's voices, which are particularly important to me, having so often been left out of history books. With a focus on South Asian voices, this cannot be a comprehensive picture of everyone's experience of 1972 and beyond, but seeks to convey the spirit of these times from this viewpoint. More than fifty interviews are supplemented by some of the fantastic testimony gathered through a range of recent oral history projects and archives memorialising this history.[9] While testimony and oral history has its flaws – memories can become muted or magnified over the years, buying into convenient, dominant or comforting narratives – taken hand in hand with historical research, it brings the past to life.

In telling these stories, I've grappled with the many challenges of language when it comes to talking about race and identity. The first and most significant is 'Ugandan Asian' itself. We are dealing with imperfect terms. I personally would never verbally describe myself as Asian, although strangers have done, and when filling out ethnicity monitoring forms, the box I tick reads Mixed, White and Asian. Until I began working on this book, I had never really used the term 'Ugandan Asian' in relation to myself either. My mother always felt uncomfortable with it, negatively associating it with the idea of the extractive entrepreneur. However, many people, particularly those of the 1972 generation, or those who have returned to Uganda, do self-identify as Asian. To use the word Asian, today, to describe people who came from the Indian subcontinent, feels reductive and wildly non-specific, given the size and cultural diversity of Asia. Even the more geographically specific terms, South Asian and South East Asian, group vast swathes of countries and varied cultures together. In that sense, while 'Asian' was the dominant descriptor for this group within Uganda at the time, in many ways it no longer feels appropriate in a global context. Because of this, I have chosen not to rely on 'Asian' on its own, although much of the contemporary literature and historiography does use this as a singular term, and instead use South Asian or East African Asian.

But why use Ugandan Asian at all, if there is a fundamental flaw in it? Ultimately, despite my frustrations with the roots of the terminology, as a descriptor, it is indelibly linked with the events of 1972 and beyond. To replace it with another word would be to sever the ties from history. While it's not a term my family have identified with personally, some in the community do. Moreover, it's for want of a better replacement. While it's true that in many ways the word Asian meant Indian, it's not as simple as to be able to swap the terms – again, due to the actions of empire. The Partition of India in 1947 meant that many first- or second-generation Ugandan Asians gained another feather to the bow of their multinational identity. Families who had come to Uganda from India now found that their roots could be described as Pakistani. And the year before the exodus, further fractures added the prospect of newly named Bangladeshi backgrounds. It would arguably be no less reductive to describe people as Indian in this context as it would be to use the word Asian.

It was actually Partition that brought the term into use, says Taushif Kara, a postdoctoral research associate at Cambridge University, whose mother and grandparents were expelled in 1972. 'The term Asian emerged before 1947, but was thrust into use after 1947 as a kind of superficial container meant to evade the problem of discursive, mixing up diaspora with the citizens of new post-colonial states like India and Pakistan.'[10] Any wording seeking to group diverse communities together will be flawed from the outset, and in this case, South Asians in Uganda were splintered into count-less sub-communities much more likely to self-identify based on common languages, religions or geographic backgrounds and castes. 'Ugandan Asian' offers a practical way of discern-ing who we are talking about within the wider history, so has been used in this book, but when speaking about people on an individual basis, you'll hear their specific background or self-identification.

A book about immigration and race relations can't help

but touch upon the more unpleasant parts of these experiences. In discussing racism, some people describe the racial slurs they had thrown their way, be it on rare occasions, or in a daily barrage of hate. Although words I'd never want to write, I've chosen not to censor them when they have been spoken to me by interviewees, as this was a part of their story – often impactful and painful – and is something that is too often sanitised from our collective history.

Another point of tension comes around the usage of the words 'refugee', 'migrant' and 'immigrant' – all hugely loaded terms, which can carry associations far beyond their intention. Some Ugandan Asian histories, and particularly testimonies, use 'refugee/s' liberally. It's the way some self-identify, and it's the way they were made to feel as they fled their homes without hope of return. It's also how the British government framed the expulsion in order to garner sympathy at home and abroad. But fundamentally, legally, the vast majority of people who left Uganda in 1972 were not refugees. They had some variety of British citizenship, and, while it was a deliberately complex landscape, this generally engendered a right to remain. They didn't come to the UK under the UNHCR refugee framework. Only those who had taken on Ugandan citizenship, or who didn't have passports, and were then made stateless, could be described truthfully as refugees. It's an important distinction, so I avoid the use of 'refugee' to refer to anyone aside from this group. However, as with other terms, if interviewees self-identify as refugees, I haven't edited their perspective.

This leaves the question of how to best describe the Ugandan Asians on the move. If they weren't refugees, were they migrants, or immigrants? I would say yes, although neither are words that sit comfortably with me, writing in a time when the word 'migrant' is usually followed by crisis, and often linked to images of boats, detention centres and cheap them-and-us political rhetoric. The word 'migrants' seems to reduce people's agency, while 'immigrants' ascribes too much. Out of the two, I've chosen to use 'migrants', as it was certainly a forced migration, a descriptor I have used along with 'the expellees', 'the arrivals', 'the Exiled'.

The British empire was at the heart of Indian migration over the years and none more so than in the Ugandan Asian expulsion. Although it occurred in post-colonial times, the resettlement struck at the core of the imperial project, with many of those coming to the UK being what Parminder Bhachu coined in the 1980s as 'twice migrants', in that they had migrated via an intermediate country to their own. Colonialism took Indians to Uganda and, arguably colonialism, or at least post-colonialism, forced them out.[11] Three generations of women in my family tell this story, with my grandmother and mother born in British colonies on two continents, which would both become independent in their lifetimes, and myself born in a former colony on a third continent. The events of 1972 created a global Ugandan Asian diaspora, from Europe to the corners of the Commonwealth in Canada and Australia, but the largest resettlement was in Britain. And in years to come, this mass settlement, during a time of considerable racial tension, would come to be held up as a shining example of one of the most successful assimilations of all times.

But what happened next? Over the past fifty years, the exiled built communities, businesses and families – children who have undertaken their own journeys to uncover their roots. Some, like myself, have discovered a yearning for something unknown but innate, and just out of reach in trying to relate to the past. This is the story of this particular mass migration, but also the story of the British empire and multiculturalism today. Uncovering how first, second and third generations relate to this period in time and to their own identities teaches us about the country's collective history. As Visram, who focuses her work on South Asian life in Britain, puts it: 'We have to extend knowledge of our history here, which is part of Britain's history. It's not an immigrant history, it's not a ghetto history; it's our history but it's also part of Britain's history because we are part of this society.'

This is an epic story, of lives wrenched apart and families torn across continents. And it is much greater than that singular story that Ugandan Asian narratives often slip into, as victims of a tragedy who overcame the odds to triumph over adversity. Focusing solely on the business winners does Ugandan Asians a disservice, overlooking the ongoing challenges of a protracted multinational migration from former colonies, as well as the complexities of life in Uganda before the exodus. This is a story laced together by the threads of colonialism, from the first part of this book, Empire, through to Exodus, and ending with Reckoning. A messy human story, which *The Exiled* hopes to give a richer reflection of. I grew up surrounded by distant memories of the Uganda years, but also with a conflicted sense of identity. I'm increasingly interested in how people with diverse backgrounds, and who call multiple places home, relate to the past. This book is but a piece of this enormous patchwork. This is the fabric of the 1972 generation – and these are their stories.

Part I

EMPIRE

Chapter 1

Where the Sun Never Sets

The continent may be a blot, but it is not a blot upon our conscience. The problem is not that we were once in charge, but that we are not in charge anymore.

Former UK prime minister Boris Johnson on
Uganda, *Spectator*, 2002 (before in position)[1]

Mathukutty and Kunjamma were married on the first day of 1953. It was a beautiful Indian winter's day – not too hot and with no rain. Sunlight shone against the yellow walls of the village church, causing them to glow a deep orange, and danced off the gold embroidery woven through the bride's cream sari, which rustled gently in the warm breeze. Outside the church the gentle whooping calls of hornbills could be heard from their perches high in the rows of surrounding palm trees. Standing before three ministers in the Anglican church close to Kottayam in southern Kerala, an area where the number of Christians almost matches Hindus, the couple made their affirmations to love and cherish, from this day forward. Lifting their voices in joyful songs of praise, the congregation raised the union to the heavens. The wedding party then descended upon the groom's family home, a farmhouse on the crest of a neighbouring hill adorned by rubber trees. Cut off from the mainland by a narrow but fast-flowing river, guests wound their way down the slopes before boarding a small wooden boat and being punted across the waters a dozen at a time. A picture postcard of Kerala, mangroves and palm trees skirted the water's edge, casting rippling reflections upon its blue surface, which was broken by the occasional bubble from the fish below. Known for its diverse landscapes of backwaters, hill stations and beaches, Kerala is one of several places in the world dubbed God's Own Country, said to have been created in the image of the Gods themselves. One seventeenth-century legend tells how warrior sage Parashurama, an incarnation of God Vishnu, threw an axe across the sea, causing the water to recede to the point his weapon struck. The land that rose from the sea was filled with inhospitable salt, so Parashurama summoned the snake king Vasuki, who converted the soil into the fertile, green lands of modern Kerala.[2]

In typical Indian wedding style, the whole village turned out for the occasion. Bride, groom and a thousand relatives, friends and the rest of the local community climbed up through the rubber plantations, past lines of trees that had been tapped to release their precious white sap. At the top of the slopes, the land flattened out to reveal a large homestead, standing proud on stilts, with stone steps leading up on each side. Here the celebrants gathered together to say prayers, read Bible verses, and most importantly, enjoy a sumptuous feast. Three courses were served on banana leaves, from rich red rice and chicken curries, to brightly coloured thoran, dry curries tossing together shredded vegetables with the flesh of fresh local coconuts. To finish, as the sky turned golden, came bowls of payasam, a sweet milky soup that infused the air with the scent of cardamom. In her diaries written looking back at her marriage, my grandmother described her new husband as both 'handsome' and a 'first-class student' – two leading characteristics for an Indian arranged-marriage partner. Before this day, they'd spent just a few hours in each other's company, reliant on their family to broker a successful partnership. Luckily for her, my grandfather was also kind, patient and, like her, in possession of a mischievous smile. They were two adventurous spirits, equally serious and humorous, and wonderfully matched for their journey ahead.

Each one of eight siblings, Mathukutty and Kunjamma – or Philip and Rachel as they came to be known in their moves around the globe – were born and grew up in India's most southerly state. Both became educators in a region where education was prized, literacy rates topped the country, and there had historically been a progressive stance on women's rights. After stepping into the new year with their new union, Philip returned to a college in northern Sri Lanka, then known as Ceylon, where he was teaching maths and science, and serving as a housemaster. Rachel remained in India, with the independence to return to work in a government secondary school near Adoor, an hour south of her in-laws' home. More than 200 miles away from each other as the crow flies, the early months of their marriage were conducted via letter. 'Though we lived together only for nearly two weeks, we became very much attached to each other,' my grandmother wrote. 'We used to write long letters to each other and thus share our love. There were no long-distance phone calls then, at least not in Kerala.' They dreamed of a future where they could be reunited. 'We were planning for a job in a place where we could be together, and God had a plan for us.'

Famously it is easier to count the countries that haven't been colonised by Britain than those that have. At its height, it was the largest empire in history and by the onset of the First World War encompassed 412 million people, making up almost a quarter of the world's population.[3] During the imperial years, the British empire stretched variously from

Cape to Cairo, the Americas to Australasia, taking in more than eighty nations and earning the moniker of 'the empire on which the sun never sets' – so widespread that at least one part was always in daylight. Or, perhaps more aptly, as Keralan politician, writer and colonial critic Shashi Tharoor put it, 'The sun never set on the British Empire, an Indian nationalist later sardonically commented, because even God couldn't trust the Englishman in the dark.'[4] Our global time zones to this day take their base from the site of the original Royal Observatory, an enduring artefact of the imperial project that was to take in both India and Uganda. The British arrived in India in the 1600s, establishing trading posts under the now infamous British East India Company, which came to rule large swathes of the country. The huge peninsula offered unparalleled shipping opportunities and from the mid-1700s, the company would account for over half of the entire world's trade, moving cotton, silk, spices, sugar, tea and opium across the globe.[5] In 1858 India came under direct British rule in the period of the Raj, which would last close to a century. India was known as the jewel in the crown of the empire until the country's schism in the dissolution of imperial rule in 1947, as Partition splintered the nation into two self-governing countries of India and Pakistan. While the Raj was no longer, British influence continued, with a new flavour.

Soon, the British were bringing people across their newly defined borders. Although a hallmark of the British empire, it can be easy to underestimate the vast scale of movement of people across the globe during these years. The millions of Africans sold as slaves and forced onto ships to plantations in America and the West Indies is the best-known example and remains one of the greatest blots on the record of humankind. We also hear readily of European convicts being sent to the new colony of Australia. These were far from the only occasions where the empire moved people like commodities, but the memory of much of this movement is lost in the vast expanse of the imperial years. Despite studying East African and Indian colonial and post-colonial history at university, subconsciously gravitating towards my distant past, I hadn't grasped the scale, depth and premeditation of the migratory paths of Indians under the empire. While Indian people already had a historic relationship with East Africa, the indentured labour system brought hundreds of thousands more people to this part of the world. Inspired by the abolition of slavery, it was an opportunity to continue accessing untapped labour, but now conceding to pay a price for it. Slavery was finally abolished in all British colonies in 1834, although emancipated slaves weren't immediately freed, instead bound to plantations in an apprenticeship system, with slavery fading out over the next four years. Indentured labour came to fill the gap in manpower.[6]

Illicit slave-trading inevitably continued unabashed but was now supplemented by increasing numbers of indentured labourers from India, moved from one part of the empire to another. Plantation owners in Mauritius, nervous about the limits to their financial gain without a regular supply of workers, were one of the early adopters, calling more than 20,000 Indians to the island in the five years after the abolition of slavery. These dubious pioneers in a new labour experiment were said to have inspired John Gladstone, father of British prime minister William Gladstone, to recruit indentured labourers on his plantations in British Guiana (later Guyana). The first 437 Indian labourers, pejoratively known as 'coolies', sailed to the Caribbean at the start of 1838 and hundreds of thousands more would follow.[7]

India's population served as a ready supply of cheap

labour, many of whom were willing to take their chances in colonies abroad in the hope of escaping poverty at home. Agents travelled to rural villages to recruit people seeking a better life. As indentured labourers, workers had to declare they were travelling voluntarily, and signed up for five-year employment terms. However, there was widespread abuse of the system, and terms could be renewed, trapping some in permanent positions. As demand grew after the abolition of slavery, indentured labour could arguably be dubbed slavery by proxy. The British shipped Indians to colonies around the world, with large numbers of workers sent to plantations across Africa and the Caribbean, working on the major commodities beyond sugar including tea, coffee, rice and rubber.[8] Mauritius and South Africa fielded tens of thousands of people, and it's estimated these countries, along with the Seychelles and the East African region, received more than 750,000 Indians across the nineteenth century. In all, more than 1.3 million Indians would be moved across the world, from islands in the Indian Ocean like Réunion to Trinidad and Jamaica in the Caribbean, through to Fiji, Australia, Tanzania and Uganda, being brought into and helping to build the colonial systems in these countries.[9]

Empire 2.0 flourished elsewhere, with the greatest nineteenth-century expansion taking place in Africa. Explorers like Captain John Hanning Speke had already been venturing across East Africa, in his case, searching for the source of the River Nile. He was the first European to reach Lake Victoria, Uganda's great lake, in 1862, and Henry Morton Stanley followed thirteen years later, documenting the region's societies in greater depth.[10] Soon, more commercial exploration was underway. Following five years of investigation and engagement in Uganda via the Imperial British East Africa Company – the British empire's commercial wing focused on developing trade on the continent – the Kingdom of Buganda fell under British control in 1894. The Uganda Protectorate was established, and borders were drawn up that roughly correlate with present-day Uganda, although the precise borders were not definitively settled until 1926 – and future leaders, including Amin, would continue to question them many decades later, claiming that parts of neighbouring Kenya should be returned.[11] Unlike Kenya, the Protectorate status garnered Uganda a level of self-government not afforded to full colonial administrations, and there remained some autonomy among local leaders. However, the new colonial system locked in inequity and misunderstandings from the start, even in the country's name. Uganda is a mispronunciation of Buganda, which arose from Swahili-speaking traders' tendency to drop the 'b' from many African place names. The British arrivals naturally followed their example, but it meant that the entire country was now named after the Buganda kingdom, despite the region containing many dozens more languages, cultures, economies and politics. This, writes Cambridge University historian Richard Reid, was 'to an extent an accident of history, or more aptly of historical geography.'[12] It's easy to forget that the borders we so faithfully respect today are arbitrary. That the clean lines on maps, which cut across diverse landscapes and undulating topography, fixed once-fluid cultural heritages in time. When travelling overland in East Africa it's always struck me how distinct a country can feel from its neighbour as you cross a border, even though these were lines drawn in the sand as the continent was carved up between empires like the spoils of war.

In Britain's now former colony of India, four months after their wedding day, a visitor arrived who would change the trajectory of my grandparents' lives. 'An education officer from Uganda – an Englishman – visited Kerala,' my grandmother wrote. 'His main aim was to recruit teachers, especially of maths and science, to work in Uganda.' The recruiter bedded down in Kottayam, staying with the local Anglican bishop who happened to know the family. The bishop wrote to my great-grandfather asking if his daughter could be interested in a teaching job in Uganda. Seen widely as a golden opportunity, as better-paid government-sponsored jobs in a land of promise, Rachel's father helped to arrange an interview for her. She took along her husband's CV to speak for the both of them, telling the recruiter that they both wanted jobs. The two highly qualified, accomplished and English-speaking teachers were an attractive prospect. 'Within a few days I received a letter saying that we were both selected,' she recalls. Writing to her husband, he was thrilled at the new opportunity, resigning from his post in Jaffna and returning to Kerala in June. Preparations got underway, with bags packed and repacked, and the kitchen full of activity as supplies were gathered for the long journey ahead. Friends and family spoke in hushed tones about the perils awaiting them, attempting to fill the couple's heads with fears. Africa was a place where snakes hung from trees waiting to kill you, Rachel's brother warned ominously. Plus, Uganda was so hot that when you put your hand on the table to write, you had to have a piece of blotting paper underneath. 'We got ready to go to Uganda without knowing anything about the place,' she wrote, undeterred. 'We were going with the idea that we would have to draw water from a well, cut firewood for cooking. We were young and ready for all that.'

The British Protectorate of Uganda was still in full force in 1953 when my grandparents and many of their contemporaries boarded boats heading towards promised prosperity in Africa. When Queen Elizabeth II was crowned in Westminster Abbey in June of that year, she came to preside over thirty-nine colonies and protectorates. It would be a further four years before the first African colony, the Gold Coast, achieved independence as Ghana. The 1950s and 1960s saw more and more countries gain independence, but it wasn't until the 1997 transferral of Hong Kong to China that many viewed the true end of the empire.[13] Having grown up under British control, my grandparents had watched their country achieve independence, but were now heading to a country still under colonial rule. The sense of progress in moving abroad for a better opportunity than those afforded to them at home cannot be separated from the fact it was enveloped in the familiarity of British authority that ran deep through the Indian continent. Preparations had involved considering the climactic and wildlife hazards, but perhaps not the implications of what willingly entering into a colonial system once more would really mean for them.

One morning two months after their encounter with the English recruiter, Rachel and Philip stood at the bustling port in Bombay, their life squashed into the suitcases at their feet. Rachel held tins packed with homemade Indian sweets that her mother had poured her love into, a way to come along with her daughter on their journey. Bodies thronged the dockside; passengers waiting to board their vessels, families flocking towards arriving loved ones, street sellers touting fresh vada pav – the city's famous fried potato dumplings in bread rolls – while porters wove at speed between them, laden with bags on their shoulders and backs. The bump and grind of steam engines thundered as they fired up, ready for the long journeys ahead, and their horns pierced the air. The heat of the engines added to the sticky Bombay summer day, as passengers queued to board a British India Steam Navigation Company ship and take the BI Line to the Kenyan coast. The fleet included ships called *Mombasa*, *Arusha* and *Uganda*, named after places where the company traded.[14] These cities and countries were just distant names to my grandparents, as they set sail on their great adventure towards them.

Saying goodbye to her parents, Rachel was hiding a secret beneath her sari. She was already pregnant with her first child, my mother, and was desperate not to have anything stand in the way of the new life ahead of them. 'My mother suspected I was pregnant, but I did not tell her as they would not let us go if she knew,' she wrote. 'My father travelled with us in the same train from Cochin to Alwaye to be with us for the last time. When he got out, he said he may not see us again, and that was the last goodbye.' Sailing across rough July seas added seasickness to morning sickness, making for a difficult voyage. The journey typically took between eight and ten days depending on the conditions, but was on the longer side as the couple found themselves tossed across their bunks by the turbulent seas each night. Unable to eat, my grandmother gazed weakly at the ceiling each night, praying for respite, and arrived exhausted when they finally docked on a new continent. Landing in Mombasa, Kenya, with their heads still swaying from the days at sea, they boarded a train to Kampala. Relieved at the more soothing movement of the train, Rachel broke into the supplies of sweet round laddoos and gulab jamun, and jalebis, twisted strands of deep-fried batter soaked in sugar syrup, as she gazed at the vibrant sights passing them by. 'The train passed through national parks with giraffes, beautiful coloured birds, lions and deer of various kinds,' she says. 'We took three days and two nights to reach Kampala, the main city in Uganda, a city on seven hills.'

Theirs was not the first wave of Indian arrivals in Uganda. In their journey of land and then sea, they were following a well-trodden path. Those who had come by choice like them, those compelled as indentured labourers before them, and those who'd come seeking opportunity long before the British empire had even been imagined. There had been a lengthy history of immigration west over the years, predating the age of empire. Indian merchants had been trading along the East African coast for up to 3,000 years, sailing into the coastal ports of Mombasa and Zanzibar on the annual monsoon winds on dhows with proud white sails.[15] The cultural impact of this early exchange can be seen in these places today, where Indian influences are visible in the architecture of Stone Town's striking antique wooden doors, originally made out of teak from Asia and sporting brass studs reminiscent of those on Indian fortified doors, and tasted in the rice and chapatis embedded within Kenyan cuisine. There's evidence of traders visiting the Somali coast as early as the seventh century BC and Indian settlements in today's Mozambique in the twelfth century. While traders mostly moved on, some settled in the region and began to move inland with their wares.

Indian migrants remained on the periphery of Uganda's economy and society until the colonial imperative sought to sustain their presence, especially in light of slow European migration to the region. The first governor of British East Africa said that the protectorate 'has everything to gain from Indian settlement', while a colonial administrator suggested East Africa should become 'the America of the Hindu'.[16] As a diaspora of traders arrived, new clientele encouraged some to stay on the continent, setting up more permanent shops near travel hubs or in growing cities. Uganda's wealthiest man can trace his family tree to such early trade routes. With an estimated net worth of $1.2 billion as of 2019, investor and business magnate Sudhir Ruparelia has built his wealth across multiple sectors spanning banking, real estate and travel. Ruparelia, his father and grandfather were all born in Uganda, but his Gujarati great-grandfather landed in Mombasa back in 1897. After setting up a trading store along the coast, he decided to wind his way inland, arriving in Uganda six years later.[17]

Trading, however, only brought small numbers of people from India until imperialism began trading lives for labour. Although Uganda offered lush surroundings and a good lifestyle, attempts to bring more European settlers to Uganda were hampered by the country's remote location. Inland, and not readily accessible like coastal British East Africa, a huge railway project was developed to connect swathes of the British regions. Tracks needed to be laid to link the Kenyan coast first with Kisumu, west Kenya, and later all the way to Lake Victoria in Uganda itself. To construct and maintain what became 1,286 miles of rail network, the British East Africa Company, instead of recruiting local people, who they viewed as unskilled and inexperienced in engineering, brought up to 40,000 Indians to Kenya and Uganda through indenture.[18] In 1875, in the wake of the abolition of slavery, Lord Salisbury, secretary of state for India, recommended Indian immigration to East Africa for settlement, colonisation, and to keep the construction delivered on budget and to deadline. Indenture was the new unrestricted labour source in the empire post-slavery. Motivated to migrate for better lives, escaping poverty and famine, workers signed up to join the railway project. Through the

1890s, mostly Punjabi Sikh and Muslim immigrant workers laid tracks in back-breaking work under the heat of the equator's sun across hundreds of miles from Mombasa to Kampala, including crossing a 450-metre-high escarpment in the Rift Valley. Cost-cutting, heat exhaustion and tropical diseases coalesced into devastating working conditions. It's believed 2,500 workers died over six years of laying train tracks – four for each mile of railway track.[19]

As well as those brought to work on the physical railway construction, the British also employed South Asians in a range of associated jobs, including surveyors, carpenters and doctors. Unlike many of the transient traders before them, some of those who survived the construction project settled and made homes and lives, with small towns along the route of the railways becoming dotted with new Indian communities and mixed-race families. Of the tens of thousands who worked on the railway project, only around 6,700 stayed on in East Africa, but they had sown the seeds of South Asian migration to the region. These lower-caste workers, indentured 'coolies', were to be the start of Uganda's settled South Asian population. Between 1880 and 1900 up to 20,000 migrants would head to East Africa, mostly to work in Kenya, but daring men took their chances further inland.[20] Some would go on to become a 'wealthy mercantile class of planter industrialists,' says historian Saima Nasar.[21] The railway brought Anwer Omar's grandfather to Uganda from Junagadh in Gujarat. After working on the railway line, he eventually settled in a small town called Mengo, where Anwer's mother was born and would later bring him into the world. 'Those who stayed back after working on the railway flourished, because they worked hard,' he says. 'They all started with little stores, or dukas as they called them.'[22] The dukawallah – shopkeeper – would become synonymous with

Indians in East Africa. As well as becoming a visible presence within commerce, opening dukas was also the route into building much larger business empires.

Back in the late nineteenth century, with business booming in Africa, the continent also caught the attention of individuals looking to start anew in a country on the up. Kausar Chaudary, who is now in her seventies and living in Birmingham, recalls how her grandfather chose to emigrate from Jullundur, India, to Uganda for the perceived opportunities on offer. 'When the railways were being built, all sorts of developments were seen to be going on in Africa,' she says from the terraced home she shares with her husband of nearly 50 years. 'My grandfather studied veterinary medicine, but he was also a farmer. He wanted to come to Uganda to keep cows and goats. Having a farm is how he got started.' Indian migrants took to all manner of professions across economic life beyond the shopkeeper archetype to include farming, hunting and trading. Kausar's mother had grown up in Kenya, hailing from another family who had chosen to take their chances across the Indian Ocean. 'My parents got married, and we never thought about what happened before that, because this was home. This was our country, Uganda, and that was it.'

By the end of the Second World War, there was a sizeable population of largely Gujarati and Punjabi immigrants in Uganda.[23] From entrepreneurs to labourers, teachers to priests, all life was represented in the Indian communities here. Hindus, Sikhs, Muslims, Christians and more had all migrated, marking the Kampala skyline with temples, gurdwaras, mosques and churches. And active recruitment continued in India, as my grandmother's experience showed. When searching for skilled workers, including teachers, doctors, and the supportive pillars of the colonial administration, the British still turned to India over hiring or training African staff. For Bashir Lalani's father, who was just eighteen in 1929 when he left Bilka in Gujarat on a steamboat to Mombasa, Africa was seen as a land of promise. 'Coming from a South Asian background to the African continent, the language was completely different, but he managed to acclimatise himself and understand the culture,' Bashir says of his father. 'The early days for my family were rough, like most new immigrants in a new country. They were shop merchants trading in local goods and cash crops. That's how they made their way – life was very peaceful under the British colonial powers.'[24]

The unrestricted immigration of the late 1800s moved into a restricted and then checked phase by 1950, as the British almost became a victim of their own success, introducing stringent restrictions in an attempt to control the flow of hopeful arrivals. By this point a local community had already long been established. Ugandan census data shows that in 1948 the number of Ugandan-born South Asians reached 16,000, compared with just 3,377 in 1931.[25] The 1949 Immigration Act, in particular, set out specific, high economic status requirements for immigrants, but this didn't stop growth, as over the following ten years, while the number of European immigrants to Uganda increased from under 4,000 to over 10,000, the respective number of South Asians grew from 35,000 to over 70,000.[26] In their journey across the sea, my grandparents joined a longstanding history of migration to East Africa from India, but it was still a leap into the dark for them and their contemporaries. Kampala had touches of home, from the Indian and British influences, to the Keralan-landscape, while containing all the components of a new adventure.

*   *   *

It is almost impossible to grasp the scale of the British empire now. Today, our world feels smaller but more interconnected, albeit still shaped by the value systems that governed the globe for so many years. As Kehinde Andrews noted in the title of his book *The New Age of Empire*, 'racism and colonialism still rule the world'.[27] But just two generations ago, it irrefutably ruled the world. For the India and Uganda of the 1950s, empire was something overwhelming. It changed everything, on macro and micro scales, down to my grandparents being recruited as imperial agents to head from Kerala to Kampala. For myself, growing up in Sydney four decades later, empire also cast its shadow, even if I didn't fully understand it. In 1990s Australia, primary school history lessons were singularly focused on Captain Cook, as much as the UK has focused on Henry VIII. I was too young to make a connection between the ships arriving in Botany Bay and the ship my own family took across the same ocean. Empire is the origin story for the Ugandan Asian exodus. My grandparents were born in a British colony, and crossed continents working under the framework of imperialism. The post-colonial structures enmeshed with legacies of inequality that were established in these years are what engendered support for the expulsion. At the start though, this was a venture of opportunity for many, with unseen costs down the line.

Chapter 2

The City of Seven Hills

A journey once begun, has no end.
Kiran Desai, *The Inheritance of Loss*[1]

The bronze-tipped minaret stands tall and proud on Kampala Hill, a lemon-hued edifice reaching towards the heavens. Ascending 304 steps to the highest point of the Uganda National Mosque, there's an unrivalled view across modern Kampala, which now spreads as far as the eye can see across hill after hill, earth-coloured homes and towering blocks dotting the distant slopes. Today, this city of seven hills is a city on the move. Opened in 2007, construction of East Africa's largest mosque began during Idi Amin's rule in the 1970s. But as his star waned, and then extinguished, construction stalled for three decades, until funding came in from Amin's former friend and one of the continent's other infamous dictators, who lent his name to the then-called Gaddafi Mosque. Inside, the mosque can seat up to 15,000 at prayers on the carpets weaving around cream towers that reach up to ivory ceilings, flanked by ornate, carved borders. As light streams through yellow and blue curved stained-glass windows in technicolour, your eyes are drawn up to the hypnotic geometry carved into the main dome, from which a contrasting dark chandelier hangs back down to the mortal realm. With a headscarf tucked over my ears and my shoes slipped off at the door, I step onto the soft turquoise and maroon patterned carpet, which my accompanying guide informs me was designed by the mosque and produced in Libya, a physical representation of the multiplicity in this mosque's construction. The geographic symbolism in the interior design goes further still. Wood from the Congo, glass from Italy and chandeliers from Egypt form a trifecta of materials representing the African, European and Arabian influences on this country. This, my guide adds with a flourish, 'is all about representing me and you'.

Kampala has long been known as the city of seven hills. Today, it's closer to a city of twenty-one hills, but its roots can still be seen within its modern expansion. From the top of the minaret, which casts its unique shadow on busy city life below, 360-degree views take in the original seven peaks – Mengo, Rubaga, Namirembe, Makerere, Kololo, Nakasero and Old Kampala – each with its own stories to tell. The National Mosque sits in Old Kampala, the birthplace of the city itself. Folklore has it that the swamp and slopes here were the perfect home for herds of antelope, which would gather in great numbers to graze on the hills and drink from pools of water. These soon became the hunting grounds of the Kabaka, the King of the Buganda Kingdom in southern Uganda, which encompasses Kampala. In the 1890s, Captain Frederick Lugard, chairman of the Imperial British East African Company, set up a fort on the top of the hill. The British referred to the place as 'the hill of impala'. In Lugandan that became *Kasozi Ka Empala*. When the Kabaka would go out hunting, courtiers would say he had *a'genze e Ka'mpala* – he'd gone to Ka'mpala. And so the name Kampala was born.[2]

The East African Rift Valley system, forged from the moving bones of the Earth, bisects Uganda twice as it cuts up Africa's eastern swathe, with the great mountains of Mount Kilimanjaro in Tanzania and its northern brother

Mount Kenya taking the limelight. But the rolling landscapes continue outside of the dramatic topography of the tectonic region. Each of the other six hills of Kampala cleaved out of the earth came to have its own unique identity, communally representing the many diverse religions, kingdoms and identities of the city. Two of the hills are adorned with the markers of Christianity's arrival in the country. Namirembe, named after the Lugandan word for peace, is topped with Uganda's oldest cathedral, St Paul's, with burnt-orange walls the colour of equatorial earth. At the pinnacle's base, royal burial grounds known as the Kasubi Tombs house the kings of the past. At the peak of Rubaga Hill sits a striking Catholic church. Once home to the Kabaka's palace, after a bolt of lightning hit it, the royals resettled on a neighbouring hill, giving this and Namirembe to the missionaries.

Atop Mengo Hill you can find the remnants of the Kabaka's palace. It was here, in 1900, that the Buganda Agreement was signed allowing the British protectorate to be formed. The country's biggest man-made lake borders the palace, while Buganda's parliament building is found across on Namirembe Hill. Getting there involves a unique quirk, which can be spotted from the bird's-eye view from the towering minaret. The road connecting Mengo Hill with the parliament – lutiiko – building, crosses a roundabout, which unusually has a gate and road also running through its centre. It was built solely for the use of the Kabaka, for whom tradition forbids the use of the roundabout. To get to the parliament from the palace, he had to go in a straight line. North of Namirembe sits the ivory towers of the country's oldest university, on Makerere Hill. The university was founded in 1922 and alumni of the hill of knowledge include former presidents and prime ministers Joseph Kabila (DRC), Julius Nyerere (Tanzania) and Milton Obote (Uganda).

Mulago Hill overlooks Makerere and is home to a leading hospital, while Nakasero Hill, now in the centre of the city, completes the septet. This was the meeting place for much of the colonial administration and today the streets are dotted with embassies and high-rise hotels reaching out into the skyline. Each of these hills once marked not just a topographical high point, but also a rise of wealth and power, where those in possession of both watched over the lives playing out beneath them under colonial rule.

At the foot of one of these hills, Kololo, a young girl with curly hair might have walked carefully across the grass towards the wall of a pale, angular bungalow. Each step, deliberate, so as not to disturb both what she was holding and what she was walking towards. When she reached her target, a fly on the wall, twitching in the sunshine, she slowly extended her arm. There was a sharp flash of movement, and then a crunch. The tiny green chameleon gripping tightly to her index finger rotated its eyes as it swallowed its lunch. When I imagine my mother, Betty, as a child, she is striding back into the porch and placing the chameleon on the large tree branch it called home. After all, her mother wouldn't allow reptiles in the house. Such were the pets of a Ugandan childhood, and the stories passed on to the next generation about a seemingly magical, far-off place. Others heard similar stories of monkeys who perched on their parents' shoulders and would gently groom you like a member of the troop, tickling your scalp with their tiny, dexterous fingers.

When I was young and still enjoying the luxury of bedtime stories, after my parents read me tales written by others, I would clamour for them to *tell* me stories. They didn't have to be creative. I always wanted to know real ones, moments from their lives. I was fascinated by all the years they'd lived without me, in countries far from mine. Bedtime stories were about transporting me from 1990s Sydney to other times, but also other places. Africa became vivid in my mind as I heard about chameleons and coconuts, the Kenyan coast and the River Nile, tropical heat and warnings of getting insects in your feet if you went out barefoot. England too was just as captivating to me, from the Second World War stories of my grandparents surviving the Blitz and the Front, to the many breakdowns of my parents' beat-up Morris Minor. The countries intersected, because Uganda was full of British memories too. It would take me much longer to appreciate the true crossover between the two countries, and to understand more than what my imagination had conjured up of these places. As a five-year-old, I would mix up Uganda and India in my head. Africa, India and England. But first, Africa.

When my grandparents arrived in Kampala they were welcomed by the headmaster and deputy of the school they were due to start teaching at. With government quarters all full at the time, they were given a room at a hotel in what turned out to be a bustling, noisy part of town. Still worn out from the choppy days at sea, and further drained by her first trimester, Rachel's initial heady days in a new country were overwhelming, although she found unexpected similarities with Kerala, from the lush landscapes to the bountiful cassava and jackfruit. Moving to a quieter, Muslim-owned hotel offering samosas and curries that further reminded the pair of home, they settled in and prepared for the working world at Old Kampala Secondary. In years to come they would return to the hotel to pick up crispy fried bhajis and delicately spiced pickles. Rachel was teaching health science in the senior school and chemistry in the junior school, while her husband was continuing to teach maths and physics. 'Teaching was not easy,' she noted. 'I had problems with some students but not very bad. The students were mainly the children of Indian traders. They all spoke English well. So we managed all right.' Her husband settled in with ease. 'People liked him very much. He was a popular teacher.' There were just a few other Malayalis, people speaking their Indian language of Malayalam, in Kampala at the time, and they gravitated towards each other, seeking community at lunchtimes at the home of fellow Malayali couples.

Preparing for the birth of their first child in the little two-bedroom home they had moved into, Rachel made white dresses and sewed napkins for the new arrival, all the while working right up until the day before she went into labour. At 7.45 a.m. my mother came screaming into the world in Nakasero Hospital. 'The nurses said, "She is such a beautiful baby, neither like the father nor the mother,"' wrote my grandmother. 'They were teasing.' After five days on the ward, they returned home as a trio. Notes in my grandmother's diary hinted at something bigger in Ugandan society though. She had given birth in the European wing of the hospital, which she wrote was 'meant for whites and Asians together'. Colonial Uganda was stratified, and here explicitly segregated, by race. Ugandan society was a triad, a triangle that saw the smallest group of white settlers at the top, the South Asians below and majority Black Ugandans below them. As in the hospital, sometimes whites and South Asians would be grouped together at the expense of Africans. This hierarchy was even reflected across the landscape. Europeans lived at the top of Kampala's seven hills, so when the city's low-lying clouds rolled in, they would still see the sun shining over the other hilltops poking above the clouds, like islands in a lake. South Asians lived lower down the slopes, with the expansive lots higher up, and the cramped accommodation lower, while Africans lived further out still. In the centre of town, South Asian shops ran along the two main roads for miles, but uniformed doormen kept a watchful eye on the European shops, a quiet segregation, which extended to white schools and social clubs.[3]

This colonial stratification with white on top, Brown as the middle class, and Black at the bottom created a geographic ghettoisation and a racial hierarchy. This class structure would have major consequences in the post-colonial era too. As well as those brought from India for the railway project, the British came to employ South Asians widely across professions. The Wahindi – Indians in Swahili – were vital cogs in the colonial machine, from people like my grandparents who came to teach, to those who worked in administrative roles, or other middle management.[4] Then there were the descendants of those brought to the continent under indenture, the second generation who carved their own path, often by starting to trade and becoming part of the landscape of ubiquitous South Asian shopkeepers. While firmly second-class citizens to the colonial rulers, South Asians were still afforded a higher status by the British over Africans on every level in society, making them a dominant minority with a greater proximity to power. While subordinate to the ruling class, they themselves had Ugandan staff, or servants, doing their cooking, cleaning, gardening and guarding their houses at night. South Asians were stereotyped, two British journalists wrote in the 1970s, 'as the middlemen, exploiters of the poor who pandered to the whites.'[5]

At the heart of the colonial playbook sits both indirect rule and divide and rule. It was seen at the very birth of the protectorate, when colonialists favoured the Buganda kingdom in exchange for their support in managing the country's other kingdoms. By splitting groups up, power remained unchallenged, and the day-to-day state functioning and expansion was done by others. Vulnerability is built into such systems to keep people from challenging authority. While occupying a position of privilege compared to local Ugandans, South Asians still held a fragile existence. They were favoured sufficiently to encourage them to keep playing by the rules, but also left fearful of stepping over the line, their lives and livelihoods reliant on their rulers.[6] With society split along racial lines, South Asians provided a buffer between the colonial elite and the colonised. They were prevented from owning land, while laws prevented Africans from trading, ensuring this sector of society would become dominated by South Asians. Europeans were the political elite and administrators, South Asians were shopkeepers, traders, or bureaucrats, and Ugandans were left working for either of the other groups, or as subsistence farmers. 'Race coincided with class and became politicised,' summarises Mahmood Mamdani, a leading Ugandan Asian scholar.[7] And unlike many other colonies, Uganda didn't see large-scale European migration, so the role South Asians played would become even more significant.[8] It has been said that 'the British had wealth and power, the Asians wealth without power and the Africans neither wealth nor power.'[9] This played out every day on city streets, within homes, and even on the maternity wards. My mother took her place within the colonial hierarchy as she took her first breaths, the layers of which would take decades to unpick.

When we talk of South Asians in Uganda, or East Africa more widely, it's usually as one homogenous group. But all broad groupings like this contain multitudes: a wealth of distinct communities, based on people's roots, religion, class or caste. Ugandan Asians had numerous ethnicities and religions, castes and sects, and spoke a wide number of languages.[10] Religious diversity included Hindus, Muslims and Ismaili Muslims – the second largest Shia Muslim group in the world – Roman Catholics from Goa or Mangalore, Anglicans like my family from Kerala and many more. Social circles were often, at least initially, built on identity markers like religion or the area in India where people had come from. As my grandparents' first days in Kampala showed, the Malayalis, gravitated towards each other, just as Punjabi and Gujarati speakers did. Some stayed in total isolation not only from Black Ugandans, but also other groups of Indians. There may have been micro-communities based on shared cultural backgrounds, but this didn't amount to sectarianism. There were distinct racial dividing lines, but from a religious perspective, schools were non-denominational, and my mother and her friends remember celebrating festivities spanning multiple religions outside their own. Kausar, whose family were Muslim, remembers it as a time of true cohesion, where she also celebrated Christmas and Diwali. 'We used to go to the Hindu temples, and they'd come with us to the mosque. We used to eat at the Sikh gurdwaras. None of our parents ever said, "You can't go there, they're different." It was a very close-knit community in Kampala. Ismailis, Punjabis, Hindus, Gujaratis, it was like one family. We used to pray together. We had education together. We never felt the difference at all.'

She, like so many, looks back on a 'lovely childhood' that brought her in contact with a true range of cultures. 'We grew up getting to know so many different communities,' she says. 'I can speak five languages because of my childhood.' Punjabi was her mother tongue, she learnt English at school and Swahili from speaking with the local population. Her family also spoke Urdu at home, and lastly Gujarati with other Indians. The East African Asian identity became something unique and altered from those who had never left India. It's something Kausar discovered when she returned to what had now become Pakistan, post-Partition, to go to university. 'We felt so different from the people there, although they were our own people and speaking our own language,' she remembers. 'It was a shock to us, because everything was so different.' She had grown up with a sense of freedom she now found herself missing, having spent her childhood swimming and playing football freely with boys, and exploring the hills around her home, picking mangoes to eat as she ran home with the orange juice running down her chin. Her early memories are full of the bright colours and flavours of a tropical country known to be so fertile that it was commonly said you could throw a seed down anywhere, and it would grow. The plump bananas hanging in the kitchen and the pawpaw bought off the back of a bicycle, sweetness that would help wash the liquid quinine down. The avocados in the garden and the guavas growing freely by the lake where her father took her swimming, which you could pluck and eat while you dipped your toes in the water. Picnics at the botanical gardens in Entebbe every other week, discovering flowers the colours of a rainbow, and seeing cinnamon, betel nuts and lychees for the first time.

My mother was also growing up among a mix of cultures in Kampala. The tables lined with chattering children at her birthday parties were loaded with Indian food, sweet jalebis and savoury samosas, but while her mother wore saris, she favoured European dresses. School was taught in English, but she learnt Swahili from chatting with Petro, who lived behind the house with his family in the servants' quarters that came as standard for many South Asians and Europeans. They had by now moved to their true family home, a modernist-looking bungalow in the suburb of Kololo, around the corner from the secondary school where my grandparents both taught for a time in the classrooms stretching back up the hill. My grandmother would later become headmistress at another school, casting fear into misbehaving students' hearts, despite her diminutive height. Perched on the corner of a residential road dotted with embassies, the garden sloped down, offering the perfect angles to practise handstands against the supporting grass. Palm trees cast their shadows over the lawn, and potted plants lined the veranda, where the roof overhung the house and created a shaded spot for their German shepherds to rest in. These weren't just beloved pets, but also guard dogs, symbols of the systemic fears of intruders that persisted among families like mine. Stories I vividly remember hearing as I grew up included the thrill of Kampala's drive-in cinema opening, where the family would head in their Peugeot 403, attaching a set of speakers to the car to get the audio for the movie, parked up in the evening breeze. But I also heard how burglars once broke in at night, stealing all the tyres off the car and casting a shadow on my mother's dreams for years. How my grandfather went down to Nakasero Market the next day and bought his own tyres back. That same car would take them tens of thousands of miles across Rwanda, Tanzania and Kenya, exploring the rolling hills, Serengeti and the edges of the Indian Ocean. In Mombasa, on the Kenyan coast, my family visited a cottage on the beachfront owned by a bursar colleague at school, who let my grandparents stay there for several weeks during the holidays. The 800-mile drive involved stopping off at a Sikh gurdwara, where everyone was welcome to a free, vegetarian lunch, and to see friends and relatives in Nairobi. Most excitingly, it also took my grandparents, mother and aunt through national parks, full of giraffe and deer, lions, cheetahs and monkeys. On the other side of the country, they drove to Queen Elizabeth National Park, renamed to commemorate a visit by the Queen two years after the park was opened, and hinting at the reverence to the monarchy in this colony. Once, navigating the water-laden paths at the northern Murchison Falls National Park, my grandfather came face to face with a herd of elephants unhappy about their arrival. 'There were dozens of elephants, and the bull elephant was tossing his head and blowing his trunk,' my mum remembers. 'Then they charged us, and he had to put the car into reverse to race away.' Close encounters with wildlife didn't stop here. Murchison Falls was a favourite haunt of family friends too, who would pile into their VW Beetle to go to national parks every other weekend. Once, when aged just six, their daughter stepped off a boat and onto what she thought was a rock. Then it started moving. The rock was a crocodile. Unlike her maths teacher, who had lost a leg to a crocodile, she was somehow able to jump off unscathed, she tells me. 'It was a miracle.' Theirs were lives full of adventures awaiting down the open road.

Driving east from Jinja to Iganga in my dusty hired Toyota Hilux a few days after my trip to the mosque, the bright equatorial glare bounces off passing windscreens as I crane my head to my left, squinting at the uniform fields, my eyes searching the skyline. I should be close. Traffic lurches past me, overtaking my slow vehicle, now keeping pace with the articulated lorries lumbering painstakingly up the highway's hills, rather than speeding past them. Soon, a large sign starts coming into my eyeline at the side of the road ahead, along with the parked-up matatus (minibuses) and boda bodas (motorbike taxis), confirming I didn't need to be searching so hard. A bright billboard shows pictures of the same blue sky above me and lush green fields, emblazoned with the words 'Kakira Sugar Ltd'. Above and next to it, are two enormous, oversized sugar packets on posts, bloated to give the impression of being full of shimmering grains. Kakira's growling lion logo paces towards me, incongruous against the slogan, 'There's nothing sweeter'. For the owners of Kakira, it's certainly an apt phrase. This business is tied to the fortunes of one of the most well-known Ugandan Asian families. Two names more than any other became synonymous with Ugandan Asian wealth: dominating the business landscape, as well as the literal landscape in fields of cotton and sugarcane, were the Madhvanis and the Mehtas.

Muljibhai Prabhudas Madhvani and Nanjibhai Kalidas Mehta both came to Uganda in the 1900s at young ages, just fourteen and thirteen years old. It wasn't long before they were trying their luck in the business world. Madhvani had come to join his uncle Vithaldas Haridas Madhvani, who had set sail by dhow for Zanzibar and Mombasa in 1893, later settling in Iganga and opening the shop that would spawn an empire. While South Asians had originally been prevented from buying land, by 1920 the British had waived this ban, maintaining the best land for themselves but allowing others to get a foothold. Within just four years, South Asians dominated the cotton industry and by 1948 owned all but twelve of the country's 195 cotton ginneries. It was the starting point for both Madhvani and Mehta too.[11] Over the next two decades, as rubber plantations were auctioned off after the First World War, they would also move into sugar, with Mehta building the first sugar factory in Lugazi, and Madhvani following suit on 800 acres of land in Kakira, outside of Jinga. The site would become known as

Madhvaninagar or Madhvani town, and grow to cover 23,000 acres.[12] According to the family, on a sunny day in the 1940s, Madhvani and his sons were arguing as they stood on a hill in Kakira looking over the shores of Lake Victoria. He wanted to plant a mile of trees running to the southern edge of the estate. His sons countered that while it had made sense to line trees along estate roads, there wasn't even a path through the marshy area he was proposing. Madhvani senior had a simple reply, 'Men are not stupid; one day there is going to be a road here.' His words ring true as I drive along the Jinja-Iganga Highway, past Kakira Sugar Works and the line of trees he planted.[13]

Based in Uganda, the Madhvani and Mehta business empires stretched across East Africa. The Madhvanis, later dubbed the Rockefellers of Africa, had more than twenty cotton ginneries, an oil factory, steelworks, sugar refinery, breweries and a string of investment properties. One descendant told me how the family pulled chips out of a hat to divide up the assets down the generations. The Mehtas, meanwhile, had extensive tea plantations, as well as manufacturing coffee and sugar. They have even been credited with introducing modern irrigation and mechanised cultivation into Uganda.[14] My mother remembers trips to visit one of the country's sprawling rural tea plantations, where the Malayali manager was a family friend. Driving past the huge processing factory, where trucks unloaded bags of freshly picked tea leaves, you then passed the fields themselves, where Ugandan women plucked leaves from the rows of greenery under the midday sun. Spending the afternoon with the friend's wife, reading books and glossy women's magazines, from *Woman's Own* to *Good Housekeeping*, 'this seemed,' she says, 'so glamorous.' These business behemoths became a huge part of the Ugandan economy – the Madhvani Group would come to be estimated to account for around ten per cent of the country's GDP.[15]

These stratospheric successes represent the highest echelons of South Asian entrepreneurship in Uganda during these years, but on a smaller scale, Ugandan Asians had long been associated with trade. Dukas, which sprung up across the country, were the most visible sign of South Asians' role in this part of the economy. As dukawallahs made more money, they expanded into larger premises, or bought factories and farms. At the turn of the century South Asians controlled eighty to ninety per cent of all trade, a figure that changed little over the years to come.[16] At the peak of the population size in the late 1960s, there were fewer than 100,000 Indians, Pakistanis and Goans in Uganda, which was just over one per cent of the population. However, their economic sway was disproportionate to their numbers. In 1952 it was estimated that 5,227 Asian retail traders had an annual turnover of £28 million, amounting to over £5,000 per trader, compared with a turnover of £10.6 million for 11,634 African traders, at just over £900 per trader. Attempts to restrict Asian business and boost African trade through governmental policy failed over the ensuing years and the wealth divide continued to grow.[17] An often-quoted figure encapsulates this: although South Asians represented just one per cent of the population, they earned a fifth of the national income.[18] This, in tandem with the racial and class separation, encouraged an image of South Asian traders as greedy, exploitative and extractive, which would gain momentum as the years passed. The remittance of earnings abroad drew particular criticism, feeding into the idea that big business was just here to take from Uganda. In the 1950s the hostility broke into the open, with attacks on some shops and a Bugandan boycott of non-African shops.[19] Taking over dukas seemed aspirational and attainable for some Ugandans. Although it was the British who restricted Ugandans' social mobility, while favouring South Asian traders, and it was the economy established by the colonial government that was fundamentally uneven, rising South Asian wealth was more visible day to day on the shopping streets than the European wealth kept out of sight within offices or behind guarded gates on Kampala's hilltops. Some small traders remained embedded in communities, but others flaunted their wealth, appearing conspicuously richer than the Africans around them, driving flashy cars as status symbols.[20] Uganda's Asians were the more public face of the inequities, and by encouraging resentment between them and the local population, the elite could remain blame-free.

The enduring association of the South Asian shopkeeper has also gone hand in hand with a particularly uncomfortable sentiment – that Uganda would have been nothing without South Asians, who developed Uganda economically. The implication is that the local population couldn't have achieved this themselves. It's something that comes out in a lot of interviews with Ugandan Asians in the 1970s – 'Uganda was nothing, it was a forest, which we turned into a lovely paradise,' said one interviewee – but is even repeated today.[21] By continuing to focus on South Asians as the sole economic drivers for the national economy, 'indigenous Africans' capacity for contributing to national development is consistently devalued and marginalised,' says Anneeth Kaur Hundle, anthropology professor at the University of California, Irvine.[22] This historic indispensability may have grown out of the ubiquity of South Asian faces on the high street, as well as the social order that literally underlined that South Asians were 'better' than Africans.[23] Perhaps it's part and parcel of an environment in which Ugandans were seen as staff for many South Asians.

Facing anti-Blackness in this period is long overdue. The focus on the racism faced by South Asians in Uganda has often overlooked the racism meted out by them. History has spoken about Ugandan Asians as pawns in the colonial game, brought over under imperialism, and moved on under post-colonialism. But they had agency too, and a critical examination needs to confront the degree to which they were active participants in the subjugation of Black people. It's something that has been explored in a recent book by historian Samwiri Lwanga-Lunyiigo, of Makerere University, published under a deliberately provocative title – *Uganda: An Indian Colony 1897–1972*. Subverting the discussion from the country as a former British colony, he explores the role South Asians played during their tenure on the continent, which he deems to be as 'deputy imperialists, sub-imperialist, privileged workers of the colonialists'.[24] A settler-colonial project led at least in part by Indians, who were by and large pro-establishment.[25]

Discussions have started on colourism within South Asian communities in Uganda, but generally with reticence. With the Indian caste system tying colour to the social order, favouring light skin, racism could be baked into people's viewpoints. Most people I've spoken with speak of friendly relations with their employees or servants, which I'm sure are genuine recollections. 'We didn't know what racism was really,' Kausar tells me. 'We children all used to play together and we never treated them as children of the house servants. They were friends.' The uglier side is an understandably difficult thing to speak about on a familial level, although one of my mother's school friends, whom she used to play piano with, told me, 'I was unhappy and uncomfortable with the way everybody treated the African servants. I thought that was appalling, and I still do. I'm quite ashamed that we had servants as well. It was their country, so it was just shocking the way they were treated.' As a child I was amazed by the idea that my mother had grown up with staff living on site. Even the idea of an occasional cleaner or gardener would have been hard to grasp compared with our simplistic suburban Sydney lifestyle, let alone the idea of a servant – which seemed to me something from the depths of history, far longer ago than within a parent's lifespan. Servants were reflective of the wider societal split. 'There was a great separation,' my mother says. 'Apart from the people who worked with and for us, we didn't have any African friends.' When my mother would visit embassy homes, to play with ambassadors' children, she saw their staff dressed in uniforms, from Fez caps and Bagandan robes to the white gloves donned to serve food. She speaks fondly of her relationship with their housekeeper and the ayahs who helped raise her and her siblings, and my grandfather was strongly liberal in his politics, but says their employees would often mention colleagues and friends suffering indignities elsewhere. The wording they used – that someone was a 'bad master' – is jarring. But a wind of change was blowing their way.

Black, yellow and red stripes wound their way across Entebbe Airport, proclaiming Uganda's national identity proudly to the world, and to the British plane touching down on the tarmac in the October breeze. The Britannia parked up before rows of soldiers in sand short suits and red caps matching the colour of the carpet rolled out to meet its Royal passengers. The Duke of Kent disembarked – the representative of his cousin the Queen – shaking hands with

Obote and the Kabaka, as children lining the runway edges waved those pocket-sized flags made precisely for events like this. In October 1962, five years after the first of Britain's African colonies won its hard-fought independence, Uganda was following in the footsteps of Ghana, Somalia, Nigeria, Sierra Leone, Cameroon and Tanzania in being released from the empire's clutches. The winds of change were blowing through Africa, as UK prime minister Harold Macmillan had said two years earlier, and the growth in African national consciousness was now an undeniable political fact.[26] In total, forty-seven countries would gain independence from European powers between 1957 and 1990.[27] The Royals were treated to displays of dancing, parades and even a canoe regatta on Lake Victoria, before crowds gathered at Kololo Stadium in Kampala for the formal handover at the stroke of midnight, when the capital would move to this city from Entebbe, where the colonial headquarters had been based. Under cover of darkness, illuminated by the bright stadium lights, the Union Jack, which had flown over the land for almost seventy years, was lowered. Applause and cheers rang out as the tricolour of the Ugandan flag were raised in its place at midnight. Independence day was 9 October, which was also, coincidentally, the duke's birthday, something he noted in his speech in which he quoted Winston Churchill's impressions of Uganda and wished the next generation the best in ensuring their new country's success.[28] In his military garb, medals hanging from his white crisp chest, and with his wife next to him draped in pearls and wearing a sparkling tiara, they looked a picture of wealth as they gazed out over crowds of Ugandans, South Asians and Britons celebrating the occasion alike. This wasn't a final goodbye, newscasters insisted, as Uganda was becoming a full member of the Commonwealth.[29]

Independence, my mother remembers, was a time of excitement. Everyone was buoyant with the spirit of it, and things were shifting societally too. As a colony, society had been stable, but fundamentally uneven. By the time my grandmother was in hospital to give birth to her third and final child, my uncle Phil, the nurses were mostly Ugandans, who she noticed would refuse to listen to the white sisters. The racial hierarchy and presumed authority that had been so fixed in place was starting to be challenged from the ground up, with a confidence imbued by independence. This, my grandmother wrote, 'was Obote's time'. But the legacy of colonialism remained visible at every turn, from the enduring three-tier societal structure, to the British systems and influence. These were so deeply embedded they were hard to shake, most of all from people's psyches, and would long outlast Britain's overt rule.

The eight years my mother had lived in a British colony had been full of the hallmarks of the mother country, which would remain in the years to come. Schools followed the British education system and term times. Some even adopted their uniforms, to the bemusement of those who had to wear them, with the Aga Khan Schools having their students wear woollen blazers in tropical weather.[30] Kampala's main department store, Drapers, sold Marks and Spencer's underwear, Sheaffer pens and Clarks shoes. A magnet for diplomats from Uganda, Kenya and Tanzania, the shop brought European products straight to the heart of East Africa. Elsewhere a specialist shop sold imported bacon and sausages. My grandfather would religiously buy *TIME* and *Life* magazines, and organisations like the Women's Institute flourished. Colonies like Uganda were part of the great British family, sharing in the institutions it prided itself on, and this colonial cosmopolitanism was felt particularly in the large cities like Kampala. You could see the British theme all the way through, says one of my mother's childhood friends, who got her Brownie badge awarded to her by the head of the organisation, Lady Baden-Powell, who was visiting from Britain at the time. 'There was a sort of deference to people who were British,' she tells me. 'My dad didn't have that, but it was unusual.' Despite independence, much of what was brought by colonialism remained woven through the Ugandan Asian experience as the country stepped into its new identity.

My family had a 'great affinity' towards Britain, my mother remembers. My grandfather had travelled to London in the 1950s to do his teacher-training qualification, supported by the Ugandan government. Doing his Postgraduate Certificate in Education (PGCE) involved a stint teaching maths and physics in an English school. He returned with a distinction in his teaching practice, and a suitcase of suits and dresses from London. The eye-catching wardrobe caught the eyes not only of friends, but also people with wandering hands. Not long after, their house was ransacked, and he was left with only the trousers and jacket he was wearing. At home, the family would gather round in the evening to listen to the BBC World Service on a large, freestanding brown wireless, taking in the British perspective on global affairs. My mother and her siblings went to English-speaking schools and primarily spoke English at home, so immersed that they all grew up with British accents. Nakasero Primary School was mostly filled with European students, my grandmother wrote, with around eight other South Asian children, and a few affluent African children, like the Kabaka's son and the children of ministers. My grandparents were always 'a little untraditional,' my mother laughs. They gave their children English names, and while my grandfather would hum songs by Indian superstar Lata Mangeshkar around the house, and even sing the Indian national anthem in Hindi, they were every bit as engaged with English culture, down to a dedication to Wimbledon. As it happened, though they didn't know it yet, their fate hung in the hands of another person connected to all things British.

Chapter 3
The Writing on the Wall

The fear was contagious, stemming not from the overt threat to yourself, but from the dark stories whirling around, caught on the wind.

The rivers of blood were in Uganda, not where Powell had spoken of.

Paul Theroux[1]

Bob Claxton was asleep when unusual sounds startled him awake late one hot Sunday night in January 1971. A gentle roar of engines, and the rhythmic click of metal. Stirring from sleep in his upstairs bedroom, the young doctor rushed to the window, where his vision brought the noise into sharp focus – a column of tanks was rumbling past his house in Kololo, just north of the centre of Kampala. 'My wife went back to sleep, didn't worry about it,' he laughs, now speaking to me from his home in Sydney 7,500 miles away from those Kampala streets. 'But I was too anxious wondering what on earth was going on.' A chance encounter with an orthopaedic surgeon in London four years earlier had brought Bob and his wife to Kampala. On meeting Bob, the surgeon's eyes lit up as he said he was just the person he'd been looking for to train Ugandan medical graduates in surgery, to save them from having to go abroad for training. It's one of many 'serendipitous moments' in Bob's life, he says, where everything seemed to come together. The couple set out to the pearl of Africa, unaware they were about to witness the making and breaking of history. In Kampala, the morning after armoured vehicles had crept into the city over-night, events took a sudden turn. 'Some of these tanks were then firing cannons over our roof from up the street,' Bob remembers. 'Which was where Amin's headquarters were.'

It was 25 January, and the country's army commander, General Idi Amin, was seizing control of Uganda in a classic coup d'état while the president was abroad. With no love lost between the two, and having suspicions that Amin was planning a move, from a Commonwealth Conference in Singapore Obote ordered the head of police to arrest him. But the message was intercepted by the army, and soldiers were mobilised. Gunshots were heard at the army barracks on Kampala's Mengo Hill. After sealing strategic positions around the capital and Entebbe Airport, soldiers and tanks filled the unusually quiet streets, which had been abandoned by the public as rumours of a takeover swirled. A flurry of gunfire was again heard at dawn. By the time Amin arrived in Kampala in the early hours of the morning, soldiers had surrounded parliament and seized the radio station, ready to enact and broadcast the new era of Ugandan politics.[2]

'We couldn't get anything out of the local radio stations,' Bob tells me. Radio Uganda had elected to broadcast martial music over any news bulletins.[3] 'We went to see if we could listen to the BBC, because that's what happened in those days. If there was unrest, you listened to the BBC to find out what was really happening. We found out that was the day of the coup and it was very tense.' In the afternoon, shortly before 4 p.m., Radio Uganda paused its relentless soundtrack of military brass bands for a soldier to come over the airwaves, declaring that it had been 'necessary to take action to save the situation from getting worse,' and reading out a list of eighteen grievances and justifications for the armed takeover. The broadcaster accused Obote of giving preferential treatment to the northern Lango region and said that his policies would lead to bloodshed.[4] 'Power is now handed over to our fellow soldier, Major General Idi Amin Dada. We have done this for God and our country,' he said.[5] After hearing the radio announcement and the sounds of guns being fired into the air, twelve-year-old Alan Kisaka ran outside. 'I thought to myself something big must be going on, so I ran from my house to the main road to see what was going on,' he later told the BBC. 'There were military transports carrying troops at high speed down the road. Some of them would stop and officers would jump out and start beating anyone who had a shirt or dress with a picture of Milton Obote on it.'[6] The sounds of tanks were soon replaced with the sounds of the city calling out in celebration of the new beginning. People poured onto the streets ahead of the nightly curfew, banging tin pans and ululating in high pitched trills of revelry, waving banana leaves and throwing flowers. Thousands of people cheered the army, chanting 'Long live Amin'.[7] At the wheel of an open-topped Jeep, flanked by soldiers wielding AK-47s, Uganda's new self-declared leader rolled through the capital looking every inch a star. Wearing trademark army fatigues, complete with epaulettes, a beret and sunglasses, Amin had one hand on the steering wheel and one waving to the crowds lining the roads and perched on top of buses in the hope of getting a better look at the general.

Idi Amin Dada Oumee remains Uganda's most famous name. Or as Amin variously called himself, His Excellency President for Life, Field Marshal Al Hadji Doctor Idi Amin, VC, DSO, MC, CBE, Lord of all the Beasts of the Earth and Fishes of the Sea, and Conqueror of the British Empire in

Africa in General and Uganda in Particular.[8] He famously also dubbed himself the King of Scotland, a nod to his country's affinity with the Scots for having both suffered under English colonial oppression, and even gave some of his innumerable children the Scottish names Campbell and McKenzie. A larger-than-life character, both physically and metaphorically, after the takeover he would go on to dominate his country's fortunes through a brutal regime across the 1970s.

Mood had soured so much against Obote's government that people across all sections of society viewed Amin as a broadly positive thing for the country. 'The previous president had been making himself unpopular, so the general feeling was that it was right to get rid of him, and now we'd have some good government,' recalls Bob. The first wave of hope within the reborn country had gradually faded over the decade since independence, during which Obote had banned opposition parties and the king of southern Uganda he had originally ruled with, the Bugandan Kabaka, and begun filling the country's jails faster than space could be found. Despite his socialist rhetoric, the Ugandan People's Conference became a dictatorial regime, and detentions, disappearances and deaths began to rise. The secret police unit, the General Service Unit, led by Obote's cousin, was responsible for much of the terror.[9] Amin's ascent to power was greeted with particular jubilation in Bugandan Kampala, as he offered a return for the Kabaka, but also on the international stage.[10] Gone were the threats of the left-leaning, cerebral Obote. Here was someone the world, and especially Britain, could do business with. The British high commissioner wrote enthusiastically that, 'at long last we have a chance of placing our relations with Uganda on a friendly footing.'[11] Some suggested Britain had been behind the coup itself.[12] With all the populism and bluster of Big Man politics, surrounded by fantastical tales and legends, Amin was seen by many as a caricature, rather than a serious contender. Seen as an 'amiable and obliging soldier,' rather than a cunning leader, he was, BBC journalist George Alagiah wrote, 'just the sort of fellow the colonial masters used to like – not so bright that they might get fancy ideas.'[13] It would soon become clear that everyone had wildly underestimated Amin.

Amin had seized a country still in its infancy when it came to its new identity, retaining many of the hallmarks of the previous decades. This included the strict social groups that had existed as the sun set upon empire in Uganda. When the stripy red, yellow and black flags started flying at independence, they brought with them new questions of citizenship. If South Asians could make their way through the quagmire of bureaucracy, they could get Ugandan passports, but in doing so, would have to renounce any previous citizenship. At the time they typically had one of the many forms of British citizenship, which was then a complex landscape including Citizens of the United Kingdom and Colonies (CUKCs), British Protected Persons (BPPs) and British Subjects. There were smaller groups of Indian and Pakistani citizens.*[14] Applying for a Ugandan visa decades later, I notice there are more UK citizenship options than usual in the drop-down menu. As well as British Citizen, there's British National (Overseas), British Overseas Territories Citizen, British

---

* The British empire was a 'patchwork of territories and identities with differentiated legal statuses'. Directly ruled territories like British India created different legal statuses for those that lived there than indirectly ruled ones like the Protectorate of Uganda. After Partition, some East African Asians' nationalities shifted further.

Overseas Citizen, British Protected Person and British Subject – remnants of times gone by. Back then, this was a system deliberately laced with complexities and getting hold of a Ugandan passport wasn't easy. It's thought only ten per cent of Ugandan Asians would have qualified for the initially tight citizenship laws that required two generations above you to be Ugandan-born on at least one side of the family.[15] CUKCs and BPPs had two years to register for citizenship, just needing to prove recent continuous residency.[16] Typically heads of households would forego their British links in order to better integrate their businesses into the country. Some saw the value in maintaining the British connection, while others approached it as a lottery, hedging their bets for the future by ensuring a mix of citizenships within a family. Uptake was deemed to be low. By 1968 under 15,000 people had registered, a number which would be used to question South Asians' commitment to the country, but by the same time some 10,000 applications had also been turned down.[17] Passports would become part of the wider discussion in the 1960s about the 'Asian question'. Independence had removed the overt shackles of the British, yet the colonial capitalist class system appeared to have stuck, and the South Asian community's position was increasingly under the magnifying glass. Many in the country felt strongly that Ugandan Asians were a 'legacy of imperialism', says anthropologist and biographer of Amin, Mark Leopold. 'They were an intrinsic part of British rule, they had been put in a superior position and regarded as more intelligent, more sophisticated, more civilised people than the local population, and local people felt that strongly.'[18]

Meanwhile, Britain was facing its own identity crisis. These early decolonising years represented a shift from being an imperial power to a nation state. There was just the small matter of the citizens of that empire, who had previously been granted free movement across it. The country was now, historian Ian Sanjay Patel writes,

> less of an invading presence in the world, exerting its will on others; now it was itself the invaded space, prone to defensive reactions as a supposedly alien presence (the 'coloured immigrant') settled itself within Britain.[19]

From the arrival of SS *Empire Windrush* in 1948 to the Notting Hill Race Riots in 1958, some Britons were feeling increasingly hostile when it came to immigration.[20] And Whitehall was getting nervous. While ideals of an open Commonwealth and a global British family were genuine, they were overtaken by concerns about what Conservative prime minister Harold Macmillan called an 'influx' of British citizens from the Commonwealth. 'I don't think anybody realised that some people would retain their citizenship of the United Kingdom and Colonies, they thought they would acquire the new citizenship of independent countries,' immigration lawyer Colin Yeo tells me over a video call. 'They didn't think that colonial subjects would retain the right to enter the UK after countries became independent. But that's not how it works.' In the year better known for the Beatles' first single release, the UK legislated to restrict their global citizens' movement with the Commonwealth Immigrants Act 1962.*[21] While care was taken to never specifically mention race, by drawing a distinction by who had issued your passport, the new bill directly

---

* The free movement of British citizens was halted and those across India, Pakistan and East Africa were among those shut out.

penalised people of colour. 'There's no controversy, I think, about saying that this is racially motivated,' says Yeo. If a colonial authority had issued your passport, then you now had to apply to receive one of the limited vouchers from the British government to travel. But the government had unwittingly left a loophole.

In Kenya, which had gained its independence a year after its neighbour, President Jomo Kenyatta was striding forward with Africanisation policies. Through the 1960s he sought to put more power in Black hands by restricting the activities of the country's 12,000 South Asian British citizens. Trading licences stopped being issued to non-citizens, meaning even South Asian business owners who had been born in the country found themselves unable to earn a living, as most weren't Kenyan citizens.[22] The shifting sands led many of those who had retained their British passports to think about heading there – which, due to a quirk of fate, they still could, despite the new laws. After Kenya gained its independence, the colonial governor had become the high commissioner, meaning that their passports were being issued directly under the authority of the British, not a colonial government. Kenyan Asians, who were charmingly described by one Conservative researcher as the 'detritus of empire', had inadvertently bypassed Britain's blockade.[23] Around 15,000 moved to the UK in one year, so naturally newspapers splashed fearmongering and wildly out-of-proportion headlines warning that hundreds of thousands of people would soon descend on Britain's shores.[24]

The prospect of unlimited arrivals from East Africa, coupled with the dawning realisation that Britain faced the same responsibility for citizens of colour far beyond Africa – including Malaysia, Singapore, Ceylon and the Caribbean

– caused reactions like that of one Labour MP, who tellingly said, 'This country cannot take upon itself the whole legacy of the empire.'[25] The British high commissioner in India warned that six million Indians living overseas could be expelled and follow in the Kenyan Asians' footsteps.[26] As new legislation was discussed to close the so-called 'backdoor entry' South Asians were using, Britain was in fact experiencing a net outflow of migration, but that didn't stop the freefalling panic.[27] A new bill was rushed through parliament in just three days. Described by some parliamentarians as 'the most shameful piece of legislation ever enacted by parliament, the ultimate appeasement of racist hysteria,' the uniquely restrictive Commonwealth Immigrants Act 1968 drastically changed people's prospects of migrating to Britain.[28] Now, any citizen of the United Kingdom and its Colonies would face immigration controls unless they were born in Britain, or had one parent or grandparent born, adopted, naturalised or registered in Britain as a citizen of Britain and its colonies, excluding some 1.5 million citizens of colour.[29] The carefully crafted grandparent clause effectively meant white settlers in colonies or newly independent nations would still be able to return. As Nadine El-Enany, reader in law at Birkbeck, University of London, wrote, the bill was 'a white Britain policy in the making'.[30]

The legislation captured the mood of anti-immigrant sections of society. The following month, Conservative MP Enoch Powell would stand up in front of his colleagues in Birmingham and deliver his infamous 'Rivers of Blood' speech. Marbled with fears of Britain's changing identity, Powell likened the acceptance of immigrant children as 'like watching a nation busily engaged in heaping up its own funeral pyre.' Warning of racial clashes, he drew his speech to a close with the words that would take root in the country's collective memory. 'As I look ahead, I am filled with foreboding; like the Roman, I seem to see "the River Tiber foaming with much blood."'[31] The two Commonwealth Immigrants Acts redrew Britain's borders and reframed the nation's view of those outside of them. 'Before 1962, if you're a part of the British empire, you are British in that story. And if you're European or American, you're actually the ones seen as outsiders,' Becky Taylor, professor of modern history at the University of East Anglia, tells me:

> So we've got this sort of linguistic sleight of hand, by posi-tioning them as Commonwealth immigrants, not as citi-zens. Because what these pieces of legislation are doing is stripping the rights of citizenship from them. What we see in the post-war period is a shift whereby immigration becomes conflated with pigmentation.

And so, people with pigmentation in Kenya were turned away from planes bound for London and left stranded in airports, or even bounced back and forth between the two countries like shuttlecocks. South Asians found them-selves placed on the fault lines of Africa's independence, says Mohamed Keshavjee, a lawyer qualified in three jurisdictions and an internationally recognised specialist on cross-cultural mediation, who was living in Nairobi at the time. 'We were trying to grapple with what Harold Macmillan called the wind of change. I always look at myself as a product of the wind of change.' Speaking to Britain's role in the fragmentation of South Asian commu-nities in East Africa, he adds, 'At the end of empire we were placed in a difficult situation, and the British govern-ment, unfortunately, didn't take responsibility and tried all sorts of legal expedients of disenfranchising the Indians of their birth right.' People who had always counted on the guarantees given to them or the generation before them by the British were left wanting. Furious protestors held up placards at Nairobi's airport lambasting Conservative MP Duncan Sandys, emblazoned with the words, 'Sandys – humanity will never forgive you!' and 'Great British Betrayal'.[32]

In their bungalow in Kololo, my grandparents were watching the Kenyan situation with interest, but without serious concern. My grandfather Philip had retained a relationship with England through his teacher-training, and although Obote was talking big on changing the status quo for South Asians, there was little material change to their lives. Kenya might have been a neighbour, but its politics felt far removed from life in Kampala. Despite the tightening of Britain's borders, as 1969 drew to a close, my grandfather was able to take my mother to Surrey, where the family had decided she should continue her final years of school. Their British Protected Persons passports were continuing to serve them for now. As my grandmother cried for days at their separation, she couldn't have guessed how soon the family would be reunited.

Across the border, Amin was taking his wives shopping in Kampala's finest department store. Walking through the grand doors of Drapers on Kampala Road, he had little interest in browsing the racks himself. While they flicked through hangers and tried on shoes, picking out the latest trends, in the years before he seized power from Obote, the general would retreat to the offices. There he would sit with the South Asian manager and chat, and the two became friendly, in part due to a mix-up with names that caused

Amin to incorrectly presume his companion was Muslim, like him, not Christian. Amin remembered the manager and when he seized power, invited the family to a presidential state dinner and fundraising event. Any animosity towards South Asians at this point was under wraps. A surprising amount of people I have spoken to have personal anecdotes of interactions like this with the president, who would drop into shops, restaurants and community gatherings, ensuring a very visible leadership, with his six-foot-four height towering over his subjects and dominating the room. Amin was everywhere, omnipotent, but also omnipresent, making his presence known as he toured across the country, often driving himself, to lead public rallies and give rousing speeches. He's been roundly described to me as an imposing figure, who had a propensity to throw you off guard with his humour.

Riding into power in 1971 promising a new era of democracy, the former heavy-weight boxing champion proclaimed, as he would throughout his rule, that he was a 'soldier, not a politician'. Presenting himself as a man of the people, Amin jumped on traffic islands to direct passing cars and stepped up the usual politician's move of kissing babies by throwing them enthusiastically into the air.[33] At the same time, he wasted little time in consolidating his personal power. A week after the coup he had declared himself not only president of Uganda but also commander-in-chief of the armed forces, Uganda army chief of staff, and chief of air staff. Ruling by decree and inflating the role of the military, soldiers were appointed to top posts, and military tribunals were elevated above the civil law system. In the years to come Amin would be known as one of the world's most brutal dictators, synonymous with savagery, and ruthless in his pursuit of personal interests. When Netflix released a series called *How to Become a Tyrant*, it placed Amin alongside Adolf Hitler, Saddam Hussein and Muammar Gaddafi.

A Kakwa man from the north of the country, Amin had long had ties with Britain after being recruited into the King's African Rifles, a British colonial regiment. Having left Islamic school with a patchy level of literacy, he was working at one of Kampala's hotels when he caught the eye of a colonial officer. Military recruiters were looking for men with large physiques for fighting, who had limited education, so as to follow orders without question, and with links to different regions of the country. Amin fitted the bill perfectly. Recruited as an army cook, he became one of Uganda's first Black officers and fifteen years after he was hired, had been promoted to lieutenant. Amin served in Kenya – including in the suppression of the Mau Mau rebellion – Somalia and across Uganda in this time, during which he was implicated in a massacre of the Turkana in northern Kenya. Despite warnings at the time from the governor of Uganda that Amin spelled 'trouble' due to his propensity for violence, Obote nonetheless made him a fixture in the military. Following independence, Amin was promoted first to captain and then progressively through to commander of the armed forces by 1970.[34]

Amin's image today is built on myth and legend, much of which was cultivated during his rule. He was a reporter's dream subject, from fantastically declaring he knew what day he was going to die to embracing a moniker given to him by British newspapers, Big Daddy. Amin awarded himself medals that he wore ostentatiously on his chest and was mostly seen draped in military uniform or safari suits rather than the politician's usual starched wardrobe. He had multiple wives and purportedly more than forty children. He praised Hitler and told a young Jon Snow interviewing him for British television that he agreed with Enoch Powell's drive to prevent the UK's colonisation from the rest of the world.[35] And later, so the stories went, perhaps Uganda's president was even a cannibal, consuming the flesh of his enemies. Truths stranger than fiction mixed with rumours to fuel a cult of personality that only served to strengthen his mystique. Never mind Amin's dreams, these tall tales were the real dream for Western journalists, who poured out copy seen through their post-colonial lens about this seemingly true-to-form African dictator who seemed to be fulfilling every cliché about the Dark Continent.[36]

Bombastic and buoyant, Amin's image preceded him then, and now. His most recent biographer found that there were 'so many layers of fantasy and prejudice in the published and unpublished material on him, that it is often impossible to penetrate beneath them.' Add to this Amin's propensity to switch moods on a dime, and it was hard to ever decipher his true feelings on a matter – something the British Foreign Office dedicated large amounts of time to, with limited success.[37] When French documentary filmmaker Barbet Schroeder asked for access to film the president, Amin played the accordion for the soundtrack, and played up for the cameras, even directing some of the scenes himself. But when the film was released, he took issue with the few critical scenes, including a voiceover insinuating his opponents were being assassinated. Amin dramatically threatened to detain Uganda's French citizens until the film was edited. The director dutifully cut the scenes, but added a subtitle to the documentary – *A Self Portrait* – to indicate its capture through Amin's own gaze.[38] He was so fascinated with his own image that after taking power Amin expanded the official photographic department to document his every move.[39]

More than 70,000 negatives of state photography[*] were found in a filing cabinet in the Uganda Broadcasting Corporation in recent years, offering an incredible insight into how Amin cultivated the image of himself and his state.[40] His public-facing image was in stark contrast to the orders he was giving. As historian Alicia Decker, who has studied gender-based violence and militarism in Uganda, put it, 'Far from the ignorant brute who has been caricatured in literature, music, and film, Amin was a calculating military man who made choices about violence.'[41] The people of Uganda were soon to learn what those choices would be.

When Lata Walter, the daughter of Gujarati traders, was growing up in Jinja, her father had given her strict instructions not to go further away from the house than the end of the street. This imaginary line drew a perimeter around their home and shop in the town lying fifty miles east of Kampala, close to the source of the River Nile. Inquisitive and wilful, she used to go and stand exactly on the denoted line, dipping her toe over into the banned territory, to try and see what would happen if she broke the rules. But danger, it turned out, could cross into her sanctuary. One day in 1972, the twelve-year-old was playing close to the house when she heard the sound of approaching footsteps. Looking up, she saw a collection of soldiers, guns toted, heading in her direction. Tearing into the compound, locking the first gate to the open area behind her, she ran into the house shouting at the top of her lungs. 'I screamed, "They're coming, they're coming,"' she tells me many years later over cups of

---

[*] Thematic selections from this vast archive have been collated by historians Derek Peterson and Richard Vokes in *The Unseen Archives of Idi Amin*, which gives a fresh visual journey through Amin's rule.

steaming tea. 'My dad said, "Who is coming?" I said, "They're coming to get us. These soldiers are coming to get us." He said, "Nobody's coming to get us," and at that point they bashed the door down and came straight in.' Pinning her father against the wall with a gun to his neck, the young men demanded the keys to the property. 'They all had machine guns against him, but my dad refused. He said, "I'm not giving you the keys," and they said, "We'll kill you then."' Lata and her mother stood desperately at the side, crying hysterically and begging him to hand over the keys. Eventually her tearful mother reached into her husband's pocket and took them out herself. The military ransacked the house, and left the family shaken but in one piece. The way in which soldiers had begun flexing their muscles like this, which included walking into Ugandan Asian shops and picking what they liked off the shelves for free, showed the changing tide. And on 1 January 1972, when my family started the new year by taking one of their visiting relatives to a Christian shrine on the outskirts of the city, the Uganda Martyrs Site Namugongo, where they were looking forward to exploring the grounds and saying prayers, they too were stopped by soldiers wielding AK-47s. 'There was a road-block and unloaded guns were doing a rat-a-tat-tat thing,' my uncle Phil remembers. 'I could clearly see that my mother was very worried.' The vocal, emotive one in the relation-ship, it would have been down to her husband to try and calm the situation. Explaining that he was a maths lecturer at a teacher-training college, he was able to appease the rest-less soldiers – educators were such a prized profession they were viewed as next to God, and at this point, still commanded respect.

Aggression had been ratcheting up against South Asians over the past year, but their position in Uganda had been becoming more precarious across the 1960s, before Amin. Then, just as in Kenya, Obote had been taking aim at the capitalist class through Africanisation and his Move to the Left policies, which included attempting to nationalise major industry and take sixty per cent shares in private companies, many of which were owned by South Asians.[42] And when Britain tightened immigration, Uganda wasn't going to watch on silently. Obote's government responded with the Trade Licensing Act in 1969 and then the Ugandan Immigration Act the year after, targeting South Asian non-citizens. The citizenship laws in both Uganda and Britain were 'a vice in which tens of thousands of Asians were squeezed,' says Mahmood Mamdani. After 1968, Ugandan Asian British passport-holders could neither obtain a work permit or trading licence in Uganda, nor gain entry into the United Kingdom.[43] By the end of the following year Obote was laying down his clear intentions to change the make-up of Ugandan society. Ugandan Asians were 'not Ugandan citizens and are not entitled to remain in our country at their own will, or because they cannot be admitted to any other country,' he said. The UK legislation, which now restricted entry to annual quotas of just 1,500 families, had destabilised the implicit understanding that people who had kept British passports could all go to Britain after independence, Bernard Ryan, professor of migration law at the University of Leicester, tells me. 'Obote starts to say, "Hang on, if you aren't going to take people, then we're going to start pushing them out." The 1968 Act, although in many ways it sits in the domestic context in the UK, would prove to be extraordinarily disruptive in Uganda.'[44] The fragilities of citizenship were starting to crystallise, with certainties cracking before people's eyes.

Obote denounced the South Asian population for having 'never shown any commitment to the cause of Uganda or even to Africa,' for focusing on making money and expatriating it abroad. Slightly softening, but retaining his resolve, he added, 'They are, however, human beings and much as they have shown every sign of being rootless in Uganda, we would like their departure not to cause either them or others dear to them, or even ourselves, any human affliction.' The government, he said, would develop systems to reduce South Asians' 'hold on and continued residence in' Uganda.[45] Although Britain marginally increased the number of vouchers it was issuing to Ugandan Asians, it would still have taken around forty years to admit them all through this scheme.[46]

Within his first year of taking power, after a gentle start, Amin was also talking tough on the future of Uganda's South Asians. He ordered a census to count the South Asian population, cancelled all 12,000 unprocessed citizenship applications and warned elders summoned to an Asian Conference that the gap between Africans and South Asians needed to narrow, or disappear.[47] Just as the colonial government had been able to pin ills on South Asians, so too could post-colonial leaders. By this time East Africa as a region was around a decade into its independence, and as Uganda, Kenya and Tanzania built themselves into new nations, there was a desire for new opportunities for all. In many ways the South Asian populations were seen as taking that space. With hindsight, these seem like clear steps in one direction, but at the time, many of Amin's initial actions were taken with a pinch of salt by Ugandan Asians who had heard similar bluster from Obote. While anti-Asian sentiment slowly rose, little else changed in people's lives. But while threats were being made in the South Asians' direction, this hid the extent of the violence the Black Ugandan population was already facing.

*　　*　　*

Duncan Laki was just nine when his father disappeared in 1972. Running home from school for lunch, he saw his cousin waiting outside the house. 'Your father has been taken,' he was told. It would take him years to piece together the puzzle of his father's disappearance.[48] Violent attacks through to abductions and murders are the hidden hallmarks of these years. While the South Asian community remained mostly shielded from deadly violence, the Ugandan population did not. What happened to them is a huge piece of the story of this decade, often tragically lost outside of the country within the myths of Amin and the fate of Uganda's Asians. Amin's greatest crime was against his own people.

After seizing power in the coup, behind closed doors there was barely pause for breath before the killings began. That same day, opposition figures were being bundled into vehicles and men began to disappear. Obote's former minister Basil Bataringaya was a particularly marked man, having been responsible for the attempt to arrest Amin on the eve of the coup. American academic and lecturer at Makerere University, Robert Siedle (of more later) wrote in his diary that he saw Bataringaya being hauled out of the Apollo Hotel – named after Apollo Milton Obote, it would swiftly be rebranded – beaten and driven off on the top of a tank. The desk manager was also detained for the crime of failing to disclose the minister's whereabouts. Personally interrogated by Amin, tortured and detained at Makindye Prison – which would become infamous for extrajudicial killings – Bataringaya was later driven by soldiers in a Jeep to the town of Mbarara for execution. He was decapitated, dismembered and his severed head was impaled on a stick and paraded around town.[49] This was to be a violent military dictatorship, which would result in the death of hundreds of thousands of innocent Ugandans.[50] Dozens of large hawks could at times be seen soaring above the capital the following month. Siedle, aged forty-six, jotted down his recollections of this in his journal, writing, 'How graceful and free they seem floating effortlessly, hardly moving their wings.' In fact, the birds were swooping over the dead and decaying bodies left in the military's wake.[51] As a sixty-year-old market vendor from the outskirts of Kampala later tellingly said, 'During Amin's time, there were not many problems apart from our people disappearing and being killed.'[52]

The dystopian-named State Research Bureau was set up a month after the coup, a military intelligence agency that served as the new regime's secret police. With state-mandated powers to operate without conducting investigations, kill squads moved in on their targets at a moment's notice.[53] Their main offices in Kampala became torture chambers, from which screams could be heard outside their white walls.[54] In stark contrast with the terror, some agents could be easily identified by their flamboyant 1970s fashion, stalking the streets in bellbottom trousers, large dark sunglasses and floral shirts. Protests, such as one at Kampala's main campus, were swiftly met with tanks, teargas and the sound and smell of shots in the air. Amin targeted the intelligentsia, payback for those he felt had treated him as inferior, with academics, lawyers, journalists and artists in the firing line.[55] And beneath the pink stucco Mengo Palace, formerly the royal compound of the Kabaka, concrete bunkers gouged into the mountainside became another house of horror. This hillside outpost had become the army's headquarters in the capital and the cells holding several hundred prisoners apiece became their underground torture chambers, where flooded waters were regularly charged with an electric current, and prisoners were murdered in front of, or within earshot of, their companions. Hammers were often used, to save bullets. If, as in Ugandan folklore, the souls of the dead stay trapped where people lost their lives, then Mengo has a lot of ghosts.[56]

Two decades before the bodies of people killed in the Rwandan genocide washed up on the shores of Lake Victoria, these same waters also hid dark secrets.[57] Amin's security forces were soon killing so many people they took to dumping corpses into the country's waterways, from Lake Victoria to the River Nile. Battered bodies were tipped into three parts of the river; Bujagali Falls, swirling waters where tourists, including myself, later flocked to go white water rafting, Karuma Falls and above the Owen Falls Dam. The latter became so overloaded with the stench of death that it is said the dam employed a full-time boatman to remove the bloated bodies from the river to prevent them blocking the dam.[58] Eventually even the country's waterways and crocodiles couldn't contain the dead, and soldiers instead took to throwing bodies into forests and marshes.[59] With most of the missing being men, it was left to Uganda's women to hunt for lost husbands, fathers and sons. Desperate women travelled between barracks, military prisons and Kampala's notorious Makindye and Luzira Prisons, searching for their loved ones. A whole cottage industry even sprung up around discovering the dead. 'Body-finders' were hired to accompany relatives into the forests and swamps commonly used to dump bodies. In a macabre money-making scheme, many of the body-finders were in daily contact with the murder squads, according to one of Amin's former cabinet ministers. 'If anyone disappears, relatives immediately contact the team and arrange a fee for the tracing of the body,' wrote Henry Kyemba. 'Sometimes news will come directly from the murderers.' The fee varied depending on the social status of the victim, anything from 5,000 to 25,000 shillings, then just under £500 and £2,500.[*][60]

Broken bodies that had evaded death were brought back from the brink in Kampala's emergency rooms, where staff worked to save men, women and children mutilated through beatings and torture. Among the staff was our family friend, surgeon Bob, who had seen a surge in violent injuries since he was woken that night by the militarised coup. 'A lot of the injured people were taken into hospital with horrible bayonet wounds and so on, which we had to repair,' he tells me. 'We used to have clinical meetings in medical school, where you would discuss different cases, and we discussed them in a way which wouldn't get us into trouble, but to try and alert the local people as to what was going on. So someone could do something about it. But of course, they couldn't really do much about it.' State violence was also dealt out to women in the most predictable and devastating way, through rape. Mass rapes took place at university campuses and security agents even commandeered a bus full of nurses, driving them directly to their headquarters for gang assaults.[61] There has always been rape in war, as conflict journalist Christina Lamb has charted in her landmark global study of what war does to women. It's hard to find a conflict without it, where it is used as a weapon, to humiliate and terrorise communities, and to attack rival ethnicities.[62] As the country became more militarised after the coup, women increasingly moved into quieter lives. Rumours of soldier assaults also fuelled fear among South Asian households, and where possible, young women started to be sent out of the country, to India and the UK.

[*] Conversion to pounds based on figures given of $600 to $3,000.

Violence often had an ethnic angle to it. Heavy boots stalked the corridors of Makerere University in the night, kicking down the doors of Langi and Ancholi women's rooms, those groups associated with the former president.[63] Attacks went beyond purges of the military to anyone deemed to be of the wrong background, including children, as Colin Grimes, former deputy headmaster of Jinja Secondary School remembers. A popular, lively school, Jinja Secondary was the biggest day school in East Africa, teaching 2,000 students, a third South Asian and two thirds African. As Amin's troops turned on alleged enemies in nearby Jinja Barracks, where many of the students also stayed with friends, they didn't escape. 'Many of them were targeted during the course of early 1971,' Colin says. 'I was witness to many of these students going missing.' One day, around thirty students came to him begging to have their caution money returned, the thirty-shilling deposits they each paid at the start of the school year to cover any damages to books or equipment. Knowing he didn't have that volume of cash on the school premises, the teacher asked them to return later that afternoon. 'When they came back that afternoon, only three of them were left alive. Two of them we took home in the back of my car and they hid in my garage until night and then disappeared, the other one decided to go off on their own. Their only "crime" was that they belonged to the wrong tribe.'[64]

After the takeover, Amin was busy travelling widely and courting the world's elite, including the Queen.[65] With media attention mostly focused on this boisterous strongman, the darkness enveloping Uganda and the actions of his forces back home remained largely under the radar. It took the disappearance of two Americans, including academic Robert

Siedle, for eyes to start turning towards the troubled waters.*[66]
Robert had arrived in Kampala with his son Edward in June 1969, a month before the first man would step on the moon. Two summers later, a trip with freelance newspaper reporter and heir to a Detroit brewery fortune, Nicholas Stroh, was to be his last. The pair set off on a 150-mile drive north to investigate rumours of a massacre at an army barracks in Mbarara. After they drove away in a pale blue Volkswagen station wagon with a hand-written 'press' sign taped to the windshield, they were never seen again. By late August the White House presumed the pair had been murdered, with Henry Kissinger warning President Nixon not to meet with Amin on this basis.[67]

Tensions were increasingly visible to everyone else too. My uncle Phil, who, despite being only five at the time of the coup, remembers the increased militarisation under Amin. 'Perhaps you don't feel the gravity or the seriousness, the mortal threat of it. But when we were driving around there were army trucks everywhere.' Authoritarianism followed him into the family home too. 'The news was very important in our house,' he says. 'It was a nightly routine and I would see everything that was on it. We saw Amin speaking. I remember seeing executions on television, people being blindfolded, tied to posts, and shot. They showed that on TV.' The regime documented such executions in their official photography.† I've also found clips in a documentary. I watch

---

* 'The international coverage reporting shifts as it becomes more obvious that Amin's government is an exceptionally brutal one,' says Derek Peterson, professor of history and African studies at the University of Michigan.

† Staff Sergeant Arukanjeru Baru was shot in front of more than 10,000 people assembled at the show ground in Tororo in June 1973. It's the only execution imagery that wasn't purged from Amin's archive.

as a figure, his hands tied behind his back, is bound by rope to a thick tree trunk at the ankles and the chest, a hood blocking his view of the firing squad taking aim. Crowds seated on grandstands show this to be a very public execution.[68] Figures vary, especially due to the fact so many people disappeared, but estimates suggest a minimum of 300,000 Ugandans would lose their lives at the hands of the military state during the Amin years. Others put the devastating losses much higher, 800,000, even one million.

Home for my family in Kampala was on the hill of Kololo, pictured in their last year here in 1972.

I grew up hearing stories from my mother Betty about life in Kampala and Simba the Alsatian featured in a starring role.

My mother Betty was the first born, seen here with the proud parents in their first year in Uganda.

Betty's parents split the parenting each day, working half-days and spending the other half at home in their flat.

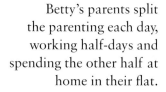

As part of their government contracts, my grandparents were entitled to an annual trip back to India – which sometimes included some sightseeing.

My grandparents, Rachel and Philip, as a young couple, a mix of suits and saris.

As part of his teacher training, Philip went to the UK and took the opportunity to travel through Europe.

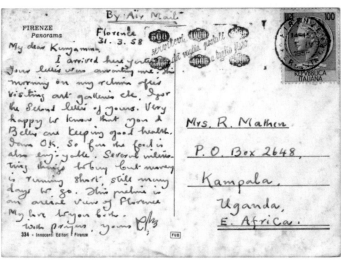

My grandmother sent letters to meet him at each destination, and he returned postcards, here from Florence to Kampala.

Kassam Majothi had worked in business since his early years, and here is seen standing proud at one of his shops in Iganga.

Fatma Majothi at work in their shop, the shelves piled high and jars of sweets on the counter.

South Indian shops lined the streets of Kampala, as documented by photojournalist Mo Amin. Though no relation to his infamous namesake, his name was handy when it came to covering Uganda. When Mo rang Amin's office seeking an interview, he was put straight through by an operator who assumed he was family. The pair built a relationship and Mo would become the only photographer officially allowed in and out of Uganda during the Amin years.

The day that changed everything – General Idi Amin seizing power on 25 January 1971, at the wheel of a jeep flanked by AK-47-wielding soldiers.

In August 1972, a year after the coup, Amin made his declaration – he wanted the Ugandan Asians out.

Kampala became a city of queues. South Asians queued for help outside the British High Commissioner's Office, while the newspapers were splashed with headlines like 'Britain is accused'.

The expulsion was kindling for the far right in Britain, who marched through London to the Home Office protesting against people of colour coming to the country. Here are porters seen leaving Smithfield Market on 24 August 1972, declaring 'Britain for the British'.

But the first arrivals touched down nonetheless on 18 September 1972, taking tentative steps into the new life they hadn't asked for.

The press jostled to get era-defining images of the first planeloads
of expellees as they landed at Stansted Airport, Essex,
on 18 September 1972, following Amin's expulsion decree.

Chapter 4
Ninety Days

My body is the protagonist watched by soldiers
in patrol cars. Roof down, the front windscreen
frames them. Amin's voice bleeds
from a radio wafting up into a window of sky.

Nick Makoha, 'At Gunpoint'[*1]

It was the summer holidays and Kausar was enjoying the
quieter times away from the classroom. Living in the
northern Ugandan town of Gulu, she taught English to a
class of chattering pre-teens at a missionary school. Each
morning, as the sun started to peek around the horizon,
casting a warm glow through the mesh doors of the small
homestead and the mosquito net draped over the bed, she
rose to greet the day. The bungalow she shared with her
brother and sister-in-law was set within the tall brick walls
of the Catholic school's compound, surrounded by land
where they could grow vegetables and mangoes. Close to
the magnificent Murchison Falls, a waterfall set within a
national park teeming with wildlife; in those days, Gulu
was a small place, where everyone knew each other. There
were just a few streets of shops, so it was a simple life, filled
with swimming, playing hockey with the nuns and

---

* Nick Makoha and his mother also fled Amin's Uganda, becoming
part of the Ugandan diaspora. His poetry explores the brutality of the
civil war, the impact of colonialism, exile and longing.

watching English movies on a projector. For anything else, you needed to head to the city. One summer's day a friend invited Kausar to go to Nairobi with her. She threw a few changes of clothes and toiletries in a bag, all you'd need for a weekend, and headed to the train station. Kausar didn't know then that it would be more than twenty years before she saw Gulu again.

The edict came soon after. Ugandan Asians were to leave the country. It was 4 August 1972 and standing on the podium speaking to troops at Tororo Barracks on a bright sunny day, citing his infamous dream, President Idi Amin announced the expulsion of the country's entire South Asian population. Accusing them of being 'bloodsuckers' who were bleeding the country of its wealth, he said, 'I am going to ask Britain to take over responsibility for all Asians in Uganda who are holding British passports because they are sabotaging the economy of the country.'[2] The next day Amin confirmed a ninety-day countdown, followed by a deadline of 8 November. The clock was ticking. This came as a bolt from the blue for many, including Kausar, then aged twenty-two. 'Everybody thought, "What is this madness?" How can you suddenly leave a place where you have lived all your life? It was a very traumatic time, because we didn't know what was going to happen the next day.' Having rushed back to Kampala from Kenya, Kausar's relatives insisted she stay put, lest she encountered trouble on the roads back north. But it seemed so fantastical that tens of thousands of people should leave a country within weeks that most simply didn't believe it. Very few people took the announcement seriously, remembers Mahmood Mamdani, who was living in the capital at the time. 'In fact, people joked about it. Conversation centred around it for an hour or so and then it was all forgotten — but not for long.'[3]

A week later, dressed in his trademark khaki army fatigues, Amin loped onto a small platform, sat down on a plastic chair and cleared his throat. Speaking at an outdoor meeting with the international press, Amin doubled down. Once more accusing South Asians of sabotaging the economy and encouraging corruption, he insisted they were Britain's responsibility, not his. 'Asians have kept themselves apart as a closed community and have refused to integrate with Ugandan Africa,' he thundered. 'Their main interest has been to exploit the economy of Uganda and Ugandan Africans. They have been milking the economy of the country.' In typical performative form, Amin had invited foreign diplomats, including the British high commissioner, to an open-air lunch twinned with the interviews. As the cameras rolled, collecting images that would be scrutinised in Britain, Amin maintained that he wasn't against the British, but it was undeniable that South Asians were in Uganda because of them. If they had only taught Africans the skills needed to build the railways, instead of bringing Indians to East Africa, this whole problem could have been avoided. 'Therefore, the British are responsible for looking after those Asians,' he said. 'I am the best friend of British, and your best friend is the friend who tells you your mistake. And that is what I said – that the responsibility of Asians in Uganda is the responsibility of Great Britain.' Despite gaining its independence, in his eyes Uganda was not yet truly independent, and would only be so after the Ugandan Asians had left.[4]

Amin's direct and unambiguous words sent panic through Whitehall. With Amin's sudden announcement, a long-held fear was turning into a reality, as a legacy of empire caught up with the incumbent government. Only this was on a greater scale and shorter timeframe than the Foreign Office had forecast. In early 1972, Amin had been 'blowing hot and cold on the Asians, sometimes threatening them, sometimes reassuring them that they were welcome to stay in Uganda,' the office's East Africa department had written.[5] Now things had swung unquestionably in the wrong direction. Ever since the Kenyan Asian migration four years earlier, Britain had feared the migratory impact of further political upheaval in East Africa, even going as far as war-gaming evacuation scenarios from the region in the instance that Africanisation led to political violence against British citizens – notably white settlers were classed as 'essential' people to help in this hypothetical emergency planning, versus 'non-essential' South Asians.[6] A new Conservative prime minister, Edward Heath, was now in position and busy with his own domestic troubles, not least of which were crippling coal strikes. Unemployment was also reaching a ten-year high, offering further ammunition to opponents of immigration.[7] Civil servants and embassy staff were tasked with drawing up realistic figures of the numbers of people Amin was talking about 'repatriating', and the cogs started spinning, searching for ways to stop him.

There was pandemonium in parliament, with some MPs suggesting that accepting the Ugandan Asians would set a precedent to other British passport holders in East Africa, or even open the floodgates to any former colony across the world. 'We cannot let in all who had any connection with the British empire, through their parents and grandparents – we just have not got room in this small island,' as a Conservative MP had said at the time of the Kenyan Asian arrivals.[8] Concerns over racial cohesion – otherwise known as the arrival of 'too many' people of colour – and fears about a public outcry during economically challenging times meant the government hoped other nations could be convinced to take on some of the number. Cables were sent to the four corners of the globe hoping to persuade countries as far removed as Japan and America to take part in a humanitarian mission rescuing refugees. Countries with ties to the expellees like Kenya and India had quickly slammed their doors shut, also fearing an influx.[9] Two weeks after the announcement, London was calling its Commonwealth brothers Canada, Australia and New Zealand to pitch in and help with resettlement, and by mid-September, leaders had been in touch with more than fifty governments. The foreign secretary was so desperate he admitted that taking in 'even a token number' would be 'of real help'.[10] Unsurprisingly, despite the frantic flurry of diplomacy, many didn't see why they should be resettling British citizens and responses ranged from muted to flat-out rejection. A Foreign Office memo sent at the end of August noted that Trinidad and Tobago were 'sympathetic but non-committal', but they had some hope 'the Swedes may be shamed into living up to their much-vaunted humanitarian principles'. There had been no response from countries including Yugoslavia, Afghanistan, Nepal, Indonesia and Venezuela.[11] Canada was the first to agree to take a few thousand people, and India would later take in around 10,000, but the offers to take in two hundred by countries like New Zealand and Sweden did little to touch the sides of Westminster's numbers problem.[12]

And so enters the most audacious part of the story, where officials proposed sending East African Asians to remote islands. In the global appeal for assistance, Britain called on island territories to take in Ugandan Asians. But classified cabinet papers from the time released thirty years later revealed that the government also hoped to set up a permanent island territory, like Hong Kong, to deport people to. In the months that followed the expulsion, the government, fearing further arrivals from Kenya, Tanzania and Zambia, launched a secret search for an island to send East African Asians to. British territories considered included the Solomon Islands, Falklands, Seychelles, the Virgin Islands, Caymans, Bermuda, Gibraltar and British Honduras. Most were quickly deemed wildly unsuitable by the Foreign Office – the Solomon Islands were reportedly 'mostly mountain and swamp', and the locals were said to have 'xenophobic tendencies', while the Pacific islands already had unemployment issues. Of the locations considered, only the Falklands offered to take qualified doctors, teachers, artisans, domestic servants and farm workers.[13] Ministers also considered paying off Ugandan Asians with £2,000 to go to India and give up their right to live in Britain. India had agreed to take 10,000 people, conditional on them retaining the right to go to Britain in the future, but the Foreign Office thought once people were there, they'd stay put.[14] It's an extraordinary thing to discover that such schemes were legitimately discussed for people like my grandparents, who had given their all to the British. It was indicative of the desire to abdicate total responsibility for their former colonies.

After several weeks of high stakes negotiations, the desperate diplomatic offensive, and the freezing of a promised £10 million loan to Uganda, the government admitted there was no presentable or workable way of turning away British passport holders. The existing quota system limited the number of arrivals from Uganda each year to 3,000 – a rate that would take twenty years for all Ugandan Asians to be admitted.[15] Having dragged their feet as long as possible while trying to make this a global issue, not simply Britain's – a strategy dubbed 'delay-and-disperse' – the government conceded defeat.[16] Standing next to Amin in Kampala, British envoy Geoffrey Rippon announced that Britain was preparing to receive the exiled. 'The real difficulty is in absorbing large numbers of people in a short period of time,' he said, speaking with a sense of inevitability and appealing to the population's sense of reason.

> But I think the British public accepts that when people have been given United Kingdom passports as a matter of history and have been given assurances by successive British governments that they will honour them if they are expelled, those assurances must be fulfilled.[17]

In Britain, the focus finally turned to the practicalities of bringing tens of thousands of people to the country within a matter of weeks, both in terms of reception and charter flights. There was also work to be done in shifting public opinion – a poll from August showed that just six per cent of respondents believed Ugandan Asians should be immediately settled. The public relations machine swung into gear reiterating the message that Britain was acting on humanitarian grounds to support a refugee emergency, not just as an obligation, and emphasising that the total numbers of arrivals had been reduced by the international efforts.[18] The brutality of the expulsion, paired with Amin's provocative statements, which included praising Hitler, helped shift the perception of Ugandan Asians from immigrants to refugees, and was persuasive in the government's efforts to resettle them in other countries.[19] This was evident in a film made by the London Television Service, the in-house 16mm newsgathering service of the government's Central Office of Information. Asked how many arrivals Britain was now expecting, Home Secretary Robert Carr shared the party line:

The total number of our passport holders who might come if they've all been expelled is, of course, about 50,000. But as a result of all the diplomatic activity which we've been taking and the co-operation we are getting from other countries to offer them other places to go to if they wish, I feel pretty sure the number is going to be very substantially less than that maximum.[20]

Offshoring isn't a new concept to me. Of the two countries I have spent most of my life in, one has a history of it, and one has aspirations. Australia's offshore processing centre in Nauru is infamous, while the UK home secretary has said it is her 'dream' to see an image of a plane taking asylum seekers to Rwanda on the front page of a newspaper.[21] But it still feels like a kick to the gut to discover that, far from the warm welcome and generous response that is often celebrated, the British government first tried to do anything in its power to avoid an ultimately small number of citizens escaping potential violence. My grandparents were directly recruited by the British colonial administration to work in Uganda, whilst living within another colony, and were expelled by a man first given military positions by the colonial rulers. And yet, down the line, the next generation of politicians would try and abdicate so much responsibility for their safety that they would beg all nations of the world to take them in instead and seek to situate people like them on remote islands. When Ugandan Asian stories centre upon gratitude towards Britain for being their salvation in a moment of crisis, it doesn't tell the whole story. We need to pause for thought and remember that if the government could have found a way to avoid their post-colonial responsibility towards the exiled, they would have.

*   *   *

Kampala had become a city of queues. People queued at embassies and immigration offices seeking documentation, visas and, above all, clarity.[22] Long lines wound out of banks, where life savings were under threat, and shelves were stripped bare as panic-buying set in – although not of the usual food staples, but of suitcases. 'Within hours, the shelves were empty,' Kausar remembers. 'People had emptied all the shops and there were no suitcases for us to put our clothes in, only the ones that were at home.' Jewellery shops were also emptied of diamonds and gold as people tried to pour their increasingly worthless local currency into transportable assets, as they would be limited to just £50 (around £540 today) when they left. The accusation that Ugandan Asians had been draining the country by sending money abroad was a central justification of the expulsion order. And certain sectors of the community had been doing their utmost to avoid paying tax, moving their business profits across borders and into foreign bank accounts. It was, in part, a relic of the top-down system under the British that had been designed to extract wealth, not distribute it. Amin was determined that this ended here. This was to be an exodus of people, not cash. Heads of families queued outside the British High Commission, even sleeping there overnight, and when the British embassy opened their doors at the end of August, it was stormed with over 1,000 people pushing their way inside, instead of the two hundred who had been called in advance to attend for processing.[23] 'We decided we needed to really seriously think about where we were going,' remembers Kausar. Her twin brothers didn't want to leave at all and were considering hiding in the countryside until it all 'blew over'. But the rest of her five brothers in Uganda at the time felt it was time to make some serious decisions. 'Everybody eventually decided that we needed to leave now – there was no other way. Everything was being done in a rush because you didn't know what Dada [Amin] would say the next day. One day, he said one thing, the next day, he said something else, so he was very unpredictable.'

Confusion reigned supreme as the daily announcements, broadcast on television and radio, contradicted themselves from one day to another. The *Uganda Argus* splashed the new decrees across the front of the paper. Soon, it was not only British passport holders, but citizens of India, Pakistan and Bangladesh who also had to leave. Then it was all non-citizen South Asians, including Kenyan or Tanzanian passport holders. The following day, professional South Asians could stay. Days later, the exemption clause was revoked. Finally, a government edict confirmed that all 80,000 South Asians in Uganda, citizens or not, had to leave.[*24] All the while, Radio Uganda tolled an ominous countdown before every news bulletin, starting with drumbeats, followed by a voiceover chanting the number of days people had left until the ever-closer deadline of 8 November.[25] The media had become central to Amin's regime, acting as the mouthpiece of the government and allowing decrees to be issued en masse. The problem was that not everyone caught the same updates. 'It all became very tense, because the rules kept changing,' remembers doctor Bob Claxton. 'You would listen to the radio every morning to find out what the rules were. The trouble was, the soldiers didn't always listen to the same things on the radio, so the rules they were implementing were not necessarily the ones that existed. There was a

* The Ugandan government continued to cite the larger figure of 80,000 people, although scholars have suggested that significant numbers of Ugandan Asians had emigrated from Uganda in the years prior to the expulsion order, in part due to Obote's Africanisation policies, making the expellees closer to 50,000.

lot of unrest and military brutality going on.' Some brave voices took a stand against the expulsion, including the president of Makerere University's student union. Responding to Amin, who had gathered students together for a speech, Emmanuel Tumusiime-Mutebile condemned the order and begged the president to reconsider. Shortly after, he was fleeing for his life. After studying in the UK, years later, he would serve as the governor of the Bank of Uganda.

For those without British passports, like Kausar and her family, who were second-generation Ugandan citizens, finding a country to offer them sanctuary was a full-time job. Their Ugandan passports had been rendered worthless. In early August, Amin had ordered citizens to bring their papers in to be checked by the immigration authorities. But on inspection, many documents were deemed to be invalid and instead of being good to go, people had their passports confiscated or torn up before their eyes. Around 10,000 people were made stateless this way.[26] Huge queues snaked in front of embassies, leading some to station diplomats on tables outside of the buildings themselves to deal with more requests. People queued desperately – and, often randomly – to take a leap into the unknown. Potential host countries were bandied about over the dinner table, as if planning a holiday, not the direction of a new life. Kausar's brothers suggested she went to join their mother in Pakistan, but after studying there in recent years, she knew she couldn't cope with the curtailed freedoms her life there would entail. There had been plans for her to marry in Kenya, and one day, while standing at an embassy filling in forms, one of her prospective husband's uncles spotted her and sounded the alarm to her future mother-in-law that her son needed to propose immediately or risk losing her. Things started falling into place quickly. Pulling all the strings they could, Kausar's family sourced a plane ticket through a travel agent they knew. Days later, and just weeks after Amin's initial announcement, she was headed for the airport, still with just her weekend bag packed from Gulu. 'Thank God, nothing happened on the way and we reached the airport very safely,' she says. 'At the airport they were looking very keenly at what sort of stuff we were carrying, and I just had a small suitcase, because I hardly had anything to take anyway.'

When news of the expulsion had broken in Kenya, as in Uganda, it had been met with scepticism. 'I remember exactly where I was in Nairobi the moment the newspaper came out,' says lawyer Mohamed Keshavjee. After a night at the cinema, he and his friends had decamped to the Hilton coffee shop across the road from his legal offices. 'A friend of mine came in and threw the paper on the table and said, "This guy is mad, he wants people to leave in 90 days," and then they started laughing. It was a moment of incredulity. Nobody believed anything serious was going to happen. Nobody lost sleep over it.' South Asians in East Africa at the time had an 'exaggerated understanding of the criticality of their position in the economic situation,' he adds, which convinced them that no one would throw them out. If it came to it, surely there would be a gradual phasing out of South Asian influence, not a sudden expulsion. As Amin issued differing missives, it did little to shore up believability. But with each passing day, worrying accounts started coming across the border too. 'We started hearing horror stories and started to see that maybe something more serious was happening here,' Mohamed says. 'Stories of disappearances and killings hit the Indian community. It was very frightening. A psychosis of fear emerged, so people in Kenya also started leaving.'

As people fleeing Uganda began arriving in Kenya, some Indian passport holders went straight to Mombasa by train to take an expatriation boat to India, while others headed to Nairobi's airport for onward flights to Europe. Soon issues arose with people staying overnight at airports or being arrested for being in the country illegally. While others in the South Asian community took sandwiches to people at the airports, a group of Ismaili businessmen asked Mohamed to put his legal expertise to work. One man, who ran one of the capital's supermarkets, gave him a wad of cash to keep on his person and use for bail and any other legal requirements. 'I consistently had about £1,000 (20,000 shillings) in my pocket, to go to the courts and help people,' says Mohamed. One night an ex-Ugandan attorney turned up at Mohamed's home with his family, having fled for his life. Seeing 'the difficulty a Black man of his calibre was having,' brought the reality of the situation into sharp relief, says Mohamed. 'He said, "Don't live in this country, get out, look at this predicament, you can imagine what will happen to you."' While people remained reassured that their president was unlikely to act in such an extreme way, the mood had shifted. 'It was a feeling that our time was coming to a close,' says Mohamed. 'People didn't have that same cosiness they'd had in the past, that their lives were going to be secure. We never belonged to the country, it never embraced us. Yes, it gave us a right of passage, it gave us salvage, but it didn't give us belonging.' Bound for that very country, leaving her siblings behind, Kausar looked down at Uganda with tears in her eyes. 'I can still remember the feeling when I looked out of the plane window at the beautiful little islands on Lake Victoria,' she says. 'I was thinking, "Oh my God, is this going to be the last time I see this place?" Because it was a wonderful place. We loved being there.'

Much has been made of why Amin really decided to throw Ugandan Asians out of the country. Was it purely spontaneous, or was it, as rumours abounded, because he had once been turned down by an Indian woman, and couldn't bear the personal sleight? These are the twin tales that accompany the expulsion – that Amin either acted on a whim, on a night's dream, or that in his fury at being rejected by the daughter of one of the wealthiest Ugandan Asians, who had refused to marry him, he had retaliated against the entire population.[27] This rejection being the final affront, demonstrating irreconcilable differences, that the South Asians were truly unwilling to mix with Ugandan society.

They're fantastic stories, now almost lore, and are regularly retold by the community.[†] But despite the shock of the announcement, and the tabloid headlines in London screaming, 'He's nuts!', the expulsion had a natural and longstanding precursor in Obote's Africanisation policies and its roots in Uganda's colonisation itself.[28] 'We are determined to make the ordinary Ugandan master of his own destiny and, above all, to see that he enjoys the wealth of his country,' Amin said, following the language Obote had set out three years earlier. 'Our deliberate policy is to transfer the economic control of Uganda into the hands of Ugandans, for the first time in our country's history.'[29] He called this his War of Economic Independence.[30] Amin's words to Britain were framed tightly around decolonising his country, with South Asians viewed as agents of empire. As English foreign correspondent Christopher Munnion, who

---

[*] It was rumoured that Amin proposed to a widowed member of the Madhvani family. Asked about it by a reporter in 1989, she simply smiled and said, 'Some people said it was so'.

[†] When interviewing people in Uganda, Aneeth Kaur Hundle often heard a 'set genre of rumours about Idi Amin', namely his dream compelling him to expel the South Asian population, and being spurned by a Ugandan Asian.

himself was arrested at gunpoint and incarcerated for four days before being deported around the time of the expulsion, wrote:

> since independence, the writing has been on the wall for the Asians in Africa . . . the general, often on record as wanting to teach 'British imperialism a lesson', has sat back cheerfully to watch his bombshell of coloured immigration explode on the British domestic political scene.[31]

As well as being part of the politics of decolonisation, the expulsion also sat within the complex framework of international law. In September the Ugandan Mission to the UN suggested Britain's Commonwealth Immigrants Act 1968 was the original sin Amin had just replicated.[32]

As September rolled around, the queues on Parliament Avenue had become a permanent fixture, as people jostled with one another for the best shot at a safe future. When delegations from countries like Canada and Australia arrived, families and groups of friends split up, each holding places in different queues to see which would pay off. Futures could come down to pure chance. Meanwhile ice cream trucks and soft-drinks stalls were doing a roaring trade, *The Times* reported, catering to those tied up in the endless bureaucracy of obtaining a route out of Uganda. People in the crowds bought peanuts from nearby vendors as they juggled piles of paperwork, waving pink, yellow and blue forms. At Entebbe Airport people were being thoroughly searched and a sign warned that 'not a single Ugandan shilling' should be taken out of the country. After waiting more than a month, the first flight to Britain would take off on 18 September 1972. Despite the fact their passengers had little choice in the matter, the flights on BOAC, British Caledonian and East African Airways weren't free – people had to pay for their own air fares. Those who couldn't were subsidised by those better off, or signed an agreement to repay the cost later.[33] The departing crowds were restricted to twenty kilograms of personal baggage, although some unaccompanied luggage could also be sent, and one ring, one watch, two bangles, one necklace and one pair of earrings.[34] In reality, most people were being relieved of visible valuables long before they got to the airport, at the many roadblocks that now dotted the country. As well as the permitted £50, the exiled were only allowed to take what they could carry in two bags.[35] Around half had some money in European banks, but the rest were now penniless.[36] Some went to great lengths to conceal what they could to get any capital out of the country. This ranged from filling teddy bears with jewellery, stripping the insides out of suitcases to line them with money and baking diamonds into fried foods. A shoemaker even made himself a custom pair of shoes with around £1,000 sewn into each sole, stitched between the leather.[37] One particularly enterprising family had their gold smuggled out of the country in the pipes of an oil tanker bound for Nairobi. A less successful ploy came from a woman who was navigating Entebbe Airport with a plaster cast on her arm, giving a convincing impression of having broken it, until she accidentally picked up a suitcase. When soldiers cut the cast open, they found her arm encircled with gold bangles.[38]

For those still in any doubt about their future prospects in the country, the arrest of one of the country's most well-known South Asian businessmen showed Amin was serious. Manubhai Madhvani was thrown into Makindye Prison for twenty-one days, where he found the walls scrawled with graffiti, plastered with newspaper cuttings of detainees and peppered with bullet holes and blood. He had taken over leadership of the family business from his father, commercial pioneer Muljibhai, and would have been seen as untouchable until his arrest. Manubhai would later say he thought his detention was entirely designed to threaten the wider population.[39] 'If the head of Uganda's biggest industrial combine, employing more than 15,000 people and manufacturing all sorts of products from steel to sugar could be arrested,' he posited, 'what hope for the ordinary clerk in a government office, or trader selling soap and sugar out at his "duka" in the bush?'[40] For most people preoccupied with the mechanics of the expulsion, detention had been far from their minds. But there was, by now, a sizeable prison population of mostly Black Ugandans, and the arrest of a high-profile member of the business community added another layer to worst-case scenario fears.

Arriving in Entebbe into this atmosphere of fear was a seemingly unlikely visitor – a butcher from a London market, who shortly before had been marching against the prospect of the Ugandan Asian arrivals. At the end of August, four hundred of the 2,500 men who worked at London's Smithfield Meat Market preparing cuts of meat took to the streets protesting against what they deemed to be an invasion on the horizon. Enoch Powell, who had almost a year earlier been declaring that 'Asian immigration was more dangerous than Black Power', had spoken out forcefully against accepting anyone from Uganda, and the porters waved signs declaring 'Enoch was right', along with chanting derogatory slogans, including 'if they're Black, send them back'. The prospect of tens of thousands of Brown people entering the UK was kindling for the far-right National Front and their vocal anti-immigration views, who waved thick, fabric Union Jack flags and carried banners declaring 'Britain for the British', calling not just for the end of immigration, but for repatriation.

Some passers-by gave Nazi salutes. The impassioned condemnation of the exiled from these East End butchers drew attention, and days after a second march of Smithfield workers, producers of Granada's (ITV) *World in Action* current affairs programme made an offer to one of the fiercest anti-immigration voices in the market. Shop steward Wally Murrell, who had spat hate from under his moustache when interviewed, stating, 'I'm not a racialist, but I think everybody has got a certain amount of racialism in them,' was given a simple challenge – go to Uganda and see the situation for yourself. Wally accepted the unusual offer and was soon out of his white butcher's garb, into a short-sleeved shirt and boarding a flight from the East End to East Africa.

Reflecting later, producer David Bolton said the documentary had been 'immensely risky' as there was no guarantee Wally would change his mind and they 'didn't really want to end up with a film that was a party-political broadcast for the National Front.'[41] Touching down in Entebbe, Wally immediately noted the poverty around him, before settling into Kampala. Ever the market trader, he headed to the central market square to start speaking to people on all sides of the debate. The level of fear soon became clear, as was the general reticence from anyone to talk about politics. Joining the throngs queueing at the Canadian embassy, he asked people what they'll be leaving behind – soon recognising that people would hardly be leaving engineering workshops, thriving shops and expansive farms behind by choice. These experiences 'made Wally recognise that the whole thing was much more complex than he had realised,' says David. The team were in Kampala for just three days before the government ordered them out, but it was enough to have made a strong impression on Wally. 'When we were out of the country and we got him to Nairobi airport and sat him down, I still had no idea of how he might sum up his time there. But that's when the warmth of his humanity came out,' says David.[42] 'After talking to these people and finding out exactly what is going on out there, I feel sure in my own mind, that if nobody accepted these people – and they have got British passports – then there would be a mass slaughter out there,' Wally told the camera, with a reflective demeanour totally altered from the defensive, swaggering one of just days earlier. 'I would help these people the same as I would help anybody, because I'm a human being, and that's how human beings should treat one another.'[43] His volte-face horrified many of his colleagues and he received a barrage of abusive phone calls after the broadcast. But Wally said that on his first day back at work, many others came up to him to say they respected him for what he'd done.[44]

This incredible transformation speaks to the strength of seeing things for yourself. We can read news and see footage, but for those unwilling to believe things that challenge their world views, perhaps it's in witnessing something first-hand that viewpoints can really shift. History unfolding elsewhere can feel very far away until you're a part of it. More than anything, Wally's experience shows the power of human connection. Once Ugandan Asians became real people in front of him, with families, homes and livelihoods, rather than faceless numbers to project fears onto, his softening was almost immediate. If everyone could see migrants as individuals like this, with hopes and dreams and fears like themselves, the world could look very different.

While the British government was busy handwringing over logistics for its passport holders, there remained the question of those who had given up theirs to take on local citizenship. With their Ugandan passports not worth the paper they were printed on, and Britain denying any responsibility for them, they were now stateless. It's remarkable Britain was able to hold firm on this, says Leicester University's Bernard Ryan. 'The stateless had not flown out of the sky in Uganda. They were British at some point. They made the pro-integration choice, and Britain punished them for this.'[45] Some were able to fulfil the stringent immigration requirements to travel straight on to countries like Canada, but several thousand were left needing assistance. The 8 November deadline applied to them too, but in order to leave Uganda they first needed valid travel documents, a country offering temporary asylum and passage there. Conversations had begun in Europe over United Nations involvement, but it was a delicate affair, due to the complex legal statuses of Ugandan Asians, the importance of not appearing to be picking up Britain's slack and the need to keep a dialogue open with Amin. By stalling proceedings until the last week of October, when most of the British and Indian passport holders had already left, the UNHCR was able to confirm that the 4–5,000 people left were not covered by any other scheme, so they could step in and grant them refugee status.[*46] Towards the end of October, a UN delegation travelled to Kampala and an emergency evacuation operation was launched. Winston Prattley, Resident Representative of the United Nations Development Programme, would head it up and be one of the story's unsung heroes.[47]

Richard Jackson had been living in Kampala for three years by this point, working in the geography department at

---

* UNHCR had to grant the stateless refugee status – a requirement for UNHCR's involvement according to its statute and the 1951 Refugee Convention – before they had crossed any borders, which was legally challenging. The delay allowed them to confirm the need and justify the rescue mission.

Makerere University. One morning, he got a call from Prattley, who he'd only met a few weeks earlier at a wedding, asking if he could pitch in with the evacuation efforts. As a lecturer, Richard had time around managing his students, so headed downtown to find their temporary office, next to East African Airways' office, already a hive of activity. Soon the twenty-seven-year-old was manning the doors and doing the initial vetting. 'My first and main job was simple and rather sadistic – I had to ask all arrivals as they came in, "Do you have a passport?"' he tells me over the phone. 'I was under strict instructions not to prompt an answer. I could see the poor people trying to guess what the "right" answer was.' The right answer, of course, was no, as the UN could only help those who were stateless, which was the official line Richard repeated. 'They drew the obvious conclusion, which was to throw their passports away and come back again. Word got passed around very quickly that there's this strange guy who interviews you, and you must never pass. After the first two days, I didn't even have to say anything, people just came in and said, "I haven't got a passport."'

Once approved, people were issued with travel documents by the International Committee of the Red Cross (ICRC) and could head next door to the pop-up airline office to arrange their tickets.[48] Despite the circumstances, these flights weren't free. 'That upset me, to think that you're being deported, but you've got to pay for your own airline ticket,' says Richard. 'Everybody in Uganda also knew the small shopkeeper from Lira or West Nile on his way to Kampala had all his money with him. They were sitting targets.' Despite the limitations on taking cash and valuables out of the country, people were naturally trying to smuggle more than their allotted £50 out with them. When it came to paying for flights, cheques could be drawn up from the

UNHCR bank account for those in need, and Richard recalls clever manoeuvres by his boss to maximise their cash, but much of the financial support came from the wider Ugandan Asian community. Ugandan shillings, after all, had become worthless beyond the borders, and people weren't allowed to take local currency with them. Meanwhile money exchanges in Kampala were refusing to change shillings into any other currency. 'In other words, it didn't matter how much money you had, it was worthless as a deportee,' says Richard. 'Nobody was accepting it, and you couldn't change it into anything.' For several weeks no one could send any mail because of this, he remembers, as enterprising people had realised Ugandan stamps were legal tender in neighbouring countries and had emptied the post offices of this substitute currency. 'People would come in with suitcases full of money,' says Richard. 'It was common for people to hand over large suitcases at the desk four or five times a day. They would say, "This is no use to me, use it to buy tickets for my poorer fellow deportees." I spent several nights at my kitchen table counting out literally millions of Ugandan shillings.' The twenty million shillings they received one day took until 5 a.m. the next day to count. As well as handing over cash, people also dropped off the keys to their cars, to the point that Richard's boss had to hire space to store all the Mercedes that had been donated for sale to fund the evacuation flights. Others donated their fleets to their Black friends, or took the more symbolic step of driving themselves to Entebbe and pouring chemicals into their petrol tanks to render them useless to anyone else, rows of abandoned, sabotaged cars left as a parting gift to the country throwing them out.

The UN mission sent planes to Austria, Belgium, Italy, Malta and Spain, five of the seven countries that had answered the high commissioner for refugees' plea for support. By the time they were nearing the end of their remit, with just days until the deadline, those still in Kampala were a cast of characters, Richard remembers, including some who'd hoped to ride out the storm but had been discovered. They included shopkeepers from remote regions like Karamoja and even an elderly ex-elephant hunter. The final planeload was gathered in a community centre, where they had been staying, and where Richard's wife Anne had been volunteering. 'They were packing their meagre possessions when in strode Idi himself,' says Richard. 'He explained to my wife that he wanted to meet everybody and to shake hands with the last Asians to leave.' To their credit, no one refused, and all lined up politely to shake Amin's hand. Then he asked Anne where they were flying to, who informed him it was Morocco. 'I nearly burst into laughter because it was a perfect double take,' Richard remembers. 'It took him fifteen seconds to register. And then suddenly he turned, with a very different expression, and said, "No, Morocco is in Africa, they cannot stay in Africa."' Amin stormed out, and Richard frantically passed the message back to his superiors. They would now head to Spain. The ex-elephant hunter was overjoyed at the thought of watching a bullfight.

If you were coming from outside of the capital, you had the added challenge of navigating countless roadblocks on the way to Kampala. Noorbegum, or Noori, who was aged ten at the time, remembers being stopped as her family made their way from Fort Portal, a town in the far west of Uganda, close to the Rwenzori Mountains that divide the country from the Democratic Republic of the Congo. 'The soldiers told us to get out of the car and strip,' she tells me over a video call from Fort Portal, where she's on her first visit back after fifty years. 'My dad was doing some serious talking with them and showing them that we didn't have anything of value. We could easily have been shot, but he managed to persuade them that we didn't have anything.' Her older sisters had been searched, but thankfully, as hoped, they'd left little Noori alone, because she was hiding a secret. 'I had a dress on, and my mother had taken some of the gold and tucked it so tight on me that nobody could see it. Luckily, they didn't look at me. As a child, you've got a sense that the adults are really anxious, but you don't know why. It was traumatic and frightening.'

Across the other side of the country, shopkeeper and merchant Kassam Majothi was watching more and more of his friends and neighbours pack up as the deadline approached. Shelves were left full of books and wardrobes with salwar kameez, as they crammed only their smallest and most beloved items into suitcases. Some were going to try their luck at customs and packed their cars full of additional boxes, tied up with string, although nothing was guaranteed. But Kassam wasn't planning to leave. Aside from the fact that he loved his life in Iganga, where he ran mixed goods shops, how could he leave the two hundred people relying on him for their livelihoods? Besides, he knew Amin and much of the military well enough to feel like things might just be okay. The family helped others travel to Entebbe, hiring a minibus so people could travel in groups and better protect themselves and their scant belongings. Kassam took on a shepherding role, acting as a liaison with the troops to ensure safe passage across the four-hour drive south. 'My dad knew how to bribe the soldiers,' his son Abdul, now seventy, tells me from his office in Bristol one morning. 'Otherwise, even if it was raining, they would open your suitcase on the road and take whatever they liked, because they knew the Asians were leaving. Soldiers would rob jewellery and cameras and clothes. They didn't care. And Amin was letting it happen.'

One day Abdul accompanied his father to drop off an auntie at the airport for her departure. Some additional flights were now being put on at the cargo side of the terminal, unfamiliar to their driver, who was used to dropping people at the usual passenger departure gates. As they tried to find their way out of the airport compound, they realised they were lost. Passing an army barrack, they were pulled over. This time, Kassam's charm was lost on the soldiers. 'They took the three of us in, my dad, the driver and myself, and made us take our clothes off and lie on the floor,' says Abdul. 'They said they were going to shoot us.' Stripped almost naked and lying face down on the dusty floor, Abdul tried to catch his breath and stay as still as possible. It seemed inconceivable that just moments earlier they had been bidding farewell to their friend and planning what to eat for lunch. Incredibly, fate intervened when one of the soldiers recognised Kassam, who was a well-known figure in the west Ugandan community and beyond. 'He told the others, "You don't know this man, he's very famous in the village and he's done so much for us. He's helped everybody, even my mother." When the soldiers heard that Amin knew my dad, they let us go.' Grabbing their clothes, they stumbled back to the car and sped away, their hearts in their mouths. The long road back to Iganga was passed in silence, each lost in their thoughts, knowing they were lucky to have got out unscathed. They could no longer stay. Kassam's status had protected him this time, but his luck was unlikely to hold much longer. His family was at risk. When they got home, he pulled Abdul aside in private and told him that they would have to make their own journey to the airport.

'There were seven days left before the deadline, so we

planned to leave within twenty-four hours,' he says. 'My dad said, "We don't want anybody to know. Let's keep it very quiet and pack up and leave." We started packing at midnight until six in the morning, while everyone else in the house was asleep."' Sneaking under the cover of darkness with just a small light on, in secret from the house staff they were all incredibly close to, felt heart-wrenching. But if the staff had discovered their intentions, they might have tried to stop them leaving, because they would be losing their jobs. 'My father was a Ugandan citizen and got on well with Amin, so he thought he'd be fine,' says Abdul. 'Until those last seven days, one of Amin's ministers said, "We can't protect you anymore." My dad never wanted to leave because he was a true African at heart.' On their final day, a soldier visited the house to blackmail Kassam, threatening to reveal the family's impending departure. With the threat of violence still fresh in his mind and fearing the worst for his wife Fatma and their children, Kassam was forced to pay him off, losing the last of his cash. And so, the evening came when the family quietly stole downstairs, with the children under strict instructions not to breathe a word, and into their waiting car. The two eldest children, Anwar and Mumtaz, would remain in Kenya, where they had been when the border with Uganda was closed. The rest of the family rolled down the driveway, the warm night breeze through the window brushing against their flushed cheeks as they said goodbye to the lives they had known.

With just two days left until his deadline, Amin appeared to be feeling buoyant in a meeting with the acting British high commissioner. Pronouncing that within a few months everyone would see the success of the expulsion, which Amin maintained wasn't racist, but simply 'Ugandanisation', he also heaped praise on Britain. Far from wanting a schism from the country, as his actions might have suggested, Amin said that he hoped to visit London again and might write to the Queen and prime minister suggesting as much. In a telex to the Foreign and Commonwealth Office, the surprised diplomat noted, 'He would like to split a bottle of champagne with the prime minister and if the population threw eggs at him he would not mind,' adding incredulously, 'It seemed as if he was proposing a state visit!'[49]

While Amin was contemplating fantastical trips abroad, in Kololo, my grandparents had been taking stock of the ever-changing situation they now found themselves in. Working in the education sector, there was slightly less urgency for them to leave, as these were protected positions that the government had realised would take time to replace. My grandfather in particular, now in a senior position helping train the next generation of educators, did not have to adhere to the November cut-off for departures. With their British Protected Persons passports, they would be able to travel to the UK, where my mother was studying for her A-levels. She'd visited in 1972, but had to go back when, as my grandmother put it, 'the trouble was looming'. In the turmoil descending over the city on seven hills, they thought they would try Canada first. Some close family friends and former colleagues had already emigrated from Uganda to Ottowa, Ontario, so a door there seemed open. My aunt remembers lots of phone calls and hushed conversations as decisions were made. Canada wasn't coming together. 'Luckily it wasn't the only option,' my mother Betty recalls. 'The options were the UK or Canada, and then the UK happened, and so that's what we did. I'm forever grateful for the family who supported us, because it was just circumstance that allowed us to come here.' Their church in Uganda had a missionary connection with a church in Cambridge, and my family was one of two who were linked to the UK. This meant they would have someone waiting to greet them at the airport, a lifeline amid the chaos. The first of their two flights were booked for 13 November, with my grandfather moving out of the family home and in with the principal to complete another month's work before following them abroad. It was a tearful goodbye to the palm-tree-lined home the children had grown up in, their housekeeper Petro who had become like family, and their dogs. Hearing that soldiers were preventing women from leaving with multiple items of jewellery, such as the traditional Indian bangles that line your arms, my grandmother carefully glued sets of thin gold bracelets together, creating one piece out of many. Her beloved books, saris and countless memories were left behind the closed door.

The vast majority of South Asian families experienced some form of violence or at least intimidation in those last weeks and days in Uganda. Many drop it into conversation so casually that it catches you by surprise – a sudden mention of seeing their father held by the scruff of his neck by soldiers, being forced to empty their pockets and strip the watch off their wrist at gunpoint or facing beatings and mock executions. For my grandmother, aunt and uncle, the journey to Entebbe driving by convoy was thankfully without further trauma. But over the dinner table years later, my grandma once dropped her own casual mention when she said, 'People tried to poison Appacha twice once we had left.' With a start, I asked what she was talking about. After dining under the branches of a huge and ancient tree in the gardens of one of Kampala's leading hotels one evening in November, as a treat from the principal my grandfather had later become very ill, vomiting late into the night. The only South Asian at the dinner table, and the only one ill despite them eating the same food. Brushing it off as food poisoning, he later stayed there for a few more days, when he suffered even worse illness. Dehydrated and barely able to move, he was found by Petro, who helped him to a friend's house for rehabilitation. There's no way of knowing if it was coincidence or something more sinister, but it's a story repeated by other people in their last days. Sentiment had turned strongly against the South Asian population and those left were being pressed to get out. Soon, my grandfather would follow his family to the airport to board a plane. His, like all Ugandan Asians', was a one-way ticket.

Part II

EXODUS

Chapter 5

Stradishall to Somerset

*History was catching up with England. The colonial child
had come to the motherland. And he had brought with him
England's colonial past. Past had become present.*
            Mahmood Mamdani, *From Citizen to Refugee*[1]

Circling down over London, Hamida Sumar pressed her
face against the cool glass of the aeroplane window and
peeked at the new life unfurling beneath the clouds below.
The bright green hills had been replaced by grey skies as she
looked down over flat fields, and bright lights. Fourteen and
on a plane for the very first time, she was bursting with
excitement; her parents' faces, meanwhile, carried more
worries etched in their furrowed brows. It was 2 November
1972, and just six days before Amin's final deadline for
departures – after which he had threatened everything from
camp detention through to unspecified escalation of violence
– the Majothi family were some of the last people to flee the
country they called home.

Speaking to me above a shop in a bustling street in the
suburb of Easton in Bristol, Hamida, now 64, beamed
beneath her headscarf at the memory of her journey. 'I was
excited, believe me. I was young, so I didn't realise where we
were going or how we would do things, I was just excited to
come to the UK.' Far from fearing the unknown, her mind
was filled with idyllic images of the country gleaned from
films, as well as from postcards sent back to her by friends

from Uganda who had moved to Britain earlier. These told seemingly magical tales of ice skating, snow and roaring fires. It would take several more days for reality to bite. Although she could sense her father's nerves, Hamida remained optimistic. 'I thought it would be okay – we'd manage somehow,' she says. 'I didn't give it deep thought.' It's a sentiment echoed by many people I've spoken to, where the journey was fun for the children, who were kept largely protected from the fears held by their terrified parents. But taxiing on the tarmac, heads were often bowed in prayer. As the planes' wheels lifted off, passengers broke out in cheers of relief at knowing they were heading to safety.[2] Others only relaxed once they were sure they'd cleared Ugandan airspace.[3] For Hamida and other children, the journey itself was the adventure, full of the new experiences of being airborne; running down the aisles and into their seats; squeezing each other's hands as their stomachs flipped as air pockets bobbed below them; eating their first food at 35,000 feet and being fussed over by everyone around them. 'I was over the moon when I went on the plane,' laughs Hamida. 'And the air hostesses were so good to us. They spoiled us, because we were kids and going through all that. So, it was a nice experience for me.'

For her elder brother Abdul, who was seventeen, excitement also reigned supreme over pragmatism. 'I'd always thought I wanted to visit England one day, and here I was actually going there – but not realising that I'm going as a refugee.' Stepping onto the tarmac at Stansted Airport, the setting sun allowed the winter chill to descend over them, marking the distance they'd travelled from the equator, and the impracticality of their associated wardrobes. 'You're thrilled to see you're in a new country, but the cold was hitting, not having the right clothing,' recalls Hamida's younger brother Rashid, who was eight at the time. Shivering in their linen and cotton layers, passengers were met by groups of volunteers who were now well-practised at dressing the arrivals, sizing people up by eye and pulling selections from the piles of donated winter wear stacked high in a room adjoining the runway. It was another first for the family. 'They gave us coats, which we had never had in our lives,' says Hamida. 'A nice warm coat. They were second-hand, but it didn't matter to us. It was just lovely to be here. I'll be honest, I was excited.'

Their arrival came almost two months after the first specially chartered flight carrying Ugandan Asian expellees touched down in Essex. Black and white photos of these initial arrivals have become the defining images of the exodus. Families are seen walking off a plane, standing in lines on the tarmac at Stansted Airport, holding small bags, or even briefcases, with all that remained of their material lives packed inside. Met by swarms of reporters and television crews, passengers told tales of high-octane journeys out of Kampala and of robberies. Kassem Osman, who arrived with his wife, two brothers and their families, told the BBC they had been stopped by soldiers seven times on the way to the airport and held at gunpoint. Another arrival, a retired government clerk, reported his losses of a gold watch taken off his wrist and 'every piece of Ugandan money stolen from my wallet.'[4]

Since Britain's begrudging acceptance of their passport holders, preparations had begun to receive the incoming passengers. At the helm of this was the Uganda Resettlement Board, which was set up in late August as a collaboration between the Home Office, Department of Environment and the Ministry of Defence. At its most basic, its remit, as described to parliament, was to 'plan the smooth and orderly reception of those who need to come to Britain and to ensure the widest possible dispersal throughout the country.'[5] The first of hundreds of evacuation flights from Entebbe landed at Stansted at 9.30 a.m. on 18 September, a watershed moment given the handwringing over the past months. The 193 refugees on board were greeted personally by the chairman of the Resettlement Board, Sir Charles Cunningham, a Dundee native who had worked his way up the Scottish ranks and through Westminster, where he was formerly permanent under-secretary of state at the Home Office. Some flights were also greeted by protestors waving placards telling the arrivals to go back to where they had come from. Britain faced an airlift of around 35,000 Ugandan Asians with British nationality, who had to fly at a rate of seven hundred a day to meet Amin's deadline.[6] Speaking in the Commons a month later, Home Secretary Robert Carr confirmed that nearly 15,000 refugees had come since that initial flight, 8,500 of whom were being sheltered by the Uganda Resettlement Board in eleven sites.[7]

When Cunningham was tasked with running the Board, he had just days to get a team mobilised. He turned to those he trusted, including people he'd worked with at the Home Office. Alan Critchley remembers his late father Tom's enthusiasm at being asked by his friend to join the resettlement mission as director. The pair would share responsibility for the operations and direction of the Board. 'He'd had a job he hated before that, so when he was asked if he would mind being director, he jumped at it,' Alan, a trustee of the India Overseas Trust, tells me over the phone. 'My father was an idealist, he wanted to change the world. This was one of those things where you could actually do some good.' Many of the rest of the hastily assembled team were made up of retired army members and, somewhat ironically, ex-colonial service officers who had been posted in India. Over the year and a half of the Board's activities, Alan hardly saw his father, who was flat out with the vast scale of the project. One Saturday, Alan accompanied his dad to the Board's bustling office overlooking the Thames and Vauxhall Bridge, curious to see what was going on. Full of people, and with the phones ringing non-stop, the office walls were covered with boards displaying flight arrival times and listing how many people were in each camp. 'It looks as if the Uganda Resettlement Board started work on 23 August and the first camps were open ready to receive people from the first flight on 18 September,' says Alan. 'So in terms of getting everything ready in three to four weeks, it was an extraordinary achievement.'

For families, the face of the Board came in the form of the volunteer reception teams who greeted them on arrival, checking their welfare and ushering them onto buses heading off into the night. Ugandan Asians who had come to the UK earlier under the voucher system also pitched in with reception work and interpreting at camps. For those with relatives or friends to collect them, journeys were simpler – but for the tens of thousands rendered not only stateless, but entirely homeless, temporary accommodation beckoned. While those on the first flight were taken to a disused RAF base at Stradishall in Suffolk, the main reception centre due to its proximity to the airport, the Majothis had a longer journey ahead of them. After the Board realised many more people would be arriving than expected without onwards travel arranged, their mission was rapidly expanded.[8] Of the 193 passengers on that initial flight, 101 had nowhere to go on arrival, giving an indication of the task ahead. The exodus had caused a schism in the usual migratory pattern from

East Africa, where the head of the family would usually travel first to get things set up for their wives and children. The Board needed to pivot from offering brief transit stops of a night or two to facilitating longer-term accommodation while families found their feet.⁹ Local resident Alan Cordy recalled the surprise he felt at seeing streams of people in brightly coloured clothes at Stradishall. Driving past the base the seventeen-year-old saw 'so many displaced people. They looked lost. They were lost, weren't they, at the end of the day? It's stayed with me.'¹⁰ Between September and November, as Stradishall started bursting at the seams, fifteen further camps opened. At the peak in early November, just over 13,000 people would be housed across all sixteen.¹¹ Somerset was home to two of them – Houndstone in Yeovil and Doniford in Minehead.

Driving into the night, leaving the lights of London behind and heading west down the M4, the five Majothi children gazed wide-eyed into the dark, winding through country roads to Minehead. After some twenty-four hours travelling by car, plane and coach, siblings Abdul, Saleem, Yunas, Hamida and Rashid arrived at Doniford. A former RAF site set along the west coast of England, fierce winds cut in across the Atlantic and fog regularly descended over the camp. The arrivals were to be housed in former barracks, white wooden buildings on stilts, which had been partitioned off inside to house multiple families, with a capacity of over 1,100. Reporting from nearby Houndstone, a journalist described the registration process and medical checks while showing images of the arrivals disembarking from coaches. 'One major problem facing the Asians is the drastic change in climate. One of the busiest places on the camp is that hand-ing out warm clothing, and, of course, a few sweets for the children.'¹² It was a dramatic change of circumstances for the arrivals used to their own homes, including those who had lived a luxurious middle-class lifestyle in Africa, and now found themselves in draughty, damp cabins.

The idea of refugee camps in Britain can seem incongruous, something found outside of these shores. But British refugee camps have housed hundreds of thousands of people across the twentieth century, says Jordanna Bailkin. From Jewish, Polish and Hungarian arrivals through to the Ugandan Asians and later Vietnamese refugees, camps have been dotted across the length and breadth of the country, ranging from 'holiday chalets and concrete bunkers' to 'military bases, prisons and stately homes.'[13] All sixteen of the camps used for Ugandan Asian arrivals were former army and air force bases, from Faldingworth in Lincolnshire, through to Kensington Barracks in central London and Tonfanau in far-west Wales, accommodating from 250 people at smaller sites up to 1,500.[14] There is a certain irony that Ugandan Asians, having been threatened by Amin with internment in camps on military sites from Nakaseke to Kambamba if they failed to comply with his order to leave, ended up in military environments in Britain. The differences, of course, were significant – these were not places of detainment, rather of sheltered accommodation. Still, these weren't holiday camps.

Minehead was a far cry from the rolling green hills surrounding Kampala or the white sands and crystal-clear waters of the Mombasa coast the family had been used to visiting. As swirls of snow dusted the cabins they now called home, the children ran outside and just about froze solid, having never experienced something so cold before. The family would occasionally venture out of the camp to explore the local area, and Abdul remembers his 'we're not in Kansas anymore' moment as the family stood on the rocky coastline, looking out over churning grey waters and choppy waves. 'We looked at the beach with the pebbles and all the muck on it and I thought, "No, this isn't like Mombasa or Zanzibar."' A photograph of the extended family standing on the desolate beach is one of their first taken in England. The children took the change in their stride, but it was undoubtedly daunting for their older relatives. Back in camp, independence and entrepreneurism had been replaced with communal living and handouts. 'It took a while to hit because I was young, I was carefree, I didn't have any responsibilities,' says Hamida. 'But it hit me that our lives have changed forever.' For her father, who had been something like a mayor in their town and always played host, the shift to queueing for food and wearing second-hand clothes, while trying to plan how to feed eight mouths, was stark. 'It was quite a blow for him,' says Abdul. 'But he took it in a good way.' The younger children were shielded from the extremities of the experience by their older siblings, parents, aunts and uncles. The fears adults had around navigating their new environment, as well as seeking to arrange housing and future security for their families, could be overwhelming.

Winter in Watchet might have been a world away from temperate Uganda, but the Majothi family, at least, had each other. Twelve-year-old Lata, who had faced the threatening soldiers back in Jinja, arrived with her two older brothers, but without her parents. Britain took in thousands of people expelled by Amin, but only those with British passports. Those who had sacrificed theirs to take up Ugandan citizenship, such as Lata's father, for better business ties, integration, or simply due to a sense of fraternity, found the door firmly closed. With passport holders let in and those without refused entry, hundreds of families, like Lata's, were split. In an agonising decision, her parents decided to send their youngest three children to the UK, in the hopes of a better education, while they temporarily travelled to India to settle Lata's older sisters and then figure out how to get her father into Britain. According to her parents' parting instructions, Lata and her brothers, aged fourteen and sixteen, would be met at the airport by family friends. Except, after stepping onto the tarmac, clutching their bags containing all their worldly possessions, no one was there. Looking around the arrivals hall, asking officials and fellow passengers, the children were at a loss. Whoever was supposed to collect them at Stansted never came. The three unaccompanied minors were now stranded in a foreign country, with no means of communication with their parents. All they had was each other.

'I don't know how long it was before my parents found out we weren't with those people,' Lata, a mother of two and support worker, told me from her home just fifteen miles from where she was first settled in the UK. 'Because communication then was useless. I wrote hundreds of letters to my family, but to this day, I don't know if they ever received them in India. I remember writing every week, but thinking back now, I never got a response.' Offering a fresh challenge to airport reception staff, the abandoned children were eventually placed onto a bus bound for the West Country. 'I didn't want to come here, and I hated it. We had no knowledge of where we were going or what Britain was going to be like. My parents packed a suitcase of summer clothes, which is all we knew in Africa. We came in October freezing to death because none of us had any knowledge. It was a big culture shock.' Without guardians, Lata and her siblings were largely left to fend for themselves at Doniford, with little help from the camp community. 'Because we didn't have parents, we'd get up and have to walk two and a half miles to school without breakfast and things like that,' she remembers. 'A lot of the aunties would come to you and ask, "Is there anything you need?" But I suppose you were in that situation where you're looking after your own and anybody else is probably a little bit of a burden. They were only just surviving within their own families.'

The issue of divided families became one of the pressing contemporary challenges surrounding the Ugandan Asian 'problem', tabled as questions in the Commons and the subject of numerous contemporary news reports. United Nations' estimates suggested that the number of people in Europe – from camps through to hostels and other temporary accommodation – with family in Britain numbered around 2,000 at the end of 1972.[15] Watching news reports and documentaries from the time shows the unfavourable view many had towards those seeking repatriation to join their families. For parts of the population, who had only just tolerated the British passport holders, those without them were a step too far. A ripped magazine tacked onto a bulletin board at Greenham Common to greet arrivals showed how important the question of citizenship had become to the public narrative at the time. 'Welcome, British passport holders,' the page of the *Economist* magazine read:

We know many of you didn't really want to leave your homes and jobs in Uganda. You know we didn't really want you to come before because we have problems with homes and jobs here. But most of us believe that this is a country that can use your skills and energies. We have worked out plans about how you should start and where you should go. They won't be perfect but they will help. You will find that we, like other countries, have our bullies and misfits. We are particularly sorry about those of our politicians who are trying to use your troubles for their own ends. And we're glad your British passport means something again.[16]

For those without them, the mood remained hostile. By vox-popping Brits on the streets about the fate of the split families, a BBC *This Week* reporter elicited the kinds of anti-immigration responses that we continue to hear today. 'See to our own people first and then we can see to the outsiders,' says one woman, with short grey hair and a leopard print scarf. An elderly man with a short grey moustache, spect-acles, and a tweed jacket and trilby accepts that some people should be allowed in on humanitarian grounds, but adds, 'You must have the numbers restricted, mustn't you? They're flooding the place, aren't they? Every town you go to.' Some agree you shouldn't split up families, while an older woman with a coiffed grey bob and a red and navy silk scarf tied above her grey coat concedes, 'I suppose we've let some in, we'd better let the others in,' before adding, 'But by and large we've far too many people here. Bursting at the seams.' For Lata, the challenges around defining who qualified to enter the UK meant it would be four years before the family were reunited in Leicester. 'Towards the end, everybody had gone, and the camp was almost empty,' she remembers, having spent six months at Doniford, during which time she had watched hundreds of families set off to new cities. She was then taken into a children's home in Minehead with her younger brother, while her eldest – then classed as an adult – was separated from them and taken to a hostel. Today, she doesn't remember how these pivotal decisions about her future were made. 'To be honest, I don't think the camp was even geared up to wanting us, let alone having to deal with kids who have no parents.'

The split families were the government's last stand, a red

line they were unwilling to cross in their determination to show that the British welcome did have limits and they weren't taking everyone in. Having insisted that current citizenship determined who received charity, those who had reneged on their British passports were simply someone else's problem. This nit-picking over small numbers of people, whose admission into the country would still have kept the total number of Ugandan Asian arrivals well below the original estimates, caused lasting damage to families like Lata's for little reason, other than making a point.

Across the country, wooden billets were now filled with families, from the elderly women congregated around bunks boiling pans of chai to the youngsters sending cricket balls flying outside. Tired, wood-panelled military buildings were taking on a new life. These camps were more than just practical housing solutions – they helped sculpt multicultural Britain as part of a 'larger project of social engineering', says Bailkin. 'From the state's perspective, camps offered a unique opportunity to shape racial and ethnic patterns of settlement. Under the guise of "resettlement", camps allowed the state to imagine the ideal map of multicultural Britain.'[17] For the government, a dispersal policy was at the heart of the ideal map, in which large South Asian communities did not develop in specific areas, but instead people were distributed evenly across Britain. The aim of the Resettlement Board was to house, process and spread people around the country. Under-secretary of state for the Home Department David Lane summarised the mission as achieving the 'maximum of dispersal and the maximum of employment, with the minimum effect on our social services.'[18] In effect, in official eyes, the expellees remained a problem to be brushed under the carpet as quickly as possible. The lord chancellor said it in so many words, telling the House of Commons that the government was 'determined to honour this country's obligation to accept those United Kingdom citizens who may be expelled from Uganda, but we are also determined to do all that is possible to reduce the scale of the problem to a minimum.'[19]

The camps, like so many things in the migration space, were largely a volunteer effort. The Home Office bore ultimate responsibility, but over sixty voluntary organisations including the Women's Royal Voluntary Service (WRVS), the Red Cross, St John Ambulance and the Society of Friends were the boots on the ground. The Citizens Advice Bureau also assisted with interviewing and documenting the new members of the workforce.[20] From young idealists through to seasoned WRVS matrons in their uniforms and local villagers, a wide-reaching volunteer movement assembled to meet the needs of the arrivals. This was no accident, but part of the government's attempt to win a tricky PR war. The Board had the unenviable task of rehousing thousands of people quickly and in a low-profile and low-cost manner. They needed, writes historian Becky Taylor, to simultaneously ensure the 'rapid and successful resettlement' of a diverse group of people 'while not being seen to offer them more favourable treatment than that received by the wider British population.'[21]

Placing volunteers front and centre of the reception and resettlement programme helped create an impression that Ugandan Asians had been taken in on humanitarian grounds, not due to any post-colonial responsibility. As well as demonstrably reducing staffing costs, this also showed a 'groundswell of public support,' says Taylor, and rebutted media criticisms that the expellees were relying on social security or the taxpayer.[22] Thousands of volunteers became the backbone of the operation, found standing on the tarmac welcoming bleary-eyed arrivals off planes, working as baggage handlers and running reception centres at the airports, through to taking up telephone operator positions and arranging transport to camps. Within the camps themselves, they worked with the arrivals on everything from health and nutrition to jobs and housing, while Gujarati-speaking volunteers became crucial interpreters for those, usually from the older generation, without English who had little understanding of their current circumstances.*[23] Ex-army chiefs and the odd civil servant aside, everything was almost entirely led by the volunteers, remembers Nancy Edwards, who volunteered at Stradishall with the Community Service Volunteers when she was eighteen. 'It had been hoped that the Ugandan Asians weren't going to arrive at all, until the last minute,' she says. 'Many of the day-to-day things, even the departures office initially, was run by volunteers. Bearing all that in mind, it was amazing it worked.'[24]

At Stradishall a school was set up in the hangars for the youngsters to continue basic English and maths, often using BBC Education Programmes to help structure the growing classes. On a Friday, head teacher Roger Sheridan had no pupils, the following Monday eighty, and that Friday 1,200 – with just three staff.[25] Young volunteers at Heathfield in Honiton remember being dressed up in saris and having photos taken together, laughing within the tangle of precious fabric saved from Uganda. Their grandmothers were busy knitting and unpicking clothes to remake for the cold

---

* While significant numbers of younger arrivals spoke English, it wasn't the same for the older generation. In a 1974 survey, the Commission for Racial Equality found that forty-five per cent of Ugandan Asians couldn't speak English and fifty-four per cent were caring for the elderly and sick.

arrivals.[26] Cultural exchanges also included introductions to Bollywood films and curries, and in some cases beautiful, lifelong friendships developed between volunteers and guests, who would go to one another's weddings and exchange Christmas presents in years to come.[27] Not everything, however, was rosy within the volunteer movement. I've heard of older men taking advantage of underage girls, grooming them within the parameters of offering care, as is so often the case during humanitarian crises. Chandrika Keshavlal, who was fourteen when she landed in Tonfanau in Wales, from their home in Iganga, recalls the 'inappropriateness' of one of the men working in the housing office. 'I can still see him in front of my eyes, a very colonial, older gentleman,' she says. 'I stood there with my father, the old English gentleman said in Hindi, "She's such a beautiful girl." But it was said in a way . . . I could see the embarrassment on my father's face and I felt the remark was inappropriate. So those kinds of things were maybe sometimes present which people probably don't talk about.'

The experience of camp life varied widely depending on what social support people had within family units or friendships, and how long their stays were. For some, the billets served as the temporary stops that had first been envisioned, days or weeks while rentals were organised or relatives were tracked down. But for others, these former barracks would take on a more permanent feel. Although 5,000 offers of private housing were made for Ugandan Asians, inspections by the WVRS found many to be unusable, either due to poor condition, or the limited time they were being offered for.[28] Councils offered up houses with varied levels of enthusiasm, some of which were not enticing prospects to families who would rather stick with the known challenges of camp life than the unknown ones of relocating to seemingly distant

places. A year and a half after the first evacuation flight
landed, five of the original sixteen centres would still be
open, housing over 3,300 people. People with additional
needs – from large families to the elderly and people with
disabilities – often took the longest time to relocate.[29] When
it seemed like the camps would be home for weeks and
months rather than days, people started doing their best to
make them feel like home, starting with the food.

The Majothis had gone from a charmed life just weeks earlier
in Uganda to communal living, including queueing up to
receive their rations. Food brings people together, but at
Doniford, it was in a very different way to home. In Iganga,
the door was always open, with friends, family and tradesmen
dropping by to talk business, politics and make plans. Kassam
was a generous host and no one would leave without joining
him for tea, snacks or, more usually, dinner seated around a
low circular table laden with chai, samosas and bhajis. Now,
he joined hundreds of men, women and children as they filed
to the mess hall to receive provisions handed out by another
state for him. Lining up to get rations in a metal tin was an
adjustment. 'They were good to us, but we had never queued
up to get food before,' says Hamida. Camp food could be
both a reminder of what people had lost, and a way to bridge
divides brought by exile and sustain fractured identities and
cultures. At Stradishall, the first Ugandan Asians were greeted
with a large Indian lunch, with attempts at cultural sensitivity
represented in over-boiled and under-spiced curries. Mealtimes
could be long affairs as camp canteens struggled to cope with
the large numbers they needed to cater for. Staggered meals
and shifts were introduced, but residents were still often left
queueing outside in the cold.

Catering was perhaps doomed to fail from the outset,

reported journalists at the time, when the Uganda Resettlement Board hired Royal Navy cooks for some camps and handed them a book of Indian recipes.[30] At Doniford, despite some of their chefs studying in an Indian restaurant to get some vital pointers on diversifying the menu, the 1970s cuisine could have used some improvement. The curry powder mixed into the baked beans was a valiant effort at cohesion but more generally English food proved tough to stomach, with the pork regularly featured on the menu off limits for the Muslims, and the beef equally problematic for Hindus.[31] It was an issue replicated across the resettlement infrastructure, with a resident at another camp writing a note to staff pleading: 'Please it is of inconvenience to Muslims the serving of pork and of inconvenience [to Hindus] the serving of cow meat. If possible, could these be eliminated. Instead chicken, goat or mutton meat would serve both these communities very well.'[32] Over time, the Royal Navy was out and a London catering firm, Taylorplan, was in, although problems remained. Newbury residents threatened hunger strikes over the food and the segregation of the camp's inhabitants and volunteers in the canteen. Similar issues at Greenham Common led the *Telegraph* to describe the situation as 'a form of apartheid'.[33] By the end of 1972, residents of Stradishall had circulated a petition protesting about the poor quality of their food, which included asking to access the kitchen to check nothing was being mixed with beef or pork and for higher quality rice to be served. The results were positive – two South Asian food advisors were appointed, along with the introduction of halal meat, Indian pickles and chutneys, fresh fruit and salad.[34] Mayur Seta, who was seven at the time, remembers his mother asking the manager's permission to cook their own Indian food at Stradishall, and the masala they were able to eat afterwards.[35]

Officially, camp rules didn't allow Ugandan Asians to cook their own food, but in practice, it became common for residents to take over sections of the catering or at least bring additional, authentic food into camp. At Tonfanau, just north of Aberystwyth in Wales, two brothers opened a shop to sell Indian spices. Another local businessman would sell food to camp residents from his van, spawning underground cooking that eventually led to each resident receiving £5 to buy their own electric hotplates. The chance to cook for themselves, or at least customise meals, restored a sense of independence to many families. 'We were getting sausages, mashed potato and gravy. Boiled vegetables. We weren't used to it,' recalls Abdul with something of a recoil even today. 'We said, "Look, this is not the food we eat." So, they let us do what we can.' His enterprising father clubbed together with others on site and would travel to Leicester to buy Indian spices and food to cater on site – returning to his roots that had seen him cater to the Ugandan elite at events, through feeding several hundred people at the camp. They were not the only family to step in to help with food preparation at scale. At Honiton, in Devon, the resident's committee met with camp leaders and asked to take over the kitchen. Outings to Exeter to buy spices and food, along with Indians in the kitchen, led to a boost in dining experiences and morale. The staff didn't always get it wrong though – catering manager Charles Buckett at West Malling was renowned for his originality. As well as catering to Indian tastes, he showcased some of the diversity of the British Isles, including plating up a traditional Scottish meal of haggis to entice Ugandan Asians to resettle in Scotland. It's not clear whether this proved successful.[36]

When it came to relocation, the official dispersal policy was built upon a deep desire to avoid so-called ghettoisation.

Ugandan Asians were told of green areas in Britain where they should consider settling, versus red areas that were deemed to be stress areas 'at capacity' when it came to immigrants, having already fulfilled any arbitrary quota of Black and Brown faces. Demonstrating the lack of racial sensitivity by those in Whitehall who dreamed up these distinctions, red and green zones were originally called black and white zones. It took the intervention of the chairman of the Community Relations Commission and South Asian leaders to drop the very on-the-nose naming in favour of traffic light colours.[37] Red zones included Leicester, Birmingham, Bradford, Huddersfield, Wolverhampton and inner London, as well as a range of outer London boroughs. The Board could only persuade, not direct, people away from areas they deemed inappropriate for settlement. Part of this persuasion included publicising information highlighting the purported difficulties they could encounter in certain (red) parts of the country, parliament heard. Reception teams were to 'emphasise the advantages of settling in the parts of the country in which social facilities are under least pressure.'[38]

Ranchhod Bhadeshia, aged forty, had left his metal and woodwork business in Masaka when a soldier came to his house waving a gun. He and his wife, three children, his parents and his grandmother packed and fled within twenty-four hours. At Heathrow he was shown a map, presumably to indicate where he wanted to go. Speaking no English, aside from the words 'yes' and 'no', the family were instead ushered onto a bus, arriving somewhere under the cover of darkness. Ranchhod told of his shock in the morning at discovering themselves at Greenham Common resettlement camp. 'We had come from a country where everywhere were soldiers. And everywhere we looked were soldiers still.' That increasingly familiar map of Britain was presented once more, with a suggestion that Scotland was nice. Remembering a friend mentioning the cold in Scotland, this was met with a firm 'no'. Two months later they were settled in a formerly condemned council house in Cheltenham, a green town that isolated them from other South Asian families and was without a Hindu temple.[39]

The very location of the resettlement camps, which were dotted around the countryside far from metropolitan centres, represented dispersal in action, although the majority of people naturally ended up moving to cities when job opportunities arose. By the time the Uganda Resettlement Board wrote its final report, it had placed people in more than 340 local authority areas. Lane told the Commons that 'if it had not been for the dispersal policy the numbers going to the stress areas would have been significantly greater.'[40] When the Board was dissolved at the end of January 1974, the total number of arrivals who had passed through their services stood at 28,608. Of this, 6,621 made their own arrangements for accommodation and settling when they arrived, meaning almost 22,000 people were accommodated, for varying lengths of time, at resettlement centres. Around half left the camps under their own arrangements, and the comparatively small number of 8,429 were resettled by the Board directly, including in 1,793 houses provided by local authorities and 2,437 in private accommodation. Reception and resettlement had cost £6.1million.[41] Those involved went on to other jobs or volunteering roles, without as much reflection as Alan thinks they deserved. 'I just don't think people realise how big a thing it was,' he says. By 9 November – Amin's cut-off date – 419 flights had brought 27,194 Ugandan Asians to Britain.[42] Doniford would close in March 1973, and by May just five of the sixteen centres remained open

– Hemswell and Faldingworth in Lincolnshire, Greenham Common in Berkshire, West Mailing in Kent and Gaydon in Warwickshire.

On a busy single-lane arterial road leading into the centre of Cambridge, after slowing my car for the traffic camera, I always almost subconsciously continue to brake as I pass a row of otherwise unremarkable terraced houses. It's here, on Newmarket Road, where my family landed after their exit from Entebbe. Just eighty miles southwest of the South Asian hub of Leicester, they were in the university town of Cambridge. The phone calls, meetings and late-night strategising had led them to the spires of King's College, the punts dotting the River Cam and the streams of bicycles challenging pedestrians for every inch of pavement. While they didn't have any connections in the UK aside from my mother, who was already studying here, they had their faith, and, on this occasion, it had come good. Through the church and friends in Kampala, they were one of two families for whom homestays had been arranged via one of Cambridge's most historic churches, the Round Church, built in 1130. This meant that when my grandmother and young aunt and uncle landed, they had people waiting to greet them, and they were one of the fortunate families not to need the services of the resettlement camp system. They were welcomed into an English family's village home, before a Methodist church offered them a more permanent and independent set-up in a currently unused home. They were handed the keys to this fully furnished home on Newmarket Road, with everything they needed to start over, down to the knives and forks in the drawers, thanks to the generosity of strangers. 'To leave a house with your silver cutlery in it for somebody you have never met, that is an example of truly helping somebody,' my mother says. One of my mother's childhood friends, who was in India at the time of expulsion, had four nail-biting weeks of silence before she received a letter from England informing her that her parents were safe. They were the other family who settled in Cambridge through the church and were accommodated in the grounds of a local private school. The comparably privileged expulsion experience that my grandparents had given them the chance to use the energy saved on logistics to launch straight into finding employment and getting their kids into school. My grandparents' experience as teachers gave them transferable skills, even if they had to take several steps down the ladder. Instead of teaching university students and at teacher-training colleges, my grandfather was now in a boys' comprehensive. But they felt British, and in many ways were. My aunt surprised her classmates with her British accent on her first day at Cambridgeshire High School, and they began settling into their new surrounds.

For the Majothis, the draughty wood and corrugated iron billets of Doniford were home for four long winter months. Attempts were made to resettle them far away in Scotland, or in Liverpool, but Kassam, like so many, preferred to head to Leicester to join extended family and the wider South Asian community. On his visits to pick up elusive Indian spices to bring down south, he'd even got as far as securing premises, but fate intervened when his children were taken on a day trip to Bristol, the closest city to the camp. After touring the streets, dreamily window-shopping all manner of clothes, toys and bicycles, the group were taken to see one of the region's highlights, a brutalist structure known as the New Bristol Centre. Opened in 1966, it brought entertainment to the heart of the city, and crucially, a rare ice rink. 'To actually see frozen ice, in a building, somewhere in the middle of the city, I couldn't figure it out,' says Abdul. 'I thought you only did it in Norway or Scandinavia, so it was exciting.' It was here that the older children 'fell in love with Bristol', says Hamida. Like the postcards of snowy scenes, replete with robins and mistletoe, which had helped colour her view of Britain, ice skating held a similarly rosy image in her mind. 'I'd never seen an ice rink in real life. I'd only seen them in the films and TV back home. When I saw that, I just couldn't get over it. And we thought, "We have to be here, and we have to learn how to do it." ' Returning to their parents, the children enthused about the lights of the big city and begged to be allowed to live there. Incredibly, it was enough to swing it. 'Our father just gave in, because we'd been through a lot, he thought, at a young age, having been uprooted and having to come here and all that,' says Hamida. 'So, he was just happy where we were happy.' It was another twist of fate that would change the course of the family's lives.

Chapter 6
White Australia to Amish Country

We wanderers, ever seeking the lonelier way, begin no day where we have ended another day; and no sunrise finds us where sunset left us. Even while the earth sleeps we travel. We are the seeds of the tenacious plant, and it is in our ripeness and our fullness of heart that we are given to the wind and are scattered.

Kahlil Gibran, *The Farewell*[1]

Kausar had always loved animals. Along with the regular household dogs and cats, her lively family home had been filled with more unusual guests. As a youngster, her uncle, who was a farmer and a hunter in the Ugandan countryside, would bring her back the exotic pets only possible in an African childhood. A vervet monkey that would sit on her shoulder and bounce across the furniture. A baby deer that would drink eight pints of milk a day and be waiting inside the house for her when she came rushing home from school to see him. But none would ever compare to Sheru – the lion in her living room.

Landing in Nairobi on 27 August 1972, carrying just her small weekend bag, Kausar approached the immigration desk cautiously, fearful of being turned away, or worse, detained. Fortune was shining on her though, and she was met with a sympathetic guard. 'He said, "We should think about the plight of the Asians, it's not a very nice thing that's happening. I'm going to put a visa for six months,"' recalls

Kausar. 'What a relief – my God, I got out. I couldn't believe that I was in another country and I was fine.' Meeting up with her fiancé's family, she let her brothers back home know she'd made it safely. They would head off on their own journeys, but Kausar wouldn't know until much later where they were going, because of their limited means of communication – a common feature of the exodus. 'We were all in shock at what had happened because we were second generation citizens,' says Kausar. 'We thought that was our country and we never thought we would be asked to leave. But then this happened, and we just hoped everybody would be safe wherever they were going. My brothers and I lost touch for quite some time, until they got settled and wrote to me.' It would be thirteen years before she would see them again. Three days after arriving in Kenya, Kausar married Ishtiaq, ending her citizenship insecurity and turning the page onto a new chapter of her life. 'From my childhood I had been very fond of animals, so it was the best thing that I got married to a wildlife vet,' she laughs.

When she wasn't teaching, her husband's work in Kenya's renowned wildlife parks – which saw him driving Land Cruisers over the bumpy, grassy paths winding their way across the plains – allowed him to take Kausar, and later their two daughters, to many of the country's finest lodges and national parks. They went with him to watch giraffes and rhinos being relocated, first darted and falling to the ground, and then re-emerging wide-eyed in their new parklands. From the plains of the Masai Mara to the foothills of Mount Kenya, they watched herds of wildebeest migrating, elephants' silhouettes swaying across the setting sun and bush-camped to the sounds of the savannah. Alongside their dogs and cat, back home there was also a ready supply of rescued wildlife to look after, injured or orphaned. 'We always had animals at home,' says Kausar. 'We had a monkey, a baby ostrich and cheetahs.' And then there was the little lion cub.

A nearby wildlife centre was home for the animals that couldn't be released back into the wild. Orphans lived out their days in sunny enclosures, with a stream of eager visitors. One afternoon during half term, Kausar and her daughters were visiting when a young lioness went into labour, and they watched on as she brought her three cubs into the world at the same time as the skies opened in the mother of all rainstorms. The smallest was stillborn, but a girl and a boy writhed around, searching for milk and teats to knead at. But the mother, exhausted from the labour, lay immobile in the rain. The rangers ran their hands through their hair as they watched her cubs getting increasingly desperate and cold in the gathering water, while the lioness refused to let them suckle. Kausar begged her husband to let them help. 'I said, "They're not going to feed because they're just a few hours old, and the mother is refusing to look after them. They're going to die. Please can I have them, bring them home for a few weeks?"' The female cub didn't make it, but Kausar's dedicated hand-rearing, which included soaking bandages in milk and pressing them into the other youngster's mouth, saved the last cub. 'I named him Sheru, because in Urdu it means little lion,' she says. 'This little Sheru was a mighty fighter.'

And so began the Born Free idyll. Alongside three dogs, a cat and a monkey, there was now a lion cub running through the yard and house like he owned it. 'He thought he was a dog, because he would put a stick in his mouth,' says Kausar, as we sit on her leather sofa underneath a painting of a lion and its cub hanging on the wall. Sheru also chewed shoes like a puppy as he scampered around their front steps. 'He would lie down and want to be cuddled. We had a lovely time with him.' They tried to teach him to hunt rabbits at home, but he would only play with them, and then go and sit in the corner and ignore his would-be prey. As Sheru grew progressively bigger and stronger, it was becoming harder to handle him. He didn't hurt anyone, but he was very playful, and both his claws and his innate strength were increasingly risky. And so, the time came to return Sheru to the orphanage where he had been born. When they visited him at weekends, he would smell their scent in the air from the gates and start roaring for them. At first, Kausar could go into his cage to cuddle him, but it took some explaining to other visitors, so Ishtiaq decided they should stop. 'But there was a little hole in the cage next door, and they did not put any animals in that enclosure,' remembers Kausar. 'We would put our hands in through the opening, Sheru would come and he would lick your fingers. He had become very tame.'

Kausar and her husband would spend twenty years together in Kenya before the wind of change blew them to the UK. Ishtiaq had a British passport, and Kausar had gained the equivalent through marriage. Two years after Sheru was rehomed in the orphanage, in 1991, they made their last big move to Birmingham, where they would tell friends about the time they raised a lion cub. Today, their house still speaks of memories of Africa, and while their photo albums show nothing from Uganda – those images just some of the many things lost to the exodus – the animals of Kenya are there as memories of an extraordinary life. Kausar's family was just one of thousands that had split. While she had remained in Africa, her brothers were now as far afield as Canada, Pakistan and Austria. This one family was emblematic of the incredible geographic reach of the schism opened up by the exodus.

* * *

There are currently 281 million people who live in a country other than the one in which they were born. It's a figure that's been growing rapidly over the years and is over three times the equivalent number from 1970. That's one in thirty people.[2] But it doesn't show the descendants of former migrants, the diaspora, whose identity and sense of belonging have been in some way shaped by their migratory background or experience. There would be billions, but no attempts to measure global diasporic populations have been made.[3] I'm part of the global Ugandan Asian diaspora, as someone who identifies with a homeland, or really, several, but lives outside of them. They can be places you weren't born in or haven't even been to, as long as you feel some kind of connection to them.[4]

The way Britain responded to Amin's expulsion created a global diaspora of Ugandan Asians. As well as following a dispersal policy inside Britain, the government also did so internationally. From the first moments of the expulsion order, the government's diplomatic offensive had seen frantic appeals made around the Commonwealth and beyond, asking countries to resettle some of Britain's impending responsibility. Some would answer the call swiftly, some slowly, and others not at all. When the expulsion order was made, all eyes turned to India. Just as market trader Wally Murrell in Kampala had asked one turbaned man why he wasn't considering going to India or Pakistan over Britain – to which he answered, 'Well we are British, we have to go to Britain with you. Because we are holding a British passport.' – so many presumed that Ugandan Asians would return to 'where they came from'.[5] But as this Sikh farmer explained, the majority of Ugandan Asians didn't have Indian or Pakistani citizenship – they had British passports. Many had never seen India with their own eyes. The connection was

generational, historic and certainly not one involving a feeling of 'home'. India was very mindful of all of this. Ever
since the potential migration of East African Asians had
reached the international consciousness with the Kenyan
exodus in the late 1960s, Britain had been trying to push
them in India's direction. However, the Indian government
was aware East African Asians were Britain's responsibility,
not theirs, under international law.[6]

The battle over citizenship between these countries is an
interesting one, says Ria Kapoor, historian at Queen Mary
University, who is exploring Ugandan Asian histories,
largely because both countries had the same concerns.
'India has a very concrete reason for not wanting this to
become an automatic recourse to citizenship based on
ethnicity,' she tells me one afternoon during a gap between
lectures and tutorials. 'And Britain has much the same
reason. Because what do you do about Fiji? What do you do
about the Caribbean? What do you do about pretty much all
of the rest of the world?' With the Indian diaspora moved
through the empire spanning every corner of the globe, the
country wanted to be just as careful as Britain. 'Papers are
what matter and ethnicity is not how you define citizenship,'
says Kapoor, which she says is consistent with India's citizenship laws following Partition. 'It's based on which
nationality you have chosen to become on paper, and I think
that's a really interesting confrontation that's going on with
the end of empire.' Britain appealed to Prime Minister
Indira Gandhi, and debate raged among Indian politicians,
but softened once they were sure the UK wasn't trying to
deny taking in any of the Ugandan Asians. India sent Air
India flights and ships from Bombay to Mombasa to collect
their passport holders, and their high commission in
Kampala eventually started accepting requests from

non-citizens to also move to India permanently. India would go on to play an important role in taking in both British passport holders and refugees.[7]

From the end of 1972 and over the coming years, people would move to places as far flung as Norway and New Zealand, Pakistan and America, Belgium and Iran.[8] The twice-migrants from India and Uganda had become thrice-migrants, or maybe more, as they navigated their way around the globe further in search of home. Some moved off the back of Britain's dispersal tactics, others because, in closing their own borders to family members without British passports, the UK had left people stranded in countries they might later call home. In other cases, personal ties or, more often than not, moments of pure spontaneity, would lead people to new shores. While the UK would end up with the largest diaspora, from the initial arrivals of around 13,000 in India, 8,000 in Canada and, 2,000 in the United States, sizeable communities have developed around the world. At least twenty-nine countries ended up resettling Ugandan Asians, forming the global diaspora.[9] The word 'diaspora' comes from an Ancient Greek usage that meant 'scattering'. And so, in the aftershocks of the expulsion's quake, Ugandan Asians scattered across the globe.

When the Canadian immigration office opened in Kampala in the first week of September 1972, it quickly became one of the most in-demand queues in town. Long lines of people holding paperwork snaked across the pavements, and shoving matches even broke out among those desperate for a shot at a new life in the north. On the first day, officials accepted more than 2,500 applications for 7,764 people seeking to go to Canada and began scheduling interviews. Lists published in the *Uganda Argus* let people know what time their interviews would take place. There would be 430 interviews within five days, when the first visas would be issued. Within days of Amin's shock announcement, behind closed doors Canadian officials had been discussing next steps. With Prime Minister Pierre Trudeau advising the country should assist on humanitarian grounds, it wasn't long before Canada was one of the first countries to step up and offer to take in some of the exiled after Britain appealed for help. On 24 August, Trudeau said Canada would 'offer an honourable place in Canadian life' for expellees, launching a resettlement programme and sending a team to Kampala. Headlines in the UK heaped praise on him for the decision, with one simply reading, 'Thank you, Pierre'.[10] While the team on the ground in Uganda was working through applications and conducting medicals, a military base in Montreal, CFB Longue-Pointe, was being rapidly converted into a reception centre that could house up to eight hundred arrivals at a time. The gym would serve as a reception space, while the barracks would be converted into an eighteen-bed hospital.[11]

Canada had introduced a points-based approach to immigration five years earlier, and the initial screenings in Kampala were to follow this framework to select around 3,000 people. But that quickly changed, says Mike Molloy, who was second-in-command to Roger St. Vincent managing the Canadian mission. 'Six days after we started, Cabinet met for a second time and told us to pull out all the stops. This is now a humanitarian effort. Process as many as you can. The 3,000 limit was off and we were told to use our discretionary authority to approve people outside of the points system, especially if they had nowhere else to go.' Despite this, Canada is widely thought to have gained some of the most qualified applicants by having moved early. There was, says Molloy, a need for urgency. As the weeks past, the security situation 'had gone to hell', and one day the office had to close when the military came and 'scared the living daylights out of everybody'. As well as broad threats to the community, some were being targeted individually. 'We had at least one case where a young man had been brought to us. His brother had been murdered the day before. We got him on a flight the next day.'[12]

The first DC-8 plane landed at Dorval Airport on 27 September, taking 148 people to Longue-Pointe for processing. The *Globe and Mail* would summarise their reception arrangements as 'Curry, Cots and Counselling' in their report the next day. At Longue-Pointe the arrivals stood under bright fluorescent lighting surrounded by their suitcases, blinking at their new reality. Like the British efforts, this was run by a mixture of government staff, the military and volunteers. Dispersal around the country was also a priority. But unlike Britain, where people would spend weeks and months in camps, this was to be a temporary stop for the arrivals. Conversations began right away about prospective locations. As a welcome gift, the children were given plastic Mountie dolls and Ookpiks – Inuit handicrafts of owls – representing two sides to their new nation's culture. Reception staff were said to be especially proud that their cooks had gone to a Montreal restaurant to learn Indian recipes.[13]

Many of those arriving in Canada were Ismaili Muslims, large numbers of whom had been rendered stateless. Their spiritual leader, the Aga Khan, who was also the United Nations high commissioner for refugees, had recommended the community take up Ugandan citizenship after independence, in the spirit of cohesion. But with Ugandan passports rendered worthless and their owners having revoked any ties with Britain or India to get them, many now found themselves stateless. The Aga Khan spoke directly with Trudeau.[14] Canada had already taken in Ismailis fleeing Africanisation in Kenya and Tanzania, and the Ugandan Asian arrivals would be a catalyst for further chain migration to Canada in years to come. Now, the community numbers around 100,000.[15] By the time the thirty-first – and final – charter departed from Entebbe, 4,420 people had travelled to Longue-Pointe, each marked by hand in a log book that shows the details of every person who flew from Entebbe to Canada. The majority of the arrivals were resettled in Vancouver, followed by Montreal and Toronto.[16] The country would go on to take nearly 8,000 Ugandan Asians between 1972 and 1974, the largest number after Britain.[17] Canada was the most popular country for re-emigration among the 1,000-plus people who moved on from the UK by the start of 1974, followed by the USA, New Zealand and Sweden.[18] Today, around one in four Canadians have come to the country as an immigrant.[19]

After the chaos in Kampala, the UNHCR airlifts had taken the stateless, now issued with paper Red Cross passports, to airstrips and camps across Europe pending their permanent resettlement elsewhere. These were the true refugees, not the citizens that Britain was painting as refugees. The stateless Ugandan Asians who didn't enter the UK became the first significant group of refugees from the Global South to be resettled in the western world.[20] Seven countries had answered the call for support from the Aga Khan, and within twelve days at the end of October and start of November, planes set off to Austria, Belgium, Italy, Malta and Spain transporting more than 3,600 people to Europe. Offers from Greece and Morocco didn't need to be taken up. By Amin's deadline, only a few of the 4,500 stateless refugees were still left in

Kampala, with the ex-elephant hunter and his final companions bound for Spain. The temporary accommodation they were taken to ranged from refugee reception centres to youth hostels, out-of-season hotels and even, as in the UK, disused military barracks. Local governments were paid by the UNHCR to provide for their needs in Austria, Italy and Malta, while volunteer organisations led the missions in Belgium and Spain. At the height of the operation, $400,000 a month was being spent on the rescue mission.[21]

In Italy, some were housed in hotels outside of Rome or Naples, while others landed in the heel of Italy's boot, in the coastal town of Otranto in the southern Apulia region. Alongside a fifteenth-century castle and coastal views, a handful of Ugandan Asians temporarily called this place home. Laila Datoo, who had lived in Jinja, was flown from Nairobi to Italy, spending six months in Otranto before a move to the similarly named Ontario across the Atlantic in Canada. In January, the high commissioner visited transit centres in Austria, Belgium, Italy and the Netherlands to reassure them of his commitment to finding them permanent homes and reuniting divided families. Laila, then in her early twenties, was invited to escort him and his wife around the site as they offered support and encouragement to the guests, including the many Ismaili Muslims on site. Seen dressed in a striking, pink, high-necked dress, Laila's photos of the historic visit also show the Aga Khan and his wife in deep conversation with the young refugees and being offered plates of fresh samosas.[22]

It was hoped that resettlement would be a swift affair, a matter of weeks. But for some, it would turn out to be months before they were offered new countries to settle in. By February 1973 almost 2,000 people were still waiting, and at the most extreme, in Italy, fifty people would remain in a transit camp until 1975. Many were hoping to go to English-speaking countries, while others were separated from their families and felt they couldn't make permanent decisions until they were reunited. The camps were home to countless heads of the family, whose wives and children had been accepted into Britain with their British passports, while their husbands, who had revoked their British citizenship, were stuck in purgatory.[23] Many such breadwinners were passing their time in a former military academy building twenty miles outside Vienna, which had been used as a camp for political refugees for two decades. Traiskirchen refugee camp continues to operate to this day, as one of the largest in the EU. Wearing thick coats and fur hats with ear flaps – unless their heads were covered with turbans – the refugees' breath steamed out in front of them in the cold Austrian winter, while they appealed for Britain to allow them in. Inside, the detainees crowded together on bunk beds, playing cards or dozing to pass the time. In the corners of the dorms, plug-in hotplates boiled water and simmered rice.[24] Around seven hundred Ugandan Asians shared the camp with nine hundred Eastern European refugees.[25] Some family divides were even wider reaching, spanning multiple countries. Hassanali and Sakinabai Fakirani, from Soroti in the east of Uganda, and four of their children, were granted refuge in Malta. Their eldest son and his family were sent to Italy, two daughters went to Canada, one to the UK, while another son remained in India.[26]

When the expulsion order came, Amita Mehta and her twin brother Anil were just two months old, so young that her passport photo shows them both lying on their mother Bhanumati's lap. As the day counter ticked down, she and her four brothers flew to London with their mother. Her father, now eighty-nine, didn't have a British passport. He joined the UN queues and was sent to Italy. Bhanumati and her husband Prabhashanker had come to marriage through an unusual route. Amita's mother was seven when her father moved the family and her five siblings from Porbandar, Gujarat, to East Africa to set up a steel manufacturing plant to help the British build those formative railroads. But back home in India, he also founded a school. On one visit, one of the students caught his attention and, as Amita says, her grandfather became 'very smitten by him'. He offered him a proposition, if he would accept it – to come to Uganda and meet his eldest daughter. 'My grandfather saw an opportunity, with this very smart, orphaned boy, who he liked and thought, "Let's see if this works,"' she tells me over a video call from across the Atlantic. 'That to me is very progressive for the time. So Dad came, they met, and found love.' They would go on to be married for sixty-eight years.

In the 1970s, now split across Europe, the family was trying to find a way back together. As they couldn't get Prabhashanker into the UK, Denmark became a working option where they could be reunited, until Prabhashanker had a visit in the camp from an American church organisation. 'They basically asked, "Are you willing to be a contributing member of society? If so, we will make it happen." And he's like, "Where do I sign? I will do anything."' The US mission was one of the quickest immigration operations in the country's history, invoking a special provision in immigration law allowing the attorney general to accept under his remit the 1,000 refugees America had agreed to take in. Once they arrived, they could apply for permanent residency and eventually citizenship. Seven major refugee agencies joined forces to resettle up to 160 people each, some organisations searching for homes and jobs, and others going to speak to the exiles in Italy. These included the United States Catholic Conference, the International Rescue Committee and the

Lutheran Council, the last of which had made contact with Amita's father.[*][27] By late autumn he was on a plane to Harrisburg, Pennsylvania, where he met a pastor and started setting things up for the family to join him. Three months later, Amita arrived in Lancaster County, and found herself living with the Amish. 'They seemed like an ostracised community, so in some ways, we had a connection,' she smiles. 'We were both outcasts and we spoke through food, exchanging recipes. It's how that worked out.' Home was a trailer where Amita shared a room with her brothers Anil, Shailesh and Sanjay, all piled in together on bunkbeds, talking into the night. They were out on their own on farmland, but close enough to a trailer park for Amita to skip down to play with the local kids. 'I loved our little red and white trailer,' she says. 'I remember the farmland, with a huge pond. I just loved being outside, it was the coolest thing. I'd lay in the grass and look up at the airplanes.'

It was quite the departure from life in Kampala, where her father had been an executive at Barclays Bank, the family owned multiple properties and Amita says she would have grown up with a silver spoon in her mouth. 'They were definitely living quite the lifestyle,' she says. 'There's a life of privilege which I've never experienced. When we arrived, we had to live on the system.' Soon her parents got jobs as labourers, with her mother going on to work as a seamstress. 'My parents' first jobs were gluing soles onto shoes at a shoe factory. And then, can you imagine being a Hindu, a

* The seven organisations were: the American Fund for Czechoslovak Refugees and the Tolstoy Foundation (each taking responsibility for one hundred people), the United States Catholic Conference, the Lutheran Council, the Church World Service, United HIAS Service (Jewish) and the International Rescue Committee (dividing the other eight hundred between them).

vegetarian, and working in a chicken factory? Dad took on these labouring jobs. People thought they were illiterate and uneducated, when in fact they spoke five languages.' Amita didn't have memories of their life before, but her parents and older brothers did, and had to mourn for their past lives. Much is often made of Ugandan Asians' financial losses, but they had also lost friendships, community and social capital. 'The socioeconomic disparity was that they didn't have any street cred, right?' says Amita. 'In Uganda, their place had been the place to be. My grandfather had elite access to music, like new records, so everyone would always come to their place to socialise and listen to music.'

From Uganda through to Italy and the UK, the family's potential future in Denmark had morphed into the slow beginnings of the 'American dream'. As one of the early arrivals, a welder called Mahmood Ilani Mughal told reporters, 'I lost everything, but I am glad to be here. My two hands are here. They are my tools and I will rebuild again, with the help of Almighty God.'[28] Meanwhile in Europe the high commissioner was keeping the pressure on for countries to step up and offer permanent welcomes to those who hadn't been able to break out of the transit centres, which included touring London, Washington and Ottawa to drum up support. The results were impressive. By late February, the British government had done an about-turn and conceded it could accept the heads of families whose relatives were already in the UK, finally reuniting the split families. Canada and the United States would also take around another 2,100 and 1,600 respectively.[29] Austria and Belgium agreed to let a few hundred remain permanently, Denmark and Switzerland expanded their schemes and Norway, Sweden and the Netherlands offered places too.[30] For Kausar's twin brothers, these additional options would come to provide an incredible twist of fate. Overall, around 12,000 stateless people had been diverted from the UK to other countries. Aside from Canada, America, India and Pakistan, who took the majority, over 4,000 were resettled in over twenty-five countries through the UNHCR resettlement mission.[31]

For Amita, growing up in Pennsylvania, life was much more about fitting in with the crowd than investigating her past. She was dismissive of her mum's suggestion of wearing a sari to her prom and prized the weekly pizza nights that meant she wouldn't go to basketball practice with the scent of curry on her clothes. 'I was just trying to be this American kid,' she says. 'I was trying to hide who I was.' But a few years later while travelling in Greece after a semester studying abroad, her family's history unexpectedly caught up with her. One day, while chatting with the house manager of her accommodation, Amos, he told her he was from Uganda. 'I said, "Oh my God, so am I," ' Amita tells me. 'He told me that's how he landed here, because they had to flee from Idi Amin mainly. And then he says, "I used to work for this really amazing couple and they had just had twins, and he worked at a bank." ' As the penny dropped, along with her jaw, Amita said her family name and they realised the incredible coincidence that had brought him and one of the twins back together in the Mediterranean. Amos and his family had to flee because they had been working for a South Asian family, one of the many traumas suffered by Ugandans after the exodus. 'He said it was the saddest day when we had to part ways, and I put him on the phone to my parents, and they were all crying.'

For some the UK proved to be a staging ground for the next, more permanent move. For Amita's family, this was taking the chance to go to the US. For my family, an even longer journey beckoned as they looked for new prospects down under. After a winter of punishing flus and recurrent bronchitis, my grandparents decided the UK was not for them and started looking into ways of returning to the southern hemisphere. As they prepared for another move, my mother had by now met my father Martin, a six-foot-tall student from Surrey studying the newly launched Computer Sciences degree at Cambridge University, and would be staying behind. She would visit him at his college, Peterhouse, and they would go for walks along the Backs, where the River Cam winds its way past the historic colleges. Despite reservations from my grandparents, concerned about the pressures of a mixed-race relationship and still adjusting to the freedoms of the next generation, four years later they would marry at the very church that had first offered my family refuge in Britain. They said their vows in front of the vicar, Mark Ruston, who had been the link drawing my family to Cambridge, the cog in the church's missionary efforts for two families from Uganda. Posing for photos as a newly married couple under the arch of the Round Church in the centre of Cambridge, tourists took their own photos too. The local paper would report the nuptials under the headline, 'Wedding guests fly in from Australia'.[32] Their reception, at a Grade I listed Tudor manor house outside the city, featured a buffet of British classics from sausage rolls and Scotch eggs to devils on horseback and scampi, a hedgehog with pineapple and cheese on sticks, rounded off with jam tarts with cream and sherry trifle. The bride wore a cream sari, sent from India by her aunt, accessorised with gold bangles and hoop earrings. The men wore top hats and tails, with grey waistcoats. The English picture was rounded off by the navy and cream Rolls Royce they rode in – my dad's father had volunteered for the Rolls Royce Enthusiasts' Club and borrowed cars from them.

Four years earlier, for the second time my grandmother would write in her diary about deciding to move to another country with little knowledge about her destination. 'We decided we would move to Australia as it is a warmer place,' she wrote. 'Without knowing anything about Australia, we depended and trusted in the Lord for moving to Sydney.' My grandfather had a series of interviews and managed to acquire a job. A few months later, in May 1974, after less than two years in Cambridge, they embarked on their final migration to Australia. Their passage on national carrier Qantas was paid for by the government, thanks to my grandfather's profession fitting in with the country's immigration needs. As they came to leave, having lived in two temporary houses, none of which felt like their homes, their boxes from Uganda had never been unpacked.

Of all the countries Britain had appealed to, Australia had proved to be one of the least willing to act. Despite repeated requests and background negotiations, the government didn't want to move an inch on its tight immigration policy, even in the face of humanitarian needs when it came to the stateless Ugandan Asians. Australia's policy was typified in the words of Prime Minister William McMahon, who, when asked in October 1972 whether immigration regarding the Ugandan Asians should be guided by compassion, said, 'I think our own interests must come first. And consequently, we should be able to choose those migrants that are going to make the greatest contribution to the development of this country.'[33] Until the 1970s Australia had aggressively pursued a policy known as White Australia, a name which really doesn't leave you in any doubt about its intentions. One of the first pieces of legislation passed by the new federal government in 1901 formally established the policy, which stated that barring entry of 'alien coloured immigration' should go hand in hand with deporting those already 'in our midst'. These, the attorney general said, were the bedrock of 'the policy of securing a "white Australia"'.[34] An openly racist policy, it was centred around the ideal of a wholly white nation. A brass protection badge from 1906 showed the spirit of the times – a white-coloured continent, labelled White Australia, circled with the words 'Australia for the Australians'.[35] Meanwhile the country's indigenous Aboriginal population, the First Australians, were forced from their land, massacred and had their children forcibly removed, in the devastating Stolen Generations.[36]

The Immigration Restriction Act 1901 also laid out one of the primary tools in an immigration officer's arsenal, which would be used to hide the outright racial motivations of the new federation's immigration policy. Potential migrants to Australia had to pass a dictation test, a technique used for the next fifty years to weed out the so-called 'undesirables', otherwise known as people who weren't white. The tests required would-be migrants to scrawl down at least fifty words in any European language. The topics changed from week to week – in September and October 1925, spring arrivals were tasked with writing down passages describing tigers, water and eels.[37] Rather than being open to a range of European migration, as it might have appeared, the multiple languages was actually a feint to ensure people of colour, primarily from nearby Asia, could be barred from entering the country. The language would be chosen by the customs officer, not the arrival. This was a test designed to be failed. If the person being tested could speak English, they could instead be asked to take down a passage in languages as obscure as Scots Gaelic or the French dialect of Walloon. In this way, the Australian government could reject people without clearly stating race was the reason and protect itself from wider judgement abroad. The test was used 805 times between 1902 and 1903 and only 46 people passed.[38] Although cartoons lampooned the tests, showing Members of Parliament scratching their heads while being read complex sentences to note down, after 1909 not a single migrant made to sit the test passed.[39]

These tests were still in practice several years after my mother had been born in Uganda. And the policy worked, shifting demographics. By 1947, under three per cent of inhabitants were born outside of Australia, Ireland or the UK. The number of Asian residents had shrunk from 1.25 per cent of the whole population in 1901 to just 0.21 by the late 1940s. In the post-World War years, Australia needed a larger population for defence and development, which it sought through immigration. The demand was dubbed 'populate or perish' and encouraged Britons to join the workforce, including through the Ten Pound Pom scheme. Up to the mid-1960s, the racial purity of the population remained paramount, with government cables bringing overtones of eugenics in their discussion of what percentage of 'coloured blood' was acceptable in a migrant. 'Persons of mixed blood coming from tropical countries do not on the whole prove a very desirable type of migrant,' wrote the Department of Immigration in 1950, while as late as 1964, admission of mixed-race people was skewed towards those with more European appearances and upbringing. Immigration decisions were very much still made on looks.[40] As a mixed-race Australian and child of migrants, hearing about the extreme lengths taken to avoid people who looked like me and my family entering the country in the recent past is extremely uncomfortable. While I grew up in an entirely different environment, these policies are within living memory. Things were soon to change, but the vitriol and exclusion can't be forgotten. Slowly the White Australia policy was relaxed to let in refugees from the rest of Europe, and by 1966, it was on the retreat.[41] All potential migrants were subject to the same rules when it came to acquiring visas, selected for their skills, not their race.[42] There were 38,800 non-Europeans in Australia by the end of that same year and around 3,000 non-Europeans would enter annually over the next five years, including 180 from Uganda.[43]

But six short years later, the White Australia mindset had not fully shifted. With elections pending, the government wouldn't budge on admitting more Ugandan Asians. The minister for immigration told parliament that applications would be considered 'on their individual merits in accordance with our non-European immigration policies'. In short, there would be no special consideration given to refugees. 'These policies reflect the firm and unshakeable determination of government to maintain a homogenous society in Australia,' minister Jim Forbes added. Australia could, however, fast-track applications from Uganda. With half of Amin's ninety-day period gone, Australia's immigration attaché in Nairobi, John Paddick, travelled to Kampala to process applications. A one-week stay turned into six, during which he became increasingly frustrated with the number of qualified people turned down by the immigration office in Canberra. Only 190 applications for 491 people were approved by the end of the ninety days.[44] Australia would turn out to be a second destination rather than a first for many, like my family.

One of the few people he did manage to get a visa for was Ashak Nathwani, a recent graduate who had fallen foul of Uganda's immigration bureau in the days following the expulsion order. Following the government's request for South Asians with Ugandan citizenship to verify their documents, Ashak took his paperwork to be inspected. When part of it was found, unfairly, wanting, the immigration official behind the desk asked him to hand over his passport. 'I thought she wanted to check something,' says Ashak, who watched her take it away. 'Literally with a pair of scissors, she cut the side and threw it in a heap. With that, I became stateless.' So began a desperate hunt for a country that would take him and his brother in. 'We went to every embassy you can think of and every queue there was, and we would stand in that queue. That became our life.' Canada was a potential option but required Ashak and his fiancée to get married first. Having heard about Australia accepting some people, he tried his luck by visiting the commissioner in his hotel. 'I gave him my application and said, "You can call me for an interview," and he says, "Sit down, this is your interview," ' laughs Ashak. Paddick was keen to help him out, so when his first answer to his profession didn't fit Australia's professional criteria (mechanical engineering), he nudged him in the direction of discussing his current role (lecturing). 'He said, "Aha, you're not a mechanical engineer, you're a lecturer. In his list, lecturer was there, so he said, "Here are your visas." He was so kind, he was the angel in all this. Not only from my point of view, all the people that I have spoken to who have come to Australia, John Paddick deserves the highest of the praise, because he was really concerned, kind-hearted, and made it possible for people like us to go to Australia.'

Arriving in Sydney on 10 October 1972, Ashak and his family were greeted with the flashbulbs of the waiting press and interviewed by eager reporters. Non-European arrivals were still a novelty and the first Ugandan Asians were proving newsworthy. Collected by a woman from the Australian Council of Churches, they were taken to a hostel – but given a frosty reception. There had been a mistake, they were told. The rooms were reserved only for British migrants.[45] The white-only policies hadn't quite caught up with the changing times yet. It would not be until the following year that the Whitlam Labor government would officially renounce the White Australia policy.

By the time my family landed in Sydney two years later, glimpsing the famous Harbour Bridge above the glittering water as the plane banked towards the runway, the hostel system had been reformed and now welcomed people of all backgrounds. Not all of those in Uganda who had been granted visas during the crisis had actually made it to Australia. Having only agreed to accept the very highest qualified candidates, Australia had put itself in competition with other countries who had also offered passage to them. By 'visa-shopping', many had applied to Canada and the United States alongside Australia. By November 1972, only 46 of the 491 approved for entry had arrived, with many choosing to settle elsewhere, or belonging to professional categories that Amin had exempted from expulsion, such as education.[46] The opposing Labor Party won Australia's elections the following month and signalled a change of direction. Incoming prime minister Gough Whitlam offered further financial assistance to the UNHCR mission, and a few months later, as the White Australia policy was officially abolished, offered resettlement places to fifty families of stateless South Asians currently in Europe. Again, few actually made it.[47]

After being greeted by some familiar faces – Bob and Monica Claxton, who had returned from Kampala – my grandparents, uncle and aunt were given a lift to a migrants' hostel in Marrickville, a suburb in Sydney's Inner West, where they unpacked into rooms alongside families from Europe and Asia. Now a popular high street with the best of suburban Sydney coffee culture and independent shops, it's a street I have walked along many times, entirely oblivious to its significance to my family's journey. Back in 1974, life at the hostel, coupled with the travel, once more showed up as trouble in my grandfather's lungs. This time, struck down with pneumonia, he was admitted to hospital, the changes of the past two years manifesting in his body. Once recovered, he had a new job waiting for him at Campbelltown High School, teaching maths in the senior school, in what was then one of the less favourable parts of the outskirts of the city, around thirty miles from the central harbour. The following month, Bob drove them to Campbelltown and gave them a beautiful surprise. His cousin John and his wife Barbara had fully furnished a rented house for them, borrowing furniture from his Baptist friends. They even handed my grandparents a casserole for their first night. Once more, my family had been welcomed by incredible generosity. Their new surroundings included a garden full of tropical plants and a pond full of fish and soon they'd bought an old beat-up Holden and could drive to work and shops. They'd stay here for four months until they found their feet and could get their own place.

As the children started school, my uncle remembers how difference marked him out. 'Back then, there were no Indians in Australia, we were some of the very few,' says Phil. 'In fact, there was almost no one with anything other than Anglo-Saxon heritage in high school. There was one Chinese boy and myself.' Naturally being the odd one out led to attention, including daily barrages of racist taunts from some of the kids, although he feels that, overall, Australians were 'warm, welcoming and tolerant' towards him. They got busy fitting in as best they could. 'The Australian model of immigration was very much assimilation,' he says. 'Multiculturalism as a concept didn't exist. It was, you come to Australia, you are a "New Australian". That was the term. You assimilate, you take on our culture and our values and that's it. And that's kind of what you did, you looked forward, rather than at where you'd been.' In contrast, by the time I was growing up in Sydney two decades later, multi-culturalism was the order of the day. We learnt about recon-ciliation between Aboriginal and Torres Strait Islanders and the rest of Australia's population, lessons seeking to acknow-ledge the devastation meted out on the indigenous, First Australian populations, and practised a slow decolonisation in saying 'Uluru' instead of 'Ayres Rock'. We even had desig-nated multicultural days in primary school, when you brought in a plate of food from your culture that would be laid out on central tables in a giant buffet. The Chinese, Vietnamese, Indian, Malaysian, Japanese, Turkish, Greek and other European specialities would far outnumber the pavlovas, lamingtons and meat pies.

But at the time my family moved, individuality wasn't celebrated, bringing with it cultural losses. While my grand-parents maintained connections through the Malayali church they attended, their children were less embedded in this community, and they didn't speak Malayalam at home. 'The connections you made were all Australian local people, so really there wasn't any need or any emphasis on maintaining any cultural identity,' my uncle adds. 'I've often thought about who I am, what my cultural identity is. And I don't feel strongly connected to anywhere much, even here in Australia.' There's a greater empathy gained from living in different situations and places, but it has impacted his social ties. 'I've often wondered how moving around and constantly breaking connections, especially in those formative years, altered things. That's the theory, that it does to some degree change the way you form relationships.' The lack of childhood friends and continuity of a social circle through the years is also something that my mother has often spoken of. Because eleven years after my relatives touched down in Australia, my mother followed them, adding another leg to her global migration. Arriving on migrant visas in 1985, my parents set about starting new lives in downtown Sydney. And a few years after that, I would join them, a child of India, Uganda, England, and now, Australia.

While my relatives were moving to the southern hemisphere, Kausar's divided family were trying to find one another across the northern hemisphere. The exodus had split families globally, with Kausar's siblings scattered across the Americas, Asia and Europe. After she flew to Kenya, three of her brothers had gone to Canada and her elder twins had been taken to the UNHCR's facilities in Austria. Several siblings had been in England at the time of the expulsion order, and her youngest brother had been in Pakistan. While she was making a life in Kenya, unbeknownst to her, some of her family were undertaking extraordinary movements over land and sea. Her youngest brother Naim had been studying in Pakistan in 1972. With a Ugandan passport, he couldn't return there, nor go to the UK or Canada. Instead, he set about reuniting with his other brothers in Austria. And so began an epic journey, in which he literally hitch-hiked from Lahore to Vienna, heading north and then joining the Silk Route west to Europe. 'He finally managed to get to Austria, but by the time he got there, the brothers had already left for Sweden,' laughs Kausar. 'Because it had taken him a long time, going through Afghanistan, Iran and all places.' Twins Inam and Ehsan, meanwhile, had ended up on their own adventurous journey featuring a fantastic mix-up. 'They knew about Switzerland, but they had never heard of Sweden,' says Kausar. 'So when the Austrians said, "Where would you like to go?", they thought they were going to Switzerland. It was only when they landed in Sweden that they realised that these were two different countries. It's really funny, as my brother Inam used to say, "How stupid were we? How ignorant? We never knew about the whole world." ' The roll of the dice stuck, and they never looked back. Both made their lives in Sweden.

The journeys these siblings made are extraordinary, but in many ways characterise the complexity of this mass migration. It moves far beyond the India to Uganda to Britain trajectory. But when I first started thinking about telling Ugandan Asian stories, I gravitated towards seeing it within this tri-continental framework, even though my own family's movements had strayed beyond its boundaries. The schism of 1972 created a diaspora, scattering people across the globe. Today Ugandan Asians live across Europe, South Asia, America, Canada, Australia and New Zealand and many more countries, as well as those in East Africa once more. While some went visa-shopping, in the panic that autumn, for many more, the first safe option was the best one. In hearing stories of the exodus, it particularly struck me how much families' entire futures rested on snap decisions, on chance or dumb luck. How the country you settled in came down to which queue in Kampala had been shorter. How chance encounters could determine the next generation's language and cultures. The sliding doors moments that would shape futures not yet conceived, and which passed by the alternative futures that would go unlived.

Chapter 7

Little Indias

So, here you are, too foreign for home, too foreign for here.
Never enough for both.

Ijeoma Umebinyuo, 'Diaspora Blues'[1]

The Diwali lights are still up as I drive up Belgrave Road. Once an ancient Roman road, today it's home to the glittering jewellers, sari shops and South Asian restaurants of Leicester's Golden Mile. Here, every year, the largest Diwali celebrations outside of India take place, and tens of thousands of people fill the streets, dancing, singing and eating under the vivid colours of this Festival of Lights. Rainbows illuminate the road from brightly adorned shopfronts, fireworks cascade in the darkened skies and the dazzling Ferris wheel carries celebrants high into the air. Where golden jewellery is bought in the daytime, on these nights the sky is lit up with the colours of gemstones, vivid lapis lazuli and garnets. The annual religious festival, originally Hindu, but now also celebrated by Sikhs and Jains, and many more, marks the triumph of light over darkness. Dancers cut shapes with their elbows slicing through the air and palms upturned to the heavens, feet stamping in rhythm to the syncopated drums. Dhols, double-headed drums, set the beat to Punjabi folk music. The recreation ground adjoining the famous street is a sea of lights, from the lasers beaming into the sky to the ornate sculptures housing balls of blue flames licking out of them. Candles hang from other installations, glowing together in a united effort of good against evil.

Leicester carries the hallmarks of the city's waves of migration, from India to Somalia. East African Asian migration became indelibly linked with the city due to strident actions taken by the then local council, but it's also visible on the streets today – where shop signs advertise Swahili or African food alongside Indian fare. The city that tried to keep South Asians out has not succeeded. Shop windows along the Golden Mile are lined with richly embroidered saris, ruby and scarlet hues ridged with golden lace and paisley teardrops raining down the hems. In other windows you see more gold, this time the real thing, as shop assistants hold out necklaces, proudly displaying them to browsing couples. Fifty years ago, these same streets looked very different. The shadow of the past can only be seen in some of the architecture, tired terraces that today have been filled with life. Back then, this wasn't prime real estate. Belgrave, Highfield and West End were areas that were unloved and unwanted – until they were picked up by migrant communities like those from Uganda.

When photographer Kavi Pujara moved back to Leicester after twenty-seven years in London, he found himself drawn to reconnecting with his home neighbourhood and his family's East African roots through his lens. Taking the Golden Mile as his starting point, he began exploring the communities and lives in the homes, temples and street corners around it, capturing portraits and street photography representing the diversity of stories at every turn. Kavi has described the project as 'both an entry point and an ending, the last mile of a long journey to Britain.'[2] *This Golden Mile* is not simply about the one-mile stretch of Melton Road that turns into Belgrave Road, he says, but about the arteries and veins that come from it, where real life hides. 'It was about re-establish-ing links with the community in the neighbourhood where I grew up,' he tells me over the phone two months after his first solo exhibition of the series closed. 'About re-defining the city for myself in relation to Brexit and this pivoting towards anti-immigration policies in this country. And rede-fining the community as one that's just as British as a white community. There's a huge community from East Africa, from Uganda, Kenya, Tanzania and Portuguese colonies, and I learned a lot from that.'

Migration and manufacturing have been the twin flames of Leicester's story, which come together on this busy street where the shadows of the former British United Shoe Machinery premises, once the city's largest manufacturing company, fall on Punjabi suit shops and Indian bank branches. When the expellees began to land on British airstrips, the resettlement teams immediately set to work with their mission to disperse people across the country, into the designated green zones and away from the red. Perhaps the reddest of all the zones was Leicester, a city that already had an established Indian community and whose local coun-cil had been explicit in wanting its size not to increase at all. The existing Indian and East African Asian population was over 10,000 at the time, and leaders panicked at the prospect of everyone encouraging their relatives and friends to join them.[3] And yet, despite their best effort to foil natural migra-tory patterns, thousands of people would head in the direc-tion of Leicester – including Kavi's family.

It's a rainy day with the first flushes of winter when I meet Leicester's long-time mayor in the council's offices in the city centre. A Leicester local since 1968, Peter Soulsby was elected as a councillor five years later representing the eastern inner-city ward of Spinney Hill in Highfields and has become a figurehead of the city's politics. Local resident and SOAS academic Gurharpal Singh has described him as a 'critical figure', whose importance cannot be underestimated in recognising the need to change the nature of politics towards embracing social changes arising from migration to the city.[4] On an upper floor of City Hall, the brightness belies the grey day, as I sit down at a long meeting table under a city map marking out Leicester's wards and councillors. I've heard Soulsby speak passionately about the impact of Ugandan Asian migration to the city and I'm keen to hear his perspectives one to one.

'The Ugandan expulsion occurred eight months before I was elected as a councillor, but I was active in the Labour Party in that area before I was councillor and I remember the anger and debate within the party about the response of the council leadership, to the potential arrival of people who were expelled from Uganda,' he starts, diving straight into the controversy that placed Leicester in the spotlight back in 1972. This is, of course, the infamous advert taken out in the *Uganda Argus*, warning people off travelling to the city. Leicester became known as the city most opposed to Ugandan Asian arrivals, conducting a vigorous public campaign against further migration. From 15 September, six weeks after Amin's expulsion order, a half-page advert ran in Uganda's leading newspaper stating that housing, education and social and health services in Leicester were already stretched to the limit. This bleak, unwelcoming picture, ran for three subsequent weeks in an attempt to stop people considering a move to the city.[5] It's come to be symbolic of the anti-immigration sentiment Ugandan Asians faced, and is something Soulsby has previously said he is 'ashamed' of.[6] But the campaign against Ugandan Asians wasn't only targeted at the expellees themselves. Leicester's own news-paper, the *Leicester Mercury*, ran scathing editorials and its letters pages were often filled with racist bile.

Not all the coverage was negative – on 23 August readers wrote in decrying the negative coverage. Reading the critical letters made Brian Herbert 'feel ashamed to be British'. A Leicester housewife wrote, 'Your leader made sorry reading. Not a word of pity for these citizens of Britain.' While Glyn Jones wrote, 'Doesn't this situation have the alarming air of what happened to the Jews before, during and after the last World War?'[7] The paper also published a purportedly inde-pendent, anonymous survey in which 303 out of 304 responses 'opposed any further Asian immigration'.[8]

Soulsby also points to the even more blatant action taken within the boundaries of British politics, when an all-party delegation travelled down to London in an attempt to directly persuade the home secretary to divert Ugandan arrivals away from Leicester, telling him the city was 'full up'.*[9] Why was there such fear of the East African Asian arrivals? 'When I'm feeling generous towards those who did this, which is not often,' he laughs, 'I think that perhaps the motivation wasn't so much, "How can these people dare to come and make their home here," but perhaps they had some concern about the genuine extent to which social services and other housing provision was stretched in the city. They were mistaken, but it at least for them made sense to try to protect what they saw as overstretched schools, housing, social services and medical provision. If they were here, I think they would say in their defence that they were legitimately concerned, but of

---

* The delegation included the lord mayor and leader of the city coun-cil, the Labour group leader, Conservative group leader and the town clerk.

course, what they came across as, frankly, was just racist.'
What he's most proud of is the fact that within a year, all
those who had supported the anti-Asian advert had been
moved out of the council.

Ugandan Asians came to the city despite these efforts,
with the majority of people heading to the Midlands or
London either straight from the airport or after a stint in a
camp finding their feet. Around a third of Ugandan Asians
who came to Britain would eventually settle in Leicester.[10]
'It's been said that putting the advert in the *Ugandan Argus*
was gloriously counterproductive,' says the mayor. 'That it
let people say "Leicester, well, everyone, seems to think we
might want to go there. That's good. Let's go and look at it
ourselves."' It's something that Mahmood Mamdani also
wrote in his memoir, explaining that, really, all these warnings served to do was put Leicester on the map. 'Most people
had by then heard of England and of London. But now they
knew there was some place called Leicester, where there were
numerous Asians. All those who had been undecided as to
where to go ... started making arrangements to go to
Leicester.'[11] Others came by chance. Ayub Ismail Majothi
found work in one of the city's engineering factories, but he
had hoped to go to London. The only reason he ended up on
a bus to Leicester is because the one bound for the capital
wouldn't take his luggage.[12]

There were of course other reasons for people to head to
Leicester. There was a healthy South Asian community
already, due to decades of migration from India and elsewhere. Many had friends or relatives here, plus there were
business opportunities. This was a city on the up. Industry
was booming in this manufacturing hub, so there wasn't a
shortage of jobs. It was also a city where women could work
– two thirds of the hosiery industry's workforce in the late

1960s was female – meaning migrant families could double their income in those crucial first years starting out. The city is located centrally in England, making it convenient for the cross-country travel that keeps migrant communities connected with their peers, and there was cheap housing to buy once you had a steady pay cheque.[13] Going to Little Indias was purely practical in many ways. The people who had come from Uganda were not, despite the way a grouping like Ugandan Asian portrays them, a homogenous group. Within them were those who already had links to South Asian communities in places like London and cities across the Midlands. Some had always planned to join relatives and the expulsion had expedited the move. But there were also those with no prior connection to the UK apart from the passports in their pockets. Such people were also likely to gravitate towards the familiar. Striving for community and employment, this would naturally take people, in a strange and unfamiliar country, towards existing networks and places full of possibility. Something in the corner of the mayor's boardroom offers a vital sign of Leicester's possibilities. While the mayor and I are speaking, I notice a black typewriter tucked on a desk, which is carving a silhouette over the Leicester skyline behind it. It's a reminder of a key part of the city's 1970s history, including when Ugandan Asians took an unexpected stand.

When pay packets were handed out at one of Leicester's largest employers, workers at Imperial Typewriter's factory eagerly opened them to check the fruits of their labour. But one morning, a mix up saw one of the factory's South Asian workers accidentally get handed the pay of one of her white colleagues. She was shocked to find she'd been getting paid less than her peer for the same job. The only difference was their skin tone. This would be the kindling that lit a fire long coming, due to low pay and poor working conditions on the assembly line. Before the era of health and safety, workers cut and stamped metal from scratch, coating and galvanising it with chemicals flying around.[14] Now there was racial discrimination too. On 1 May 1974, thirty-nine South Asian workers, the majority women, led a walkout. Their strike would soon have the backing of hundreds more workers, with 500-plus joining them on the picket line.[15]

Leicester in the 1970s was a manufacturing hub, with tall factory towers reaching out into the city skyline. It was known for its knitwear and hosiery factories, printing and food manufacturing, and leading companies like Imperial Typewriters and British United Shoe Machinery, which at its height employed 4,000 people. These factories offered opportunities to generations of migrants, including Kavi's Ugandan-born mother, who worked as a lockstitcher her whole life after arriving in the city in late 1969 from Kenya. The family had, he says, 'seen the writing on the wall', as Africanisation policies brought their work to a halt, so they moved to Leicester to start anew. 'My mother didn't speak English, but she found accommodation, established herself here and got a job. It was quite a shock to her, navigating all the cultural codes, because she was so young, only nineteen.' Three years later, Kavi was born, and he has early memories of spending school holidays lying in factory aisles between rows of industrial sewing machines scrawling on scraps of paper with his set of colouring pencils.

After being bought out by an American company, Imperial Typewriters had set about a rapid expansion of its workforce, doubling it between 1968 and 1972. There was also a specific change in recruitment tactics. Until 1968 all employees had been white, but searching for cheap labour, managers now focused on hiring migrant labour, looking for workers from India, Pakistan and the Caribbean who they could get away with paying lower wages to – one of the many inequalities new arrivals faced. After 1972, a large number of Ugandan Asians had made it onto Imperial's assembly lines.[16] Ishvar Rohit started work as a change hand sprayer in the factory in autumn 1968, getting paid £16 for a 52-hour working week. He had promised he would send his mum his first wages, and she used the money to make a gold ring that she proudly wore for the rest of her life.[17] Chandulal Karsandas Thobani and his wife Indira both got jobs at Imperial as assembly line workers after passing a short and simple test of doing up some screws. It was far from difficult to get employed there at the time, as he recalls. 'I was watching through the window, the people who were working at Imperial Typewriters. Most of them were from my town in Uganda, so they would say hi and one day I came out of the house and they said, "What are you doing?" I said, "I am doing nothing." So they said, "Come and join us at Imperial Typewriters, you will get the job." '[18] By 1974 the workforce of 1,600 was two thirds South Asian, and many of them were women.[19]

The strike at Imperial lasted more than three months. Marching under banners reading, 'Support just demands of Imperial workers', and 'Imperial Typewriter is slave labour', young women, some wearing flares and others dressed in saris, strode past Leicester's terraces, shouting slogans into megaphones. The strikers, however, were never supported by the Transport and General Workers' Union (TGWU) and went for weeks without pay. The local press took a harsh line on the protestors, with the *Leicester Mercury* using it as an opportunity to present the South Asians as a threat to the community. The wider insinuation was that immigration itself was a problem – just look at how these immigrants were stirring up trouble.[20] The 1970s was the time of the trade unions, as spiralling inflation and the resultant drop in real wages saw widespread strike action across industries. The miners' strikes of 1972 and 1974 were set within a wave of industrial action, including in the iron and steel manufacturing and ship building industries.[21] Recession combined with the decline of traditional industry fuelled nationalism and racial tension, particularly in more multicultural cities like Leicester, as rising unemployment caused increased competition for jobs and made the working migrant classes appear to be a visible threat.[22]

The strike at Imperial didn't end in typical success. After a long summer of picketing, arrests and racial abuse, the strikers won some concessions, but just five months later, owners Litton Industries closed the company and moved production overseas. But this had been a crucial step forward in labour history, showing how South Asian migrants were willing to stand up for their limited rights, and raise their head above the parapet. The stereotype of the submissive Asian woman, rife in newspapers during this time, had been subverted. And two years later, it would be once more, when an even larger strike began by workers at North London's Grunwick film-processing factory. At its helm? A young woman from Gujarat who had moved to Tanzania before coming to Britain, Jayaben Desai. Like Imperial, Grunwick had hired many female migrant workers, mostly from East Africa and many from Uganda. Their factory was based in Willesden, in northwest London, close to where large numbers of Ugandan Asians had settled in other designated red zones like Southall and Ealing.[23] As Jayaben said, 'They got more work out of us. Asians had just come from Uganda and they all needed work. So they took whatever was available.' The factory dropped leaflets through people's doors offering jobs. What they hadn't advertised were the degrading working conditions, fearsome management and summary dismissals. The Grunwick strike, unlike previous industrial action from minority groups, gained the broad support of the labour movement, and it became a watershed moment. They were popularised as the 'strikers in saris'.[24] However, the challenges of the 1970s and 1980s for the Ugandan arrivals would go far beyond labour disputes and workplace discrimination.

Every afternoon when ten-year-old Kavi left the safety of the school gates, he would look left and right, before glancing over his shoulders as he set off determinedly in the direction of home. He needed to make it to Laura, the local lollipop lady. This mission wasn't the dedication to road safety it might seem to be. Because as well as helping kids cross the road, she had also proved a potent defence against the racists wanting to kick his head in. 'I knew, come home time, that if I could get to Laura, I'd be safe,' he wrote on Instagram, next to a recent portrait of the now elderly Laura gazing gently off camera while seated in her kitchen.[25] 'I didn't always make it, but on the days I did, she never failed to send the skinheads packing.' It's an astounding daily threat for a child, but was so normalised, Kavi tells me, it's just what life was like. But it's taken many years for him to confront the violence of these formative years. His childhood salvation, now snowy-haired and her face lined with the years that have since passed, was one of the first people he asked to sit for a portrait when he returned to Leicester. 'She reminded me what used to happen to me,' Kavi says. 'Just walking to the park or to the newsagent was running the gauntlet of possible threats. I didn't realise, because it had all seemed so normal, that when I left aged eighteen to go to university, this had affected me. I buried it away in my subconscious for the next twenty-seven years.' Coming back to the streets that held painful memories forced him to face the trauma of 1980s Leicester. 'When I was showing my children around, I'd be thinking, "That's where I got my nose broken," or, "I remember getting kicked in at the bottom of this hill." All of this came back to me and I understood at that point how we embody traumas, how they are still in us, even if we don't think about them.'

The 1970s and 1980s in Leicester and beyond were an era of what was then called racialism, moving far beyond casual racism to the skinheads with close-cropped hair and heavy boots ready to assault you for the colour of your skin. Racial attacks had become so commonplace, they were known as 'Paki-bashing', where groups of young white people would attack Black and Brown men on the streets. The late 1970s were 'fairly troubled years' for Leicester, Soulsby agrees, when the National Front was at its most active and even came within a very small margin of winning a single seat on the city council – notably in a part of the city where few Ugandan Asian arrivals, or previous immigrants, had actually made their home. 'The letters NF were plastered and graffitied in all sorts of places across the city, and occasionally offensive slogans as well,' he recalls. Or as celebrated Leicester community leader Manzoor Moghal, who had been a deputy mayor in the town of Masaka and fled Uganda in the middle of the night after discovering he was on a hit list, put it, 'In the 1970s, racism is so rife in the country that you could cut it with a knife.'[26]

The preceding years had been a time when 'No Blacks, no Irish, no dogs' signs could still be seen in windows when advertising rooms or jobs. Although the 1965 Race Relations

Act had made racial discrimination illegal, there were notable exceptions for landlords and employers. It took a second act in 1968 to bring legal equality into the housing and employment markets. Public information campaigns around the second Race Relations Act leant on Britons' sense of sportsmanship to try and encourage 'fair play' when it came to people of colour, with one advert saying, 'Funny crowd, the British. We'll shout our heads off demanding fair play in a game of football, but outside, some of us stand by watching others being kicked around, just because of their colour or race.'[27] Another animation culminates in a young South Asian couple moving into a new house while eating ice cream, having previously been denied a house viewing and overlooked in the soft scoop queue in favour of white customers.[28] But prejudice went on, and despite films like this also being issued in languages like Urdu and Hindi, many arrivals didn't know their rights or have the agency to fight for them. And for youngsters, schoolyards became battlefields when bullies seized upon race. Pramilla Dattani remembers girls threatening that, 'if they had knives, they'd kill us,' while teachers turned a blind eye.[29]

Ugandan Asians were far from the first visible foreigners to settle in the city, or the country, but much of the opposition to their arrival was framed around classic anti-immigration tropes of the city being full, and jobs, housing and social services being overloaded. There was a broader fear of the arrivals too, sometimes framed around the idea of cultural cohesion, but at its heart, sitting squarely on race. 'I don't like them at all,' a young brunette with piercing bright blue eyes told an *ATV Today* presenter. 'I don't seem to get on with them. Have enough of the coloured ones as it is.'[30] Afro-Caribbean communities had started settling in the city from the 1940s, with the 1950s and 1960s seeing arrivals from

Punjab, Pakistan and Gujarat.[31] Leicester's white communities were used to people of colour, but that didn't always equate with favourable views of them. And the public branding of Leicester as a red zone against further migration had perpetuated the idea that Ugandan Asians were a strain on society.[32] 'I remember walking down the street with my mum as a really young child, probably six or seven, and people spitting at my mum because she was wearing a sari,' Kavi says. 'I've heard stories while photographing people for the book about how some other early residents weren't able to hang saris up in the back garden to dry, or neighbours would throw coal dust over them, because they felt this "Asianification" of the area was a problem.'

Attitudes of the time were exemplified by what you'd see in popular culture, including across the three – and later four – television channels. 'Growing up in the 1970s, you'd turn on the TV and see very few Asians on there, but you'd see really quite racist stuff on the BBC or ITV,' Kavi remembers. 'Comedians like Jim Davidson, who were completely xenophobic on mainstream television.' The family used to watch the sitcom *Mind Your Language*, set in the classroom poking fun at learners of English as a second language. 'It was completely racist, but we would be so delighted to see a Brown face on TV. I remember watching the shows with my parents and squirming, but we were so starved of representation that it was a wonder to see at the time.' His reflections on representation remind me of a question I hated in high school – which celebrity did you look like? While other girls picked between singers and movie stars, in the years before the crossover of Bollywood actresses into Hollywood, there were just one or two recognisable Brown faces on British television who I could even slightly claim to resemble. 'In the culture we were in it was normal to be the butt of jokes on mainstream television,' says Kavi. 'It's taken many years to slowly move away from that, but that's the culture my family were going up against every day.'

Racism wasn't limited to areas of high immigration. While the larger numbers of arrivals in the Midlands' cities fanned the fire of right-wing extremism, those isolated in rural areas faced the opposite problem of standing out from the crowd so distinctly that they could become sole targets. 'Everyone was white,' remembers Lata of the years she spent after Doniford Camp in a local children's home. 'The whole of Minehead was white. I was the only Asian girl in the whole of West Somerset at that time. People would look at me as if I had two heads.' Her classmates stared at her so much in the shower after sport, to see the colour of her skin, that she stopped playing sport, which she'd previously loved. And from the earliest days, kids would also hurl racist slurs at her. 'They would call me names, and I had no idea what they even meant. So I'd go back to the children's home and say, "Can you please tell them my name's not 'paki' and my name's not 'nigger', my name is Lata?"'

It was in Bristol, a widely multicultural city, where I was first called a 'paki', and when, one evening, toiling up vertiginous Park Street past wine bars and restaurants on my way home, a group of guffawing boys chanted monkey noises at me. I was so surprised by this one, that I stopped to turn and stare, rather than push on to avoid intimidation. Racism in the UK today is mostly quiet, in the second glances, questions, micro-aggressions and lost opportunities, but sometimes, it's as overt as it ever was.

Many Ugandan Asians I've spoken to seem to have faced the prejudice of these years with remarkable stoicism. There can be a reluctance to speak about the difficult times, full stop, before you get to the indignity of admitting you've been

the target of often violent racism. There's something embarrassing about being the subject of racist words or actions,
that can still turn your stomach cold at the memory years
after, despite knowing you did nothing to warrant it. Focusing
on the hard work and the upwards trajectory is a more
comfortable space to inhabit. 'My parents' generation are
really a much firmer generation and they just got on and
don't particularly like to discuss these things, because they
think if you raise them, you're challenging the country that
they envisage has given them sanctuary,' says Kavi. 'They
seem to feel that it's insulting to talk about these things. As
a person who was born here, I think it's important to talk
about these things, but there are very distinct generational
differences about how much we want to engage with some of
these issues. If you talk to my parents' generation, they're
very forgiving.'

The division of Britain into red and green had also split
migrants into those bedded down in communities and those
out on their own. In places like Cambridge, where my family
had landed, things were more isolated. This was a distinctly
different experience to being in a town where you had speci-
ality food, others speaking your mother tongue, and general
social support. Some people lived in even more remote parts
of the country, like Chandrika Keshavlal Joshi, whose family
remained in Wales after their initial stay at Tonfanau Camp.
'I would say the early five years of our lives were really tough,'
she says. 'And unlike a lot of Asian people who went and
settled in places like Leicester, Birmingham – where other
Asian social support is there – we were housed in a small
estate in South Wales.' Only ten families were housed in
Rhondda, the most South Wales said they would accept.[33]
Kamala Sharma's family was the first of just four families to

settle in Hull, but remembers welcoming neighbours who stopped by with offers of help, had them round for Christmas lunch and rushed her to hospital when her appendix burst.[34] The corners of the UK people ended up in would in many ways determine the trajectory of people's cultural lives. For those embedded in community, South Asian culture thrived in some homes in Britain, while other families became masters of assimilation, throwing off markers of their heritage and adopting the high tea and tweed of the British upper classes.

By the time Lata was reunited with her parents four years after arriving in the UK, she had changed so much they barely recognised each other. 'We were very excited to see them, but when we got there it was almost like we were strangers. We didn't recognise them, and they didn't recognise us. My mum said, "These are not my children." We'd forgotten our language as well, because we hadn't been speaking Gujarati and my mum couldn't speak English. I was just sitting there not being able to talk to her.' The harsh years in children's homes and being taunted in the school yards had forced Lata and her brothers to blend in as much as possible. They hadn't realised it would be the thing that tore them from their parents for a second time. After the initial meeting at a relatives' house, like so many, Lata's parents settled in Leicester, and called the children to return to the family home. But the years apart came between them as sharply as shards of broken glass. 'My dad was very, very angry, because we'd Westernised,' she says. 'And my brother and I were getting frustrated because we'd Westernised. They wanted to have the children they left behind, but we'd been living with white families.' As well as having lost many cultural connections, there was now a language barrier between the generations too. 'My dad refused to let us speak English. He said, "Until you can speak in Gujarati, you're not speaking another word of English in the house." ' Lata gained the language back, but picking up British culture had come at a cost and the family clashes left a permanent mark.

Thinking about these different migratory experiences speaks to broader questions of assimilation and identity. I've often seen Ugandan Asians praised for their cohesion, for fitting in with their new surroundings. In many ways this came naturally, because despite the obvious cultural differences, Uganda had been a British colony, and that Britishness extended across many aspects of life, from the curriculum to the royal reverence.

Masters of disguise, they couldn't disguise their skin colour or accents, but many spoke English and had an understanding of, or even an affinity for, parts of British culture, which primed them for assimilation. But there's a more sinister side to this, where I've seen praise heaped upon Ugandan Asians for their ability to squash their circular selves into square British pegs. 'What sweetened the pill for the white population was that most of these people were middle class, often bringing capital with them. They were experienced businesspeople, and well-practised at blending in,' a piece in the *Guardian* read, pointing out that many were coming to Britain on the second leg of the generational journey from the Indian subcontinent. 'They had already developed strategies for integrating, as a minority ethnic culture, into an alien society.'[35] While it's true that having already moved from India to East Africa, and having found a way to navigate those changing societal situations, Ugandan Asians were in many ways dexterous cultural navigators, this emphasis on the positives of integration and assimilation can overlook the pain caused by being severed from your identity and culture. In that sense, an expulsion becomes an erasure of not only everything you knew, but also who you are.

Six years after the expulsion, people of colour in Leicester were estimated to number 50,000, of which 10,500 were Ugandan Asian. By 1984, surveys put the South Asian population at twenty-two per cent, with close to eight per cent giving their place of birth as East Africa.[36] Despite its best efforts, the Resettlement Board had been unable to stop people gravitating towards the city, as only a third of people were rehoused directly by them. Although the Board was credited with resettlement, as per its name, the majority of Ugandan Asians found their own accommodation. Some have suggested it's more appropriate to consider the onward movement of those the Board did accommodate as a relocation rather than a resettlement, as little was done beyond sourcing limited homes, with no actual assistance in settling.[37] The benefit of many moving of their own volition was the support they gained from being embedded within South Asian communities within cities like Leicester and London.[38]

The arrival of a disproportionately entrepreneurial and upwardly mobile group had dovetailed with the decline of Leicester's traditional industries. 'The big trees in the forest were collapsing, because they were undermined by globalisation,' says Soulsby. Established industry stalwarts would be shuttered throughout the 1980s, with the formerly mighty British United Shoe Machinery Company collapsing within a decade of the expulsion. Soulsby remembers a trip to China during the 1980s when he spotted a single British United machine on a factory floor. 'I said, "Oh look, that's made in Leicester." And all around it were machines that looked absolutely identical but were made locally. That's when it really hit me.' It was easier, of course, in the immediacy, to blame the arrivals for the toll global trends were taking. But many of the South Asians in Leicester picked up from that manufacturing heritage, and the city today remains a manufacturing centre in a way out of keeping with other British cities, with a focus on textiles and clothing. It's estimated East African Asians created 30,000 jobs in Leicester.[39]

Leicester's mayor has been part of the city's politics for six decades. So what does he think has worked in that time? How did people come to settle 'successfully' in the city compared to other places in the country? 'It's always struck me that there's two factors that I think led to a comparatively rapid progress in engagement in the life of the city,' Soulsby says. 'One was that those who came were able to and did engage in the political life of the city. They came with the right to vote and that mattered, because their votes mattered.' Within a few years there were a significant number of councillors with Ugandan Asian origin, as well as others with East African Asian and Indian backgrounds. Gordon Palmer, the first East African Asian lord mayor of Leicester, came from Tanzania.

As well as this clear demonstration of engagement with political and civic life, he credits the role of housing in cementing a sense of literal ownership within the city. Rows of Victorian and Edwardian terraced houses in suburbs like Highfields had been abandoned during the war years and were for the taking, offering a way out of cramped and poor quality rentals, as well as close proximity to the foundries, mills and factories many worked in.[40] Despite being little-wanted property in run-down areas, deposits were often out of reach for the new migrants, who not only lived crowded together in small buildings, but also clubbed together with extended families and even the wider community to get onto the property ladder. Some of the early migrants lived fifteen to a house, or even organised themselves into a day and night shift to share overcrowded spaces.[41] Thanks to the incoming home-owners, Leicester managed to avoid the fate of many of its contemporaries and retain its vintage terraced housing across districts, with buyers saving condemned suburban housing, deemed no longer fit for habitation, from demolition during slum clearances. 'It's one of the reasons why Leicester was amongst the very first councils in the UK to stop the bulldoz-ers,' says Soulsby. 'The extent to which they literally bought into the fabric of the city was something that I think produced a remarkable sense of belonging.' It's a feeling echoed by Dharmesh Lakhani, who lived in Belgrave. 'Ugandan Asians came and ended up buying a lot of these properties, so the council didn't have to knock the whole area down. Instead, the Asians rebuilt it. But what they built around this area was a community. It wasn't just about bricks and mortar.'[42] And it wasn't just the residential skyline that shifted with the demo-graphics. Mandirs, mosques and gurdwaras developed to cater for the arrivals' many religions, starting in small empty premises and even garages. Meanwhile in 1974 the Natraj cinema on Belgrave Road brought Bollywood to the East Midlands. 'We thought we must open a big cinema which gave you a variety of films,' says Musa Juma. South Asian cinema became a place of connection for the diaspora across the country in the 1970s, from Liberty Cinema in Southall to the Odeon in Ilford.[43] Leicester's 700-seat cinema, the first funded by a South Asian community, opened with romance *Aap Ki Kasam*, starring Rajesh Khanna, a superstar of Hindi film.[44]

In the years since then, Leicester has been held up as a model of multiculturalism, where diversity has become its strength, although this idyll was shattered in 2022. I'm speak-ing to Soulsby in the wake of Leicester's darkest moment in recent history – when riots broke out between groups of

Hindu and Muslim men, as parts of the British South Asian community turned on one another. 'I've always said that what is now fashionably described as community cohesion is always a work in progress,' he tells me. 'We do things better than a lot of places, but that doesn't mean we're in any way a model of perfection. We've got a lot from which people can learn but that doesn't mean to say that we've got everything right. In general, Leicester has enormously benefited from those who have chosen to build their future here. Every aspect of the city's life has been enriched by that – the political, the economic and the social and cultural life of the city.' In the latest census, the fears of the 1970s have in many ways been realised. This is one of the first cities in the UK where people identifying as white are no longer the majority. The latest census data showed the number of white people had dropped by ten per cent since the previous collection a decade ago. The Asian population, encompassing South and South East Asia, is forty-three per cent.[45] The beauty of the community, as captured in *This Golden Mile*, is that people didn't have to assimilate and leave their generational history behind, nor stay in isolation from the city they called home. They could hold both truths at once.

As Ugandan Asians settled around the country, whether following the directions of the Resettlement Board and heading to cities and towns less populated by immigrants or gravitating towards South Asian communities, they were part of the shifting social and racial landscape of Britain during these years. For those in cities like Leicester it was a starkly different experience to those in more isolated environments. But those living in green zones would also have new opportunities, many leaning on the same cultural traditions of the generations before them and bringing them into modern Britain.

Chapter 8
Hope on the High Street

*There is no place on earth we can historically and unequiv-
ocally claim to be ours, and so we have become adept
wayfarers who settle but cautiously, ready to move on if the
winds change.*

Yasmin Alibhai-Brown, *The Settler's Cookbook*[1]

A spring day on St Mark's Road can feel very far from its
setting in the West Country city of Bristol, the home of
Wallace and Gromit, Banksy, Massive Attack and Isambard
Kingdom Brunel. The cars parked along one side of the pavement bear British number plates, but your senses are otherwise transporting you east and west across the globe, from
the strains of reggae carrying through the air to the scent of
mustard seeds frying in hot, crackling oil. Coloured bunting
weaves across the street, red, blue and yellow flags fluttering
on the breeze, evoking prayer flags of the Tibetan peaks.
Interwoven with the triangular colours are rows of string
lights, lighting up the street at night with the warm glow of
their bulbs. Even on an ordinary day, there's a festival spirit
here. And every spring, the street is transformed into something else altogether.

The first time I walked into Sweet Mart, one of the largest
shops on the road, I felt a strange sense of coming home. It's
not something I vocalised, or even gave much thought to
until many years later, when I came back to speak to the
owners. But now I can see that this sense of homecoming

was tapping into my subconscious, across my senses, nudg-
ing deep childhood memories and cultural connections that
I had long forgotten. Today the displays of fresh produce
lining the footpath entice you closer. Pulling open the dark
brown wooden doors lets out the scent of warm spices being
cooked in the kitchen above. Turning right, you enter an
expanded fruit and vegetable section, a kaleidoscope of
colours, from the apples and oranges long stocked on high
streets like these, the now regular mangoes and passion
fruits, to the still unusual dragon fruit, soursop, custard
apples and feared, pungent durian.

I'm always looking for one thing in a fruit selection like
this, scanning the trays for the small, green globes of guavas,
an enduring symbol of my formative years. In the back
garden of my grandparents' very Australian sprawling
suburban home, behind the Hills Hoist washing line and
across barbed grass, dry from the searing summer heat,
which would spike my bare feet, stood a lofty guava tree.
Laden with fruit, my visits would be punctuated with trips
to the tree to pluck a fresh snack. Biting through the hard,
tart skin and into the soft white interior, you'd invariably
end up with its seeds stuck in your teeth. I never thought
about how this tropical fruit, originally from Mexico but
now produced in the greatest numbers by India, came to
grow in my grandparents' Sydney garden. Now, it's clear to
me that it was a piece of home. You leave so much behind in
other countries, but recipes and ingredients are precious
things you can bring with you. A few years ago the house
went on the market again. Like anyone with a healthy curiosity, I looked through the listing, armed with equal doses
of hopeful nostalgia and ready judgement. The interior
renovations had stripped the place of any character, as is
modern minimalism's want, but the greatest tragedy came

in the photographs of the garden. The guava tree had been ripped up. A hot tub stood in its place.

Adding guavas to my Sweet Mart basket, as a small attempt to right this wrong, I continue past fresh herbs and spices, many of which I don't recognise myself, and into an Aladdin's cave of goods from around the globe. With origins as an Indian shop, the emphasis remains on the subcontinent, but there are spices from as far and wide as Cambodia, Morocco and Guatemala on offer here, across rows of alphabetised packets. There are more than thirty types of chilli, and over one hundred different chilli sauces. Bombay mix, dried peas, sugary gulab jamun and jalebis all go in my basket. The latter is one of the sweetest foods on the planet, twisted and fried batter which is then drenched in sugar syrup. After the first bite, you think you can't have another, but you will soon find your hand is empty. At the hot food counter, tucked in the far corner of the produce maze, sit samosas fresh from the fryer and the young staff prepare you chaat, boxes of the traditional northern Indian street food, layering spicy potatoes, chickpeas, tangy chutneys and mint, and topping it off with crunchy sev, fried spiced chickpea flour scraps.

For serious matters, you need to speak to Rashid. Coming down the stairs and round to the tills, is a smiling and now greying man replete in a branded Sweet Mart T-shirt. In total command of his space, it's a far cry from the eight-year-old who stepped bewildered off a plane from Uganda into a new life in the UK. Following in the footsteps of his father, and then his brother Abdul, Rashid has now taken on the mantle as head of the family's thriving business. Upstairs, passing by the kitchen where huge pots simmer dhals over low heats, we sit at a table not dissimilar to the ones pictured in black and white photographs framed on the walls around me. Then, Kassam sat and talked shop with associates in

Uganda. Here, the spirit of Iganga carries through in Easton. This too is a table where strategising, planning and community cohesion takes place. The mayor of Uganda has even visited and sat down to chai here too. While chatting to Rashid, it turns out that my initial moment of disjointed connection many years ago, and the ongoing feeling of ease within this space, is not unique to me. It's easy to view shops for their commercial side, as mere places of enterprise, capitalism and money-making. But for marginalised communities, and certainly East African Asians, they are so much more than that. 'There are plenty of shops, so what brings people here?' he poses. 'It's that interaction. If a customer comes in and speaks in Swahili, and someone else can too, then they love that. He feels at home. Multilingual people can come in and speak different languages and find a connection here.' Their unique perspective, bringing both South Asian and East African cultural influences into the premises, has helped sow an inclusive and overwhelmingly welcoming atmosphere here quite unlike other places I go to buy food.

This was the first Indian sweet shop in Bristol, a legacy that remained in its name, even as it expanded into a food emporium. Sweet Mart was a popular name for Indian shops across Uganda, with numerous Sweet Marts seen shuttered on the streets of Kampala in the wake of the exodus. But in 1970s Britain, specialist food stores were not a common sight. Although immigrants had been coming to the UK from India for years, the communities that had developed remained mostly in certain pockets of the country, such as London and Leicester, and the menu elsewhere was still firmly British. The 1972 forced migration that saw families like mine head to the UK was not the first. Historian Rozina Visram has shown evidence of a considerable South Asian presence in Britain from the seventeenth century. As the East

India Company cemented its authority over the broadly termed East-Indies, so began light migration of Indian citizens back to Britain. This included servants and ayahs brought by British families returning from India, as well as the sailors who crewed the ships and later diplomats and visitors. The number of Indians travelling to Britain increased from the mid-nineteenth century. Some as a result of the social changes imperialism had brought India, while others, says Visram, came 'out of a sense of adventure'.[2] This included students who would go on to shape the region, from non-violence protest leader Mahatma Gandhi, who studied in the UK from 1887 to 1890, to future leaders Muhammad Ali Jinnah, the first governor-general of Pakistan, and Jawaharlal Nehru, the first prime minister of independent India. Small communities were established by the mid-twentieth century, with a notable surge in the 1940s and 1950s, when migrants were recruited directly from India to fill post-war labour needs in Britain.[3] Workers and families uprooted by Partition set off for Britain, along with those migrating from East Africa, growing the South Asian population to over a million by 1981.[4]

During those more recent years these migrants started taking on struggling corner shops, seeing the business potential between the four walls.[5] By the 1980s, the Ugandan arrivals had changed the high street. A *Daily Mail* report published in 1976 estimated that Ugandan Asians were running 4,000 grocery stores, 1,000 newsagents, 500 sub-post offices and 300 pharmacies under two years after their arrival.[6] It's a huge number when you consider what the majority of these people were starting with – the clothes on their backs and a desire to create a better life for their children. The business stereotype was a part of what had driven them out of Uganda – the archetypal dukawallah – but for many it was to be their salvation in their new lives. They were ready to take on a dying trade – general store numbers had fallen by over half across the late 1950s – and attempt to make it their own.[7] On arrival into Britain, many enterprising people immediately spotted a gap in the market when they noticed the shuttered shops on Sundays or in the evenings, vowing to open newsagents that would cater to weekend essentials and late-night whims. One Gujarati who spotted the closed shops on the way from Stansted to his temporary camp accommodation later opened a mini supermarket in Leicester that opened beyond 5 p.m. – his son Jaffer Kapasi would go on to become an OBE-awarded businessman.[8] As Manubhai Madhvani, who had continued to build the family's Ugandan business empire, once said, 'you can take someone's money, but you cannot take their know-how.'[9]

After Kassam and Fatma's children had persuaded them to stay in Bristol, they began working with resettlement staff to look for accommodation options locally rather than in the north of the country. The fact they were now willing to stay in a designated green region, as opposed to the glaring off-limits red of Leicester, was seen as a win and something to be supported by the Board. Weeks passed and eventually, as their patience was starting to wear thin when it came to communal living, a home was found through a church. A two-up two-down in a post-war housing estate in Lawrence Western on the outskirts of Bristol, it was a long way from the ice rink, but was close to Blaise Castle Estate, where the children could run through the grassy hills of the grounds, and around the Gothic-style folly. It was here, with the support of a host family, that the Majothis could take the first steps to rebuilding their lives, searching for a permanent home, schools for the children and work. Kassam took just a couple of weeks' financial assistance, determined not to take handouts. It's a characteristic shared by many of the people I've spoken to and has fed into the independent and 'successful' stereotype of this wave of immigrants. Pride reigned supreme among many of the exiled, who seem to have not wanted to have considered themselves needing or deserving of signing on. At job interviews employers recognised Kassam's entrepreneurial spirit, his daughter Hamida remembers, and told him that he wouldn't be happy working for someone else given the clout he had in his former life. True as that may have been, branching into a new venture was easier said than done when you had no money and broken English.

His first break came after taking up the suggestion of their hosts to do some catering at a local festival in the centre of Bristol, on College Green, next to the cathedral. The evening before, Fatma carefully mixed spices, potato and onion, rolled out pastry and wrapped and deep fried 100 parcels for their experimental first sale. Without a car of their own, or another's to borrow, it was the bus for Kassam and his elder children. 'Can you imagine, in the 1970s, taking 100 samosas, on a bus? The whole bus was smelling of samosas,' says Abdul. 'It was quite embarrassing at that time, because the culture was different. You'd get passengers saying, "Who is this guy coming with such a big smell?" In those days, people weren't used to curries.' Hearing the embarrassment about the transportation of the samosas made me laugh, because it reminded me of a similar story my mum had told me. One of her defining memories of her childhood is travelling by train – across the famed Indian railways on the way to the Taj Mahal built by the generations of Indians before her – and the snacks my grandmother would pack for them.

Possibly one thing more pungent than samosas, boiled eggs. As her mother would enthusiastically peel them, releasing their scent far across the carriage, my mum sank lower and lower into her chair, cringing deep inside. For her part, my grandmother advised her to stop caring what other people thought, which was, as always, salient but hard-to-action advice.

Leaning on traditional food provided a lifeline for South Asian arrivals, even if they had to field years of tropes surrounding curries and other spiced specialties being smelly, messy or dirty. But that day on the bus the discomfort was worth it for Abdul and his brothers – they sold out within the hour. Finding a phone box, Kassam rang home and his wife raced back into the kitchen to prepare another 100. Two more bus journeys, and he was back selling the food of his forefathers to Bristolians for the first time. 'He saw a niche in the market, that nobody was doing proper Indian food,' says Abdul. After the success of the festive samosas, the family continued to mass produce them for sale at other markets and events, including St Nicholas Market in the heart of the city and St Paul's Carnival, celebrating Afro-Caribbean culture in Easton, as well as branching out into full-scale catering for Indian weddings and a range of other events. It wasn't only samosas that you would have struggled to find in 1970s Bristol. The Majothi kitchen lacked the basic ingredients needed for much of their Indian and African flavours. Rashid laughingly remembers the time one of his elder brothers, who moved back to Kenya, posted the family two pineapples. 'It must have cost him £30 or £40, which was a lot of money then, when the pineapples only cost pennies. And they came by air, not sea. But we treasured them when they came, the smell, the taste – we had missed it so much.' This was a time when you could find bananas in some shops, but not everywhere. Sourcing coriander leaves was a challenge, let alone anything more specialist. Getting hold of spices and Indian vegetables and pulses necessitated a journey too, albeit a shorter one. 'When we came here, we couldn't get anything,' says Abdul. 'Chillies, chapati flour, okras, gourds, nothing. We used to go to Leicester and buy these things in larger quantities and sell them. Soon, we got known as the spice people.'

Food offers a cornerstone for many immigrants starting afresh in a new corner of the world. For Ugandan Asians, food had already been a fusion, tying together Indian flavours with Ugandan produce and traditions at the true intersection of these two cultures. It's visible to this day in Uganda's diverse menus, particularly the country's most famous street food, the rolex. Named not after the watches, but a play on words on the rolled eggs (rolex) inside these popular street snacks, they're made with a base of Indian chapatis, topped with a vegetable omelette, which is rolled up into a wrap. Alongside fried bread mandazi you'll also find Indian samosas on street stalls, while Indian curries sit alongside Ugandan matooke (green plantain), groundnuts and beans. Recipes contain memories, as Yasmin Alibhai-Brown showed in her seminal Ugandan Asian memoir, *The Settler's Cookbook*, which showcases the fusion of Ugandan and Indian cuisine in dishes like chili matooke, coconut cassava, fried green tilapia (fish) and posho (or ugali, a porridgey dough made from maize flour) and rice.[10] Such recipes are interspersed throughout her prose, picking up on relevant parts of the story and infusing them with flavours, all the while showing how interwoven food is with the immigrant experience. Food certainly remained my main cultural link to India, despite not otherwise growing up embedded in a South Asian community. Without the Malayali language or church, it was the food cooked by my grandparents that provided a connection to this part of me, from the chicken curries and appams (fermented rice flour pancakes) to biriyanis and samosas. The extended family would head in the direction of Sydney's Harbour Bridge to go to a South Indian restaurant to devour crispy masala dosa, larger rice pancakes filled with potatoes and onions, and dip flaky, buttery parathas into vivid coloured curries. Similarly, when food writer and chef Meera Sodha, author of *East* and *Fresh India*, asked her mother to show her their family recipes, it turned into a journey into her parents' past lives in Uganda through to their own parents' in Gujarat. 'I realised that each dish was in fact an ode to a particular time, place or memory,' she wrote. 'Every recipe had a family story embedded in it.' Meera's grandfather had moved from India in the 1950s, starting a printing press, timber yard and Pepsi-Cola Bottling factory. Years later, working as a lorry driver transporting steel around Lincolnshire, plantains reminded him of home. Food, she found, is 'history, no matter which country you happen to be in.'[11]

The fledgling catering venture was keeping the Majothi family sustained in their council house, but like so many former business owners, Kassam was dreaming of building a shop once more. But without a mortgage or long-term finances, he couldn't find a single bank manager who would loan him money to cover the rent of even tiny premises. For now, their home, or more specifically, their garage, would have to do, as Rashid remembers. 'The garage we had at home was like a little shop with old sweet jars containing nuts. There was a teacher in my school who wanted to get things like pistachios and cashews, which you couldn't buy anywhere then. Those kinds of things were just not avail-able. My dad would buy things wholesale and bring them for us and the extended family, but also sell some of it.' Teachers would drop Rashid back home from school to stop off and do some garage shopping. For six years, catering got them by, although money was tight, leading to tough choices between clothes and putting food on the table, as Hamida remembers. 'I once wanted to buy a pair of shoes and my dad didn't have enough money to give it to me. Then after two weeks, he gave it to me. He gave me £2 to buy this pair of shoes, which was expensive then. Milk was only a penny, chocolate was half a penny, so to spend £2 was a lot. I was so happy, but then I felt it, that he's given me his week's money to buy it.' As soon as she was old enough to work, Hamida became a Debenhams girl, working in the department store on weekends to be able to buy her own shoes, and help her siblings out too.

Over the years, the family's food became well known, particularly in Bristol's South Asian communities. Others too started hoping Kassam would open a shop, says Rashid. 'A gentleman who loved my dad's food always said to him, "You make beautiful food, why don't you start a shop?" And he would reply, "How can I start a shop when I haven't got anything to start it with – I don't have a reference, I don't have a house, what can I do?" And he said, "I can do something for you."' Their friend was an entrepreneur himself, who had pivoted from working as a bus driver to running a clothing business. Now well-established himself, he was willing to lend a hand and offered Kassam a small building that he was currently using as a storeroom. For a little rent and the investment of adding kitchen facilities, 82 St Mark's Road was his. 'With the help of a few friends and the full support of my mum, they started the takeaway there selling Indian sweets and samosas,' says Rashid. 'So that's why the name came – Bristol Sweet Mart.'

For just £12 a month, Kassam had his own four walls and could stock them with sweet laddoos and sandesh, kaju katli and mysore pak. The stalwart samosas, his ticket to ride, were always available on the counter. Cash flow still remained a problem though. To grow the business the family needed to expand their offerings, but without the chance of a cash injection from the bank, it was proving hard. Ever the creative thinker, Kassam leant on his business nous in the way so many migrants do when starting something from absolutely nothing. 'My father used to buy rice, sell it cheaper than what he bought it for, raise the cash, go to Leicester, buy spices and chillies and vegetables and chapati flour, come back, sell it and then pay this cash and carry back within a month,' says Abdul. 'So that's how we used to raise money.' In the spirit of loss-leading, Kassam was turning grains of rice into hard cash, making more than he'd originally paid for it, but only after initially making a loss. It was reminiscent of the way businesses got started in East Africa, where goods were often supplied on credit. Gifted at complex calculations, he 'would know the weight of something without having a scale,' remembers Rashid. In an interview for a local magazine in the early 1980s, Kassam challenged the reporter to test his mental arithmetic, 'eyes twinkling and ostentatiously putting away his pocket calculator.' The journalist dutifully named the price of a pen an awkward 13p. ' "Now ask for a large, odd number of pens, like 79 or 63 or 87." At random I chose 73 and within the next breath, "They will cost you £9.49. Go on, check it if you like." He was right every time.'[12] Described by Kassam as a 'gift from God', this skill had previously proved highly useful in his Ugandan merchant days, when he could also tell what sacks of maize, peanuts, chillies, coffee and beans weighed at a glance. As Abdul says, 'Amin took everything from my father, but not his business mind.'

Back then St Mark's Road was a far cry from the gentri-fied, dynamic multicultural quarter it is today. Partly a red-light district and partly congregated by street drinkers or petty criminals, it was, as the Majothi's family friend and fellow Ugandan Asian Bhanu Bharania told me, a 'no-go area'. Taxis would refuse to drive down the street after dark, insisting on dropping you off at the very top before doing a U-turn and wheeling away at top speed. This was in part due to scepticism towards areas where immigrants were living. Unlike those red zones of London, Leicester and Bradford, Bristol hadn't been a huge magnet for the Ugandan Asians – around six hundred East African Asians would come throughout the decade. Although their arrival was still met with dismay in some areas like Totterdown, where residents of the brightly coloured houses that zigzag the hills objected to the idea of fifty to one hundred families moving into the neighbourhood. The small numbers of arrivals from the Caribbean in the 1950s and 1960s had put some sections of society on alert to further 'coloured' migration, although the tiered approach to racism presented South Asians as more palatable migrants than those that had come before.[*][13] Bristol had also seen Irish migration during this time, people who, amongst other things, contributed to building the city's artery M32 motorway. The ten Chinese restaurants on Bristol's streets by 1966 reflected the presence of people from Hong Kong and China. By this time there were only around 2,000 South Asians, which by the 1980s would have only grown to 6,000, and by 2001 at least 10,000.[14]

* A local newspaper reported a prejudiced perspective expressed at the time that, 'Community workers in Bristol recognise that Asian immigrant families tend to be more stable than West Indians, as the entire focus of their culture is on respect for father and mother and support for the relatives.'

When teachers Hariprasad and Harbala Joshi arrived in Bristol, they were desperately seeking community. They'd previously spent fifteen years in Kampala, their final days in Uganda dogged by drama. One day they were flagged down by soldiers, dragged out of their car and Hariprasad had shots fired over his head. The soldiers sped away, leaving the family deserted by the roadside. They too had ended up at Doniford Camp, but bespectacled Hariprasad's teaching experience allowed him to be immediately recruited to help teach the camp's one hundred children who had joined the local comprehensive school. This meant that just ten days after arriving, he had a job and the family had moved into a flat in Minehead. When the camp eventually closed, Hariprasad started looking for other jobs and the family moved to Bristol. But soon after, he had a stroke, and things became harder for them all. 'When I came home I found it difficult to cheer up,' he told a local reporter. 'We had had so many friends and such a nice social life in Kampala, and here we knew no one and were terribly lonely.' He took a creative step towards fixing this problem. Going to a greengrocer run by South Asians, he asked them for the names and addresses of some local South Asian families. He was given a list of seven. Writing to them, he said he'd hired a hall to celebrate Diwali, the Hindu festival of lights, and although he could only afford tea and biscuits, he'd love to see them and any of their friends there. On the day, as the Joshis waited nervously at the hall, soon the first people took tentative steps inside, and before long, more and more people kept coming in. Over one hundred people came. 'There were Sikhs, Muslims, Hindus, Asians from Uganda and Kenya – it was wonderful,' said Hariprasad. The family had found their community. Six months later he was elected vice-president of the Bristol Indian Association and would later become its president.[15]

As in Leicester, South Asian migrants also changed the built environment, converting a terraced house and grocer's shop into the city's first mosques and a disused school and post office into the first gurdwaras.[16] Hariprasad and other East African Asians involved in the Bristol Hindu Association fundraised to get a site for the city's first Hindu temple, which was founded in 1979 and officially opened two years later in a late Victorian Gothic church, which had previously been a Methodist chapel.[17]

The South Asian corner shop revolutionised shopping in Britain. Gone were the strict opening hours and the regimented Sunday closures. For people starting out, there was no time like the present to be making money and many found ways around the 1950s Shops Act, which rendered it illegal to open after 8 p.m. and on Sundays. There was a loophole that allowed later trading if you sold perishable goods, which included newspapers, magazines and vegetables. With such goods being the mainstays of the corner shop, this enabled many to operate outside regular trading hours. Local authorities by and large turned a blind eye to the very much non-perishable cigarettes and snacks that were also flying off the shelves out of hours.[18]

On St Mark's Road, Kassam was working eighty-plus hours a week, in the shop from sunrise opening as soon as anyone knocked on the door and staying late into the night for passing taxi drivers seeking food. 'He was the kind of person that if he was in the shop, the shop was open,' says Rashid. 'And in the evening, you'd have drivers coming by. You couldn't get Indian-style kebabs at night then, so they would finish their shifts and want to get ten to fifteen kebabs together. They would knock on the door and ask, "Can you make us kebabs?"' Never one to turn someone away, Kassam would fire up the fryer and offer takeaway late into the night. The family were building a dedicated customer base, but that didn't mean it was always plain sailing. Like anyone of colour in 1970s Britain, there were racist jibes to deal with, and where not outright racism, certainly stereotypes flung their way. On one occasion, the sons remember, a customer lost patience with having to wait in a queue and opened a bottle of milk and threw it around the shop, shouting abuse at Kassam.

For Kavi's family in Leicester, the threats of violence they faced daily came closer to home in the 1980s when, after ten years working in factories and with machinery, as labour-intensive industries began to decline, they returned to their shop-keeping roots and took on a corner shop. 'I think a lot of Asians at the time thought it was better to work for yourself, and it's a business my dad knew really well,' Kavi says. It was a full-time job, and more, working from the early hours preparing papers and doing deliveries, through to shutting up shop at 7.30 p.m. at night six days a week, and working half days on Sunday. 'That was the only time they had off, except for Christmas Day. They worked every day for the ten, twelve years they had the shop. The work ethic was incredible. What I find so fascinating, so beautiful, with that generation is that there was no safety net. When you're a migrant, there is no fallback, so they just had to make it work, with all the sacrifices that entailed. They just stepped up and got it done.' Making it work also meant fielding more than just long working hours. 'It wasn't the easiest time to be a shop owner,' Kavi remembers. 'My dad had renamed the shop The Corner Shop. I don't know if it was a sense of humour, but because there was a trope of Asians and corner shops, it attracted a lot of attention. We would have fireworks through the door at Bonfire Night time, bangers lit and posted through the letterbox.' As corner shops became indelibly linked with South Asian communities, the term 'Asian shopkeeper' became commonplace, firmly tying the ethnic grouping with this profession.[19] The less savoury words 'Paki shop' would also be both hurled at proprietors and used conversationally, placing racist language into the lexicon as if it were an acceptable day-to-day descriptor.

When people talk about their experiences opening shops and starting businesses, hard work is always front and centre of that story. Ugandan Asians as a group have come to be known for their work ethic. It's something that has always sat uncomfortably with me, feeding into the 'good immigrant' line of thinking where migrants, despite their often-traumatic histories, are expected to behave as well as, or indeed better than, the majority communities they join. It's a point exacerbated by the negative narratives about migrants espoused by British politicians like Priti Patel, herself the daughter of a Ugandan shopkeeper Sushil Patel, or in the opposite way by former prime minister David Cameron who celebrated Ugandan Asians as 'one of the most successful groups of immigrants' of all time, casting the subtle undertone that other immigrants might like to do their best to step up to match these heady heights.[20] There's no doubt that as Britain became a nation of South Asian shopkeepers, some Ugandan Asian entrepreneurs went on to achieve stratospheric financial success, reaching *The Sunday Times*' coveted Rich List. These multimillionaires include the Madhvanis, who we have met, working across commodities, PR Patel in pharmaceuticals and Nazmu Virani, working in the financial services. Abdel Shamji built a business empire within a decade of arriving that included a large share in Wembley Stadium; Zul and Nazmu Virani have a property empire and Rupin Vadera became a global investment manager. Rumi Verjee founded the Domino's Pizza franchise in the UK, while investment banker Shriti Vadera was the first female head of a major high street bank, Santander.[21] Fortunes were also made in less glitzy surroundings. Clifton Packaging, founded by four brothers in the 1980s, became a leading food packaging company, while the Leicester Paper Company was later sold for £42 million.[22] Artist Zarina Bhimji has exhibited in the Tate, and Shriti Vadera chairs the Royal Shakespeare Company.[23] On a smaller scale, hard work has been a big part of many people's stories. But not everyone had conventional or financial success.

Moreover, while success on the high street has generally been equated with indisputable progress for Ugandan migrants, there's also an argument to be made that the ubiquity of the South Asian shopkeeper arose as a result of racial exclusion. Shut off from many other professions they were qualified for, and forced to take on low-paid shift work, migrants were slotted into professions that didn't threaten the status quo, forcing them to diversify by default rather than design. Exploring South Asian enterprise in Leicester, Michael Freeman posited that the arrivals had 'frequently limited themselves to markets where they cannot be perceived as a threat by white people.' In short, headway was made in spheres considered undesirable by pretty much everyone else. 'Grocery shops, newsagents, taxi-hire, off licences predominate for Asians; areas in which white entrepreneurs have long been in retreat.'[24] Behind the hard work there was humiliation for those forced to take jobs far below their experience and former status, joining the workforce on the lowest rung. A survey of the first 1,500 arrivals found just twelve per cent were unskilled workers, despite what their subsequent employment might have suggested.[25] For many, it was a lack of economic opportunities that drove them to establish their own businesses, to make something for themselves outside existing employment frameworks that didn't accept them or recognise their qualifications. Entrepreneurism was at times borne out of structural racism people faced, not ingenuity. This lack of opportunity was exacerbated by the decline in British manufacturing in the 1970s and 1980s, which badly affected South Asians who were working in factories. Significant numbers switched to the service sector at this point, borrowing money from family to set up businesses and leading to a boom in East African Asian-owned corner shops and restaurants. By becoming shopkeepers or restaurateurs, they could evade the discrimination holding them back by working for themselves. By 1991 about one-quarter of Britain's South Asian community was self-employed.[26]

The enduring association between Indians and corner shops shows no sign of letting up. One day, returning to my parents' quintessentially English village for a weekend visit, I was walking through the church grounds, surrounded by chocolate-box cottages with thatched roofs, when an elderly lady I didn't know stopped me. We made some usual small talk about the weather, before she said what it seemed she'd wanted to ask, 'You work in the shop, don't you?' It took me a minute to work out what she was talking about. I had indeed worked in a shop, but not since I was eighteen. Then it dawned on me – she meant the village shop, run by the only other people of colour in the village. 'Oh, no, I'm the other Indian family,' I managed to say with a weak smile. It was a simple misunderstanding, but one which, in an instant, had reaffirmed the way I stood out for my skin colour. Despite the multiculturalism of its cities, rural Britain remains overwhelmingly white, with South and South East

Asian shopkeepers still often bringing the only diversity to villages. I can only imagine the isolation that came from the dispersal policy where so many of the arrivals were placed into remote locations like this, without easy transport or the communication methods we can today rely on for remote community.

After the peak of the late twentieth century, South Asian-owned shops went into some kind of decline. By 2002, just fourteen per cent of people in the community were self-employed, as the next generation became more highly educated and qualified for professional jobs in Britain and saw a future outside the family path – along with being less willing to tolerate the relentless working conditions that their immigrant parents accepted. The numbers of family-run South Asian corner shops had dropped twenty-five per cent in ten years by then to under 12,000.[27] The advent of the superstore and the well-stocked petrol station shop, both often with twenty-four-hour trading, further squeezed their trade. But smaller shops have been making a comeback, with supermarkets branching out into convenience stores, with 'pop to the shop' habits on the up.[28]

These kinds of businesses have become the heart and soul of their communities. Every shop has its story, which the National Trust has hoped to capture in their Corner Shop Stories social history project, led by Sadiya Ahmed, founder of Everyday Muslim Heritage and Archive Initiative. 'Corner shops are more than sites of exchange where goods and services are sold,' wrote organisers. 'Underneath the façade, they have come to symbolise integration, cultural exchange and perhaps most of all, entrepreneurial flair. Yet these every-day spaces are seldom thought of as remarkable and we rarely pay homage to the people who work tirelessly to keep our beloved shops open all hours. As a result, the rich social history of the corner shop remains largely untold.'[29] One voice capturing memories of shopkeeper life is BBC presenter Babita Sharma, whose accounts take you into her parents' shop near Reading and into daily life when your home is shared with customers. The corner shop sits at the centre of any community, she says, serving as a 'nerve centre of information,' which is at once 'the butcher, the baker and the candlestick maker'.[30] She bristles at the idea of South Asian shopkeepers being responsible for the corner shop concept – 'if we had been, perhaps we could have stomached the stereotype' – pointing out her parents 'merely occupied a space that had originally been created by the finest architectural minds of post-war Britain.'[31] The corner shop is a 'quintessentially British institution', says Babita. 'Though its face has changed from a very white pre-war incarnation to the ideal entrepreneurial gym for hard working immigrants, the passing of time has not altered its unique place in our lives.'[32]

Shops like these have become hubs for Britain's migrant communities, representing safe spaces that offer solidarity and even friendship.[33] At Sweet Mart, it's been a labour of love and a family affair. Kassam's children, grandchildren and their extended families continue to man the tills today. The relationships made in business have been a huge part of their integration but also that of the next generation of arrivals. 'He was the old-fashioned guy who believed that whatever good he did would come back to him. And it did,' says Abdul. 'Even in Covid times we had loyal customers coming to us, so we didn't suffer as much as a community. My father got on with every new group of refugees that came in and he would make them feel welcome. He would tell someone, "Don't worry, pay me when you can", and they suddenly felt that there was someone in England that they could trust.'

Their produce pulls together their roots from India to East Africa while adding in the flavours of the local Afro-Caribbean community, and a diverse range from elsewhere around the world. It's become a two-way, participatory process, says Rashid. 'In the early days I remember my dad, my mum and my brothers would advise people on what ingredients they needed for different recipes, and what would go well together. Today we get people coming to us now and educating us, and asking, "Can you bring paprika from this particular source or this country?"'

The story of these shops is not only how migrant communities were established, says Ahmed, a daughter of a Walthamstow shopkeeper, but how they 'introduced new spices, fruits, vegetables and ingredients that have impacted the British palate and food industry'.[34] By finding their way, Ugandan Asians changed British tastes, introducing them to foods that have now become commonplace on menus at traditional pubs and in the aisles of supermarkets. Marks & Spencer is about as archetypally British as you can get. Founded in 1884, the retailer has now gone global, exporting its particular brand of Britishness in the middle-aged plain knitwear and reliable undergarments it was always known for. But today, its Food Hall is where the crème de la crème of ready meals can be found, and its Indian range is a good indicator of how far that palate has come. M&S today stocks more than thirty microwaveable or oven dishes, from chicken dhansak through to peshwari naan and bhajis. The changing flavours of Britain have been further illustrated by chicken tikka masala topping the nation's favourite dish polls for a decade. 'My father took a risk with Indian food, but he was sort of certain that he was going to succeed because it's different food,' offers Abdul. 'Food here was pies and fish and chips and, not being funny, quite boring. He brought a lot of interesting food, Indian dishes, African dishes. You can't beat Britain for that. People want to try anything new.' Migrants have reshaped not only the nation's tastes, but also the economy. More people are now employed in Indian restaurants than in the once-leading industries of coal, steel and shipbuilding combined.[35]

Return to St Mark's Road during the final week of Ramadan, and it's a street transformed in a culmination of community cohesion in front of where that first Indian sweet shop stood. A red carpet snakes its way down the road, which has been closed off to traffic, with white fabric on either side, forming a two-tone carpet on which hundreds of people take their seats. The iftar is usually for Muslims to break the fast together, but the Majothis and other key players in the local community, including the street's mosque, and the city's large Somali community, have invited everyone to break bread together in Bristol's Grand Iftar. In 2018 it was dubbed Britain's biggest street party, as throngs of people ate hot pots of curry and rice.[36] 'It was so busy, I've never seen so many thousands of people on the main road and the side streets,' remembers Hamida of the inaugural iftar. 'It was amazing. So many people joined in, even if they weren't Muslim. That's when you realise, my God, this is a multicultural place completely.'

Heading back to my flat with bulging shopping bags from Sweet Mart, unpacking is like pouring into my past. The Bombay mix and dried peas conjure up memories of small crystal dishes set on doily napkins to snack out of before dinner. When I slice the chillies later I will be transported back to hot Sydney kitchens, where sunshine and spice meld together into a warm hug in my mind. Biting into the Indian sweets takes me to South Indian restaurants, aunts and uncles and cousins crammed together enjoying the last of the spoils of birthday meals. But it is one of the most innocuous items in my bags that sparks the strongest memory, pulling me seemingly physically through time and space. Translucent rectangular chips of sugar, looking closer to candy than the granulated sugar cubes of the west, were the mainstay of my childhood treats. Hard sweets that hurt the roof of your mouth if you sucked too hard, your tongue twisting over the glucose, and which risked your baby teeth if you crunched too soon. Held within a heavy glass jar in my grandmother's dark brown kitchen cupboard, just the sight of them brings back the scent of the cupboard hers were stored in – and much more. The feel of the pebbledash porch and the burning hot terracotta tiles on the driveway, scorching the bare feet of a southern hemisphere childhood. The smooth round wood of the banister lining the speckled white carpeted stairs, the Mavis Beacon typing game on the earliest vivid orange Apple Mac. This is food, for sure, but it's something more, setting the five senses alight. These are the markers on the map of my childhood memories, triggering sight, smell, taste, touch and hearing and bringing thoughts out of archives I thought had been long forgotten, crisper and clearer than my recollections of yesterday.

Part III

RECKONING

Chapter 9

The Returnees

Exile is a dream of a glorious return. Exile is a vision of revolution: Elba, not St Helena. It is an endless paradox: looking forward by always looking back. The exile is a ball hurled high into the air.

Salman Rushdie, *The Satanic Verses*[1]

The Fairway Hotel in Kampala cuts a sleek shape in the Nakasero district, a sprawling white jigsaw of balconies bordered by palm trees and other tropical greenery. Turning off the main road opposite the city's prestigious golf course, you have to navigate through a complex intersection where traffic police wait gleefully to catch out unsuspecting drivers. Rounding the corner, a patchwork stone wall comes into view, flanked by lines of boda boda motorcycle taxis parked outside. Under a golden arch, your vehicle briefly frisked for explosives, a quick check underneath with a mirror on a stick, and you're out of the street noise and exhaust and into a comparative oasis of calm. It was within these walls that many South Asians took refuge when they started taking their first tentative steps back into the country they had been exiled from. This is a site at the centre of the Ugandan Asian story, from its owners to its clientele. Originally a family home belonging to Indian cotton trader and ginnery owner Bandali Jaffer, it began a new life in the late 1960s when his son, Sherali Jaffer, a member of the first Ugandan parliament, turned it into a hotel ahead of Pope Paul VI's first historic visit to Africa in 1969. But just a few short years after the highs of the papal visit, Amin had taken over and Sherali had received a 6 a.m. message from a friend in government that he needed to get out of the country that same night. Fleeing on a plane to London, he thought it would be a brief hiatus. But five months later, the expulsion came, and everything turned on its head. Fairway was taken over, its rooms occupied by soldiers instead of guests.[2] His former travellers' retreat was now an army base.

When Amin ordered the South Asians out, their properties and possessions were left for the taking. It had been practically impossible to sell things in the run-up to leaving, as everything had lost its value in a crowded market as desperate people tried to make back anything before they left. Some handed over their cars, valuables and cash to their African friends or staff, representing a more personal transferral of wealth during the exodus. Homes and businesses were seized by the state. The Departed Asian Property Custodial Board was set up the following year to organise the expropriation and reallocation of the newly acquired cache of more than 5,000 South Asian properties, which ranged from people's family homes to schools, factories, shops and even religious sites. Larger homes were gifted to affluent military men and those in Amin's inner circle, and the premier properties were redistributed over time to those favoured by the government, such as those hailing from Amin's West Nile region, like the Kakwa and the Nubians, or those practising Islam, his religion. Many of the large old Indian shops, dukas, were split into smaller sites and rented by four or five Ugandans where one business had once stood. Community centres, hotels and restaurants became late-night haunts for the military, with some even being turned into discos.[3] Nepotism led to formerly thriving businesses being handed out to soldiers and officials with no relevant experience, with predictable results.[4] Kampala's photographic studios were passed to members of the military, while the central Kodak agency, which processed the majority of colour film, was given to a senior army officer. This placed the state in even more control over the imagery created within it, and authorities even arrested people for taking photographs that had not been officially sanctioned.[5]

The Amin years continued in the same vein of tight control, and countless Black Ugandans fled the country in the wake of the expulsion. The country was also dogged by spiralling economic crisis – having expelled people accounting for much of the country's tax revenues, there was an immediate crash.[6] By 1978 Amin was declaring himself the 'conqueror of the British Empire', to roars of laughter and claps. Speaking at the summit of the Organisation of African Unity in Khartoum, Sudan, on 20 July, he said he had 'uprooted British imperialism from Uganda'.[7] He would rule the country until April 1979. In the year the Soviets invaded Afghanistan and Britain elected its first female prime minister, Amin fled after a disastrous foray into war with Tanzania. Uganda's politics remained conflicted over the coming years of civil war, which included Obote returning for a second tenure. These were even bloodier years for the country. It's thought the lives lost during Obote's cumulative rules dwarfed those during Amin's, the broken bones discovered in mass graves testament to the regime's atrocities. Instability reigned during these years of civil war, until one Yoweri Museveni seized control and made an interesting move – to call the exiled back.

After leaving in 1972, almost twenty years would pass before the Jaffer family recovered Fairway Hotel, during which time they had resettled in Canada and farmed chickens. But today the hotel, which is bustling with visitors from across the world, is back in the family, run by Sherali's Canadian-born grandson Azhar Jaffer. The thirty-five-year-old remembers how it fast became a hub for the returning South Asian community in those early years after Museveni's amnesty. 'My grandfather and my father were very hospitable. I think at the very beginning they understood the suffering people were going through, because we were some of the first Asians to come back,' he tells me. 'I remember my dad saying how tough it was. It had taken them years and years to recover their property. So when they got the hotel back, they felt obligated to help. They thought it was good when people came back to Uganda.' Being offered flexible rates and payment terms meant many families settled in for long periods while they tried to find their feet and get their homes back. I lost track of the number of people who mentioned they had stayed at Fairway then. It was less a hotel in those days, more catered apartments or communal living, which for some even included keeping goats on the balconies. 'I've heard stories from my grandparents' friends saying when they first came back, they would all sit around tables and make things happen, so it became like a community,' says Azhar. 'I think that's why there's so many memories.'

Walking around the balcony corridors that led to the rooms, or by the Spanish-inspired bright mosaics and fountains in the lushly planted grounds, where several resident cats wind between my legs, I think about the ghosts within these walls. From the army occupation years, when the sound of heavy footsteps would have reverberated around the grounds like the drilling of new construction does today, to those first flushes of youth as the South Asian returnees lent a feeling of resurgence to the grounds. Just behind Fairway, on a nearby road, is my mother's primary school, still full of life and where children's voices peal out during playtime. Checking into this hotel, whose motto, fittingly, is 'your home away from home', is where I start to meet the past.

Museveni is one of the continent's longest running states-men, his longevity only rivalled by his peers in Equatorial Guinea, Cameroon and the Republic of the Congo. He has held Uganda in an iron grip since he rode into Kampala in 1986, and in the years that followed, in a signal of a firm departure from times gone by, he encouraged Ugandan Asians to return to reclaim their homes and restart their businesses. Most had by now moved on, committing their hearts and minds to new lives far from East Africa. But for others, there was an irresistible pull back to the country they had always called home. They were willing to take their chances at making it home again. Museveni's call for Uganda's Asians to return was not just a grand gesture of reconciliation, journalist George Alagiah wrote, but a 'sensi-ble act of self-interest too'. Over lunch in 1997 at the presi-dent's sprawling farm, surrounded by his beloved longhorn cattle, Museveni spoke pragmatically about the returnees to the then BBC Africa correspondent. 'I like my Asians,' the president said. 'They work hard. All the time they are work-ing. And me, once a year, I collect my tax. That's all. They make some profit, I collect my tax.' Today's returnees are investors. The Uganda that Museveni sought to preside over was, in his own words, 'a new order', stepping out of the shackles of colonialism into something more self-deter-mined, ready to weather the geopolitical storms ahead. 'Uganda is a new place. We still have links with the old colo-nial powers, still have pressures from Europe, but they are pressures on a healthy body, not a sick or sycophantic body.'[8] Within this, South Asians could again play a financial role, but this time benefiting the state more directly. That same year, within the auspicious surrounds of Neasden Temple, London's largest, Museveni spoke of Uganda's need for economic regeneration. 'You can keep your money,' he told the South Asians among the 8,000 gathered under the intricately carved marble domes. 'But you can help us rebuild our country. Your country.'[9]

When Jayjayvanti Madhvani Popat arrived back in Uganda with her mother and sisters in 1995, they stayed at Fairway. Their room at the back of the hotel had a little lounge and kitchenette area, so once they had bought an electric cooking range, they would go down to Nakasero Market and buy fresh produce to cook in their temporary home. 'We were happy there,' she tells me as we sit on her balcony in the afternoon breeze in Kisementi, Kampala. 'We would walk to the lawyer's office and then come back and make a simple meal and swim. People started coming back and we were meeting more people. My mother was full of stories because she knew this family or that family and, as some people came back, she was happy to connect with them.' Jayjay's grandfather Vithaldas Haridas Madhvani was the inaugural member of the family who had started their empire in Uganda, setting off to Africa by dhow in 1893. Since then, her father had been managing properties in Jinja and Kampala. 'He just loved this country,' Jayjay says. 'He never thought that he'd have to leave this part of the world.' Growing up in Jinja, Jayjay went to school in Darjeeling and spent her younger years between Uganda and India. As the family took their first tentative steps towards finding their houses again, it was within the walls of Fairway that Jayjay was also first introduced to the man who would become her husband. 'The first year we came was very nostalgic, very sentimental,' she remembers. 'A lot was new to me, because

I didn't know Kampala well, I only knew Jinja as a child. I felt very lost, and like I didn't belong, because I didn't know anybody from the old times there. It took me a while to settle in.'

Those with some of the biggest financial motives were some of the first to return, including the Madhvanis and Mehtas, as well as several hundred owners of larger properties. Under the Expropriated Properties Act, they could set the wheels in motion to repossess what was formerly theirs. When Manubhai and his brother Mayur returned to the former Madhvani estate in Kakira, they found it taken over with elephant grass, returned to the land in their years of absence. Their company, which first began trading in Uganda in 1914, was supported by the World Bank and the African Development Bank in getting the factory back on its feet. The slow work of bringing their sugar estate and oil and soap refineries into action again paid off and today the Madhvani reach extends far beyond sugar, to construction, flowers and luxury tourist lodges.[10] Mahendra Mehta, now ninety, was personally escorted out of Uganda in 1972, but returned when he could in the 1980s. 'Everything had to be started from scratch,' he says. Today the Mehta Group employs more than 8,000 people. 'I have spent most of my life in Uganda and feel deep affection for this land of my adoption.'[11]

Some quarters of the returnee economy appear to exemplify the claims levelled against South Asians in the 1960s – that they were exploitative and extractive, using Uganda to make easy money that was then sent out of the country. With South Asians back in business, and once more a pillar of the economy, could history be repeating itself?[12] But free markets and foreign capital were at the heart of Museveni's drive to recall the South Asians, as well as encourage a new generation of Indian and Pakistani workers, who have no links to the East African Asians of yore, to migrate. They have come purely for business opportunities and once more dot the streets of Old Kampala. And philanthropy sits within many South Asian business models today. The Mehta compound in Lugazi and the Madhvani one in Kakira also offer schools and hospitals for their workforce, indicative of the efforts being put back into supporting Uganda.[13] Power couple Sudhir and Jyotsna Ruparelia's business wing – which grew from a single store again in the 1980s to take in investments, forex and banking, as well as hospitality and agriculture – is paired with their own foundation, working across education, health and the environment in Uganda.[14] Some, like Bharat Gheewala, returned for work but alongside their portfolio of properties, also run charitable enterprises. His father ran the drive-in cinema in Kampala where my family used to spend their weekends. Today, he and his son run a vocational college near Tororo in Uganda's east, where three hundred students learn everything from carpentry to hairdressing.

Museveni has namedropped successful Ugandan Asians for providing their talents to the country, including former high court justice Anup Sing Choudry, Olympic swimmer Supra Singhal and academic Professor Mahmood Mamdani.[15] One of those who was quick to return was Vali Jamal, who had grown up in Uganda in the 1950s. 'I always kept thinking about Uganda and our life there,' he wrote, remembering sneaking across the border from the wedding he was attending in Kisumu, Kenya, in 1982 with a guest who had returned to live in Uganda. 'I saw the utter devastation of the countryside as we drove in and saw plantains and cassava growing outside our house in Kololo.' In the years that followed, Vali dedicated his life to producing a monumental testament to his people, telling Ugandan Asian stories in a book he was still completing when he passed away in 2021. Last estimates put his work, which others are set to complete, at 2,895 pages and two million words.[16] Carrying the manuscript around in an old-fashioned doctor's bag, it weighed more than ten kilograms and was twice the length of the King James Bible.[17]

Beyond business impact, history appears to be repeating itself in other ways too. There are no Ugandan Asians in parliament, once more keeping out of politics and focused on economics, aside from broadly backing the president. Uganda's constitution preserves South Asians' status as outsiders, and has limited citizenship since 1995 to sixty-five indigenous communities. Despite the business privileges afforded to them, Ugandan Asians can't become citizens by birth, leading to a lingering sense of instability. Not enough to put people off returning to their roots or trying their hand in a thriving business market, but enough for there to be calls to add the Bahindi – Indians – into the constitution, something Museveni has said he is open to.[18]

He was an imposing figure, striding down the road in downtown Kampala, his tall stature casting a long shadow under the afternoon sun. His presence was felt by those around him far beyond those behind the cameras following his every move. Idi Amin was back on the streets of the capital, and not everyone was happy about it. It was 2005 and Hollywood had come to Uganda, as the cast and crew of *The Last King of Scotland* decamped to Kampala to film some vital scenes. So convincing was Forest Whitaker's portrayal of the commanding general that rumours abounded of the fear Amin's reanimation was striking into some locals. Friends of anthropologist Anneeth Kaur Hundle told her how some of Kampala's youth, born after Amin's era, 'imagined the ghost of Amin was "being made to return to Kampala, and that his

appearance on Kampala Road was an inauspicious omen." '
The film's production managers recruited South Asian
extras, asking those walking by the set if they'd be happy to
don some traditional lungi, carry bags and otherwise look as
if they were fleeing the expulsion order. Going full circle, in
some cases their recruits were the actual children of the
expellees, recreating vignettes of their parents' generation's
expulsion.[19] The film's release brought Amin and 1970s
Uganda into the limelight and to global audiences for the
first time on this scale. It redrew Amin for international
crowds, but also for the new generation of Ugandans who
had lived without him. Historian Alex von Tunzelmann
scored the film a B+ for entertainment and a C– for history.[20]
Meanwhile, Whitaker's punchy portrayal of Amin, which
was by all accounts an accurate depiction, would win him an
Academy Award. Accepting the Oscar for Best Actor, he
thanked the people of Uganda 'who helped us film and have
its spirit' – perhaps thanks were also due for tolerating the
awakening of Amin's spirit.[21]

The picture of expulsion that reappeared on the streets in
those weeks was a stark contrast to usual, when this chapter
of history is kept firmly hidden from view. Uganda's national
museum is more preoccupied with ethnography than
contemporary politics, with displays focused on traditional
musical instruments, cars and the fading feathers on head-
dresses and a collection of stuffed birds. Kampala has no
museum exhibits dedicated to Amin's crimes, or even his
rule, and no memorials to his victims. You can visit the
cavernous remains of the army's torture chambers at Mengo
Palace, but there's otherwise no obvious markers of what
happened to Uganda's population across the 1970s – and
dwindling memory of it today. Uganda now has the second
youngest population in the world, pipped from its former

top position by Niger. More than three quarters of Ugandans are under thirty-five, and its young population is projected to double over the next twenty-five years.[22] What happened fifty years ago might be fresh in the diasporic community's minds, but it is out of living memory for the vast majority of the population. 1972 is a pivotal year in my world, but not of any relevance or meaning for the Ugandans I chatted to. Mentioning Amin's name would yield recognition, but with a sense of something from long ago. After fleeing the country in 1979, Amin eventually took up residence in Jeddah, Saudi Arabia, where he lived out his days quietly on a Riyadh government allowance. He spent around two decades there, dedicated to Islam, enjoying swimming and fishing in the Red Sea and kept with a ready supply of his Ugandan favourites, including cassava and millet flour sent from his hometown of Koboko. His Maserati of the 1970s had been replaced with a white Cadillac.[23] When Amin passed away in 2003, his precise age unknown, aside from missing his home country, he appeared to have been without regrets.[24]

While Amin never returned to Uganda, the years without him have prompted a more critical examination of the histories of his era, including the Ugandan Asian expulsion, and the support for it. 'It's easier to point to their expulsion as a singular tragedy from which they recover, they are victims of a horrible dictator and then go on to build new lives,' Richard Reid, professor of African history at the University of Oxford, told a radio programme:

And slightly trickier to think about a different narrative, which is what led them to be on the receiving end of such anger, not just from Idi Amin, who of course is a relatively straightforward target, but from millions of Ugandans, who did see them as a problem – as obstacles to economic advancement, as condescending and patronising and even more racist in some ways than white administrators. That's a more complicated historical reality to get to grips with.[25]

While it can be argued that South Asians lacked the power to marginalise Black Ugandans, as they were operating within the niche carved out for them by the colonial government, it's also true that there was no wide scale challenging of this status quo. The expulsion was a 'nationalistic moment' for Uganda, writes journalist Andrew Rice, and Amin is not viewed with a solely negative lens, despite the brutality of his regime. 'These twin histories of Amin's regime, one that says he was a devil, and one that hailed him as a saviour, ran like parallel threads through Uganda's fragile patchwork peace. If you pulled one frayed strand of truth, you never knew what might unravel.'[26] Rice spent years digging into justice in the post-Amin world, including tracing one man's very personal journey towards retribution.

After Amin, there was no equivalent of South Africa's Truth and Reconciliation Commission, seen at the end of five decades of apartheid, or the gacaca courts that met in the wake of Rwanda's devastating genocide. These court-like restorative justice schemes, each greeted with varying levels of enthusiasm and success, at least attempted to look the past in the eye. Museveni had launched his new leadership with bold ambitions to do the same, creating the Uganda Commission of Inquiry into Violations of Human Rights. Supreme Court Justice Arthur H. Oder was appointed as chair overseeing investigations into abuses across all leaderships since independence. While Justice Oder's request to extradite Idi Amin and Milton Obote from their respective exiles led nowhere, he remained hopeful about what else could be achieved. 'Ugandans should not think that the incidents which concern them happened so long ago that it is useless to raise [them] now,' said Oder, who himself had hidden in friends' houses and a bat-ridden attic to escape a roundup by the secret police in 1977, before managing to escape to Kenya.[27] The commission, which included a lawyer, a doctor and a professor of history, swiftly got to work documenting atrocities from arbitrary arrests and forced displacement through to disappearances and killings, with the aim of recommending prosecutions. In its first year the Oder Commission heard hundreds of testimonies in almost every region of the country – 608 people gave oral evidence. Testimonies and reports on the commission's work were broadcast on radio and television, and the written records of the evidence charting the violence of Amin and Obote's regimes filled eighteen volumes. But just a year later, proceedings had already ground to a halt. Officially, this was due to financial problems, but it was really due to what Rice deemed to be a change in 'policy and tone', from justice to reconciliation. Museveni had cut a deal with rebels in the northwest of the country, many of whom were Amin's former soldiers, to lay down their weapons in exchange for being granted an amnesty. Where further investigations took place, nothing came of them.[28] Museveni later hired many of the people who could find themselves with questions to answer, perhaps in his own attempt at reconciliation or at least strengthening of his power. When the commission's report was released in 1994, few were even aware of its publication, let alone facing justice.[29] In the years since, when people sought answers, few found them. In the absence of official channels, two men took their own journeys towards the tragic mission they shared in common – finding their fathers who disappeared during Amin's reign. The pursuit of political compromise showed 'the idea that unity and reconciliation was a higher

227

value than justice,' Rice said.[30] If you wanted to find your father, you'd have to do it yourself.

In the years that passed after Duncan Laki returned home from school to find his father Eliphaz missing, his family had survived by staying quiet, and not asking questions. Although the nine-year-old had vowed to track down his father, it would be many years later before Duncan got a clue into his father's 1972 disappearance. At the heart of his mission to piece together the truth was his father's Volkswagen Beetle, which had also been taken the day his father went missing. He had been the first man from his village to ever buy a car. The family still had the spare key, which Duncan kept. In high school he heard that a man from the army barracks now had the vehicle, but he was fearful that pushing further might end up with him taking two steps back. 'It was a tightrope,' he said. 'If I show interest in the matter, someone might hide the evidence. So even if someone I knew worked in the car registry, I could not bring myself to tell him, "Let's look for this."' He would be married and with a family of his own before he investigated the records. Before that, and two decades after Laki's disappearance, the family finally held a memorial service, which was attended by the new president Museveni. 'His presence acknowledged a secret and personal debt,' writes Rice. Laki had been part of the resistance, a martyr, not a victim. After spending the 1990s living between America and Uganda, always keeping his father's precious car key with him, in 1999 when working as an attorney for the Uganda Revenue Authority, Duncan finally traced the number plate. He found a name. Then he found the man. 'Muhammed Anyule was arrested, and when he was asked by the police investigators, he said, "I know the owner of the car, of the Volkswagen. He is dead, but I'm not the one who killed him." At that point, I felt that I was under a very big shared weight which was removed off my shoulders,' Duncan said.* And so began his slow journey to discovering the truth of 1972, which would lead to one of the first trials of crimes under the Amin years.[31]

Not all those that returned came to settle. Some came to seek answers to decades-long questions. Edward Siedle landed at Entebbe in 1997. It was twenty-eight years since he'd landed here for the first time on his fifteenth birthday. Uganda was just the latest in a string of places his father's work had taken him to, from Trinidad to Venezuela, Peru to Panama. In the space of two years this equatorial country would prove to be definitive in shaping the course of his life. Arriving in the midst of the seasonal grasshopper swarm, they watched locals shaking white sheets beneath the bright streetlights where the insects flew, capturing them as a delicacy. The latest move was borne out of his father Robert's new job teaching at Makarere University, although he didn't solely concern himself with sociology, says his son. Edward later discovered his father was also involved in the intelligence community. 'His work was very clear,' he tells me on a call from home on the east coast of the United States. 'What I was going to do there aged fifteen was entirely unclear.' A year after their arrival, they were joined on campus by another American family, with whom they would become forever intertwined. A freelance newspaper reporter and heir to a Detroit brewery fortune, Nicholas Stroh threw himself into covering violence in the Ugandan Army following the coup. This drew Stroh and Edward's father north, where the

---

* For Duncan's full story, see Andrew Rice, *The Teeth May Smile but the Heart Does Not Forget: Murder and Memory in Uganda*, Picador, 2009.

pair disappeared in the summer of 1971. In the years that followed, Edward had returned to the US and tried to process his grief, but always wanted to find out what had really happened. It was a mission that brought him back to Kampala and would take him out into fields with a group of gravediggers to search for his father's body.

'I view Amin through a very complex lens,' says Edward. 'Yes, he was an evil guy but a lot of strange things were going on in Uganda at the time. I brought a lawsuit against Amin for the murder of my father, and there was a settlement, which enabled me to go to law school and things. And then I went back to Uganda to dig for his body.' Surprised by the team's enthusiasm for the task, Edward later discovered they didn't know they were looking for bones, but had presumed, based on his part-Indian appearance, that they might soon find some of the South Asian treasure rumoured to have been stashed in the soil during the exodus. Edward had become a forensic expert and used his experience to piece together formerly classified documents from the CIA with the information he gathered as he made his way around Uganda. His painstaking investigation suggested his father and his companion found the evidence they were looking for – hundreds of soldiers' bodies, killed by brute force when newly commissioned officers under Amin turned on the existing troops, would have been lining the roads. From former army members, he heard how the pair were captured at the barracks and killed too. Edward didn't find his father's body, but he met and interviewed one of his killers in prison, finding answers, if not everything he'd been looking for.[32]

The day Jayjay and her mother got back to Jinja in the midst of an electrifying thunderstorm, they hardly recognised the town and had to ask someone to show them to their old plots. 'When we reached the last home where we had lived, we weren't allowed to enter, and the occupants threatened us,' she remembers. It was a crushing blow after spending two decades dreaming of this moment. 'Mum was so disappointed, as she had built up such high hopes of finding her home as she had left it in 1972, that on the return journey to Kampala, we stopped at the old Owen Falls Bridge, and she threw away her home keys into the Nile.'

When Jayjay's mother had left, she hadn't taken any of the title deeds or documents for their properties with her, because she thought she would soon be returning. 'She escaped in the nick of time, because the next day, they went around to all the Madhvani properties and took all their cars,' says Jayjay. The luxury vehicles were sold for just 100 shillings. 'We never dreamt we would ever, ever get to come back.' As the pair explored Jinja in 1995 and pieced together what had happened in their absence, they learnt their home had been allocated to an army officer in the 1970s and that other members from the barracks had occupied every inch of space – with different soldiers living in the kitchen and even under the staircase. Working with the Custodian Board, lawyers, and fending off opportunistic agents looking to make a quick buck, the returnees began the arduous process of repossession, including the uphill struggle to prove ownership. For those that couldn't repossess their properties, small compensation fees were made available, but most eventually succeeded. 'There had been no maintenance, not even a lick of paint, so we got back properties in a very dilapidated state,' says Jayjay. 'It was quite a task to put it all together.' Over the following years, they would regain fifteen properties, although they had to take one person to court for fraudulently repossessing one of them before they had got to it. After years of chasing the army head office at Bombo, Jayjay got the call she had been waiting for. 'A young and dynamic officer called me up one fine afternoon and asked me to come and take over my house! Lo and behold, it was actually empty, as he had taken the initiative to put all the occupants in an army truck and take them back to Jinja Barracks.' Jayjay would move permanently to Kampala. 'I think it was just God's will or my karma to come here,' she says.

By inviting South Asians back and giving them the opportunity to recover their property and land, Museveni was offering an olive branch to the expellees. This 'post-expulsion reconciliation' was not without its challenges, as reclaiming homes obviously necessitated relieving someone else of theirs. Ugandan tenants and squatters were displaced by the returnees claiming back their former houses, shops and factories.[33] A fraught process, it could take anywhere from a few weeks through to months, or even years when there was a dispute or a valuable site involved. There was also the small matter that many of the finest premises had been gifted to army men and government figures. When sixty-five-year-old Safdar Walji returned, who had left behind the family coffee and tea plantation, two factories and more than 6,000 cattle, he found Uganda's attorney general was living on the plantation.[34] Knowing the right people could expedite recovery, while some took advantage of the system to gather assets of expellees who hadn't returned, or by passing on just a fraction of the profits made from sales or rentals to oblivious clients abroad. A murky network of agents sprung up to blackmail people over unpaid fees. Watching on were the select few who had never left Uganda. Although almost all of Uganda's Asians had departed in autumn 1972, a small minority of chancers remained, some sanctioned and some adventurous, all finding ways to make the system work for them. As the expulsion deadline rolled round, up to 5,000

Ugandan Asians remained. Some would stay the course, but most slowly drifted out to Kenya as things became progressively harder. A small community of several hundred stayed throughout the Amin years.[35]

In his office on the top floor of a grey residential building just streets away from where my mother grew up, Ali-Shah Jivraj draws me a sketch of the stratified society in the British years – three concentric circles denoting the hill of Kololo where we're sitting today. The smallest where the white people lived at the top, then the South Asians, and then below – and often far beyond the circle itself – Black Ugandans. Today the hills are mixed but wealth still dominates in the upper echelons. A century ago, Ali-Shah's relatives had been early arrivals, involved in agriculture from the 1920s, before moving into mining in the west in the 1950s, and staying the course in the 1970s. 'A few Indian people stayed back and my father was one of them,' he tells me. 'My father and his younger brother didn't leave. This was home, they'd never see themselves anywhere else. Uganda is one of those places – it's home. And they were young, they were single. They thought it would blow over and things would normalise.' Mining operations in Kikagati continued – one of the industries that was perhaps suited to enabling South Asians to stay, as it required specialised, technical knowledge, and was lucrative for the state.[36] Like other South Asians who managed to balance life in Uganda after the expulsion, his father played nice with the government, particularly when war broke out with Tanzania. 'Idi Amin and my father sort of became friends,' says Ali-Shah. 'Because our mines were in western Uganda, they were on the border with Tanzania. Amin had to become friends with my father so he could get free fuel and food for his troops. It became a friendship of convenience. It's interesting, if you hadn't got on with the regime in some way, things might have gone differently if you stayed.'

Ali-Shah and his brother were born in Uganda and the family navigated the next challenging decade together. 'The 1980s were the worst years for Uganda,' he says. 'Because there was all this confusion of who's in power, who are the rebels, who is securing you. They stayed all through those tough times and things were hard economically.' Ali-Shah remembers a simple childhood, of cycling and playing outside, navigating a lack of electricity, and the day the first ice cream shop opened in the early 1990s. 'I had a great time growing up here. People were always so nice, and everything was calm. We didn't have much exposure to the world, but at least every couple of years we would go to the UK to my dad's family.' After studying in Malaysia, Ali-Shah's been in Kampala ever since and has no intention of moving from his home. Having lost most of their money in the BCCI bank scandal, over the years the family continued working in business and now invest in real estate, helping convert the skyline with luxury apartments and rentals. Growing up, Ali-Shah went to local schools and speaks the Ugandan pidgin English that he says offers an instant connection with some Ugandans. 'There's very few of us who are still able to do that and connect very well with locals. Lots of people have their family history here, but they weren't born or raised here, so when they come, they're very mzungu.'*

Most of those who remained after 1972 were men. Some like Ali-Shah's father, managed to keep hold of their businesses, but the majority lost their shops and other ventures, instead working as contractors for the government,

---

* Mzungu is the Swahili word for white, and is used broadly to refer to foreigners across East Africa.

merchants or in the informal economy. The South Asian presence during these years was 'tenacious and imperilled', says Hundle, and roughly fell into one of three groups, each with their own form of protection – 'powerful businessmen with industrial know-how and personal connections to Amin, small-time traders who cultivated relations of protection with more powerful Indian and African men, and civil servants who worked in ministries.'[37] Personal ties and connections allowed people to navigate the turbulent environment they found themselves in, while specialist expertise afforded them a protective advantage.

After sitting tight in the 1970s, Amirali Karmali would grow his business to be one of the biggest conglomerates in Uganda, the Mukwano Group.[38] From the petrol station owner in Buganda keeping himself afloat with cash, to the Sikh industrialist with a platoon guarding his sawmill or the traders crossing in and out of Uganda importing sanctioned goods, tenacity was on show across the country.[39] A trader living twenty-five miles southwest of Kampala not only continued supplying government departments, but was also the goalie and the only Indian in the Mpigi Stars football team.[40] Muslims, Sikhs and Hindus who remained also tried to protect their places of worship from repossession and damage. In the process, religious sites even became homes. Ram Singh, Amin's chief engineer in the Ministry of Defence, had his team of construction workers and civil servants live together in the gurdwara. It was affordable, secured the premises and provided the men with a safer communal living space. Sites like this could also offer sanctuary to family members or returnees.[41] Those who remained 'managed to fit themselves within successive regimes without overtly politicising themselves,' says Hundle, making them 'both victims of 1970s racialised state violence and complicit collaborators in authoritarian state regimes.'[42]

Climbing through Kololo, taking my first glimpses of the same roads my family used to drive along, I drive up Elizabeth Avenue. I've just passed Philip Road, and higher up will meet Prince Charles Drive. These nods to the imperial years are seen across the country, including the sprawling Queen Elizabeth National Park in the west bordering the DRC's Virunga mountains, where famed tree-climbing lions lounge, overlooking savannahs once home to the Basongora people, before the colonial administration drove them off their grazing land to create the national park.[43] Elizabeth II's reign was deeply connected to the continent; she'd been staying on the foothills of Mount Kenya in 1952 when she got the news that her father had died and she was now Queen, a pivotal event in many Ugandan Asian childhoods.[44] Despite the sixty-odd years that have passed since Queen Elizabeth II was no longer the head of state and Queen of Uganda, and calls for change, the capital's street names have yet to be decolonised.* But in other ways, Kololo is changing. Once the preserve of embassies and sprawling bungalows, the skyline is growing vertically, as developers eye the sky and build apartment blocks high above the treeline.

---

* Barbara Angopa, 'Ugandan campaigners seek to decolonise Kampala's streets', *Al Jazeera*, 25 June 2020. In the wake of Black Lives Matter protests, a campaign was launched online to remove the names of British colonial figures, including Major-General Henry Colville and Lord Frederick Lugard, from Kampala's streets. In the early years of his rule, Amin had renamed a number of these streets – but they were reversed when his regime fell. Malcolm X Avenue is one of the renamed streets that remained.

With a white hard hat perched on my head, Bindu Thakar walks me through construction of her new home and the adjoining block of flats, where once their single property stood. A common sight across the hilltop, enterprising families are adding apartment blocks within their home grounds as an easy earner. There's similar towers going up at neighbouring properties, some so high they cast shadows over others' homes. Over tea and cake at the nearby Acacia Mall, which is home to a cinema, shops and even a cascading waterfall feature over the stairs, we catch up about what brought her and her family back in 1995. Bindu was twenty-three when she married a man in the UK who, as fate would have it, had been born in the same small hospital in Uganda as she was. They were brought into the world two years apart by the same midwife. Bindu grew up in Iganga, where her father ran a shop, until they fled to the UK when she was eleven. Her grandfather had come from Gujarat to Uganda years earlier, like many, seeking 'greener pastures'. Around ten years into Bindu and her husband's marriage, a holiday to Uganda to visit family sparked thoughts of moving back and trying their hand at new business. 'I hear a lot of people who are still wary of coming here because of their experiences leaving, but in that sense, I think I had moved on,' she tells me, having been able to put the strip search she was subjected to at the airport back in 1972 out of her mind. Some things remained the same though. When she visited her family's former home in Iganga, where several families were living together, she noticed the very same sofas they had left twenty years earlier, their cushions now ripped at the seams.

Swapping London for Kampala was a major adjustment. 'My initial five years, I hated it,' Bindu confesses. 'I found it really hard to adjust to Africa, life was very slow. And I had

two young children, who were four and three. I kept thinking, "This is not for me."' The infrastructure challenges of
the 1990s as the country recovered, including intermittent
power and water issues, added to the frustrations. Those
early years were similarly challenging for Jayjay. 'I didn't
know a soul, and had to get used to the very, very slow pace
of life, because I was used to living in Bombay where you're
in the fast lane, life is buzzing,' she says. Joining a few
women's organisations and clubs gave her familiar faces to
wave to on the streets, and she soon started slowly building a
life as more and more people returned. After a slow start in
the 1980s, by 1997, around 4,000 properties had been
returned, and a further 1,500 sold.[45] Bindu eventually moved
back to London, and as her husband's distribution business
boomed, the family spent the next decade living between the
two countries. 'When I moved to the UK and we bought the
house, the idea was my husband was going to move back to
London,' she says. 'But he kept reaching better and better
targets in his business, and I was enjoying it every time I
came back.' Bindu returned to Kampala, escaping the 'rat
race' of London for a quality of life she now says can't be
beaten. Her son is based in Uganda too, while her daughter
works in London. 'If you asked me after being here for
twenty-five years, Uganda is my home. We do come and go
to London. But I love it here.' Criss-crossing the globe has
left her feeling like a 'multicultural being', she says. 'I'd say
I'm an Indian, for sure, and referred to as an East African
Asian, but I have a lot of British in me.'

Splitting life between Uganda and England is a feature of
many returnee lifestyles. Taking a boda boda across town,
along a busy shopping street I find Rishi Tailor's office, at
the back of a small showroom stacked with car tyres. To the
sound of the road noise outside, he tells me how his family

makes it work. When Rishi's father came back to Uganda from Leicester in 1978 for a two-week holiday, he ended up staying three months. His former home, where he had previously imported alcohol and rice and his father had worked as a tailor for Amin's army, was calling him back. These were the Obote years, and basic commodities like sugar and salt were sparse, with huge demand for importation. Rishi's father moved over in 1979. 'When you landed, there were no phone calls, so we didn't know what was happening,' Rishi tells me, sat behind his managerial desk piled high with papers. 'My dad was away for about nine months and my brother was born. He hadn't even known my mother was pregnant.' That first trip cemented his father's decision to return permanently. 'He said, "I'm going back to Uganda, that's where my work is, and I can get everything back."' Moving back on his own, he was soon bringing in produce from across East Africa; Kenya, Tanzania, Congo. After Rishi's arrival, his mother put her foot down about the split family and brought her two children to Kampala in the spring of 1982. They were challenging years, he says, of coups, curfews and shortages. After a few years, his mother took him and his brother back to the UK. Since the 1980s the family business has mostly been in tyres, including fulfilling government contracts. After boarding school in Kenya, O-levels in Uganda and then university in England, Rishi was living in Leicester when he decided to commit to Uganda in 2005. 'Things are very different to when my mum was here,' says Rishi, now forty. Life here involves long hours at work, but is paired with koroga (barbecue) nights, trips to the Nile and off-road biking. 'You can get anything you want here now. It's much safer than other places and my wife and kids are very happy to be in Uganda.'

Looking out over Kololo from the bare bones of Bindu's

construction site, concrete girders jutting out into the skyline, I think about life in this quarter of Kampala now and then. It's a city transformed, and on the rise, literally and metaphorically. There was never any question in my family's mind that they would return after they left. Living in a government-owned home meant there would never have been property to reclaim. And each migration drew a line under the country before it, not to be crossed again. But I can't help wondering what life might have been like if, like the returnees I met, it had been on the table for my family. Running alternate futures through my mind like tapes, merging my mother's memories with stories I'd heard in recent days, I was lost in my thoughts. I sense I would have felt conflicted about forcing a new generation from their home if the family home had been ours, but enamoured with reconnecting with the recent past. Shaking my head, I returned to the cement floorplan I was walking around and focused on visualising the kitchen island and herb garden that would one day fill these spaces, rather than alternate timelines.

Reflecting on the expulsion in an opinion piece for the *Daily Telegraph* fifty years later, Museveni described the forced expulsion as a 'shameful chapter of Uganda's past' and reminded readers how his administration had welcomed people back. The Ugandan Asians had helped build the nation's economy, he wrote, and were needed again for this. 'After the war in which Amin was defeated, Uganda's economy and international reputation was in tatters,' he wrote. 'Integral to rectifying this was bringing our Indian community home.' The anniversary was a 'sobering week to reflect on the historic ties that bind Britain and Uganda' and looking to the future, he took a positive view on one legacy of empire. 'Still today some balk at using the Commonwealth to its full potential because it was born from colonialism. But the past is gone. What remains is our shared inheritance, and it is for all the Commonwealth's members to rebuild, reshape, and take ownership of our historic club. We should use it to trade closer and better, and make it what it should be: the vehicle for our shared futures.'[46] A few months later, the president told Indian business leaders that he wanted children of citizens to automatically get Ugandan citizenship, as well as easier access to permanent residency and multiple re-entry visas for Indians.[47] The elder statesman, approaching his eighties, has been favourable towards South Asians, while cementing his authoritarian rule and arresting opposition politicians. It remains to be seen what will happen next. There are fears in some quarters about what a new leader could spell for their future. New generations of migrants from India and Pakistan now eclipse the Ugandan Asian returnees.[48] Some of the returnees criticise them for a lack of commitment and attachment to the country, for coming to make money but not a home – ironically, what they had been accused of all those years before.

In whatever direction Ugandan society continues to develop, its South Asians will always be seen as different, says Azhar. 'When people first see me, the first thing they'll think is that I'm an Asian. Then I'll open my mouth and talk, and I'll sound like I'm a mzungu, like, I'm American or whatever. And then as soon as I introduce myself, they'll say, "Ee, you're Ugandan," because my name is known. So I always say whenever I meet someone, I go through this identity crisis. I think people will always see us as different, unfortunately. I don't see that changing for at least a couple of decades. But I see the newer generation of Ugandans that have more exposure to social media, who are travelling more, that demographic does not discriminate at all.' Ali-Shah also relates to the complexities of the way he is seen when it comes to his identity. 'When I tell Ugandans I'm a Ugandan, they're like, "No, you're Indian,"' he says, noting that the constitution doesn't describe how you look. 'When I travel, you go to the white countries, you're Indian. And then I went to India many years ago and I was in this taxi and this guy asked me, "Where you from?" I said, "What do you mean, where am I from, I look like you, don't I?" And he said, "Your skin colour is of the soil, but you're not from here." So I told him, "Listen, when I'm in Africa, the Africans tell me to go back to India, white people tell me to go back to India, I'm in India and you ask me where I'm from."' There's a difference, he says, in how the different groups of South Asians are seen in Uganda. 'People can tell if you're from here, or from outside. I was born and raised here, my family's history is here.' The young generation are making a commit-ment to the country, as Azhar adds, 'The East African Asians like us, we're here because this is home. I have a choice. I could literally pick up and leave and go anywhere I want. I choose to be here. I like being in Uganda.'

Chapter 10

Good Immigrants and Glass Ceilings

Sometimes the past seems to be a foreign country and eerily familiar at the same time.

Klaus Neumann, *Across the Seas*[1]

When you pick up a newspaper or turn on the television, you'll see two kinds of stories about migrants in the UK, and elsewhere too. The ones shouting the loudest scream of invasions and swarms and new but invariably still tired terminologies, conjuring up visions of Biblical plagues, casting humans as vermin to be eliminated from sight. Contrast this with the feel-good stories of individuals who break the mould, be that winning sports championships, saving lives in hospitals or becoming best-selling chefs. Welcome to the binary of the bad and the good immigrant. Bad immigrants are illegal, daring to come by boat across choppy waters uninvited to our shores. They're stealing our jobs, or scrounging benefits. They're terrorists and criminals. There's no more room on this island for them, refugees or not. Good immigrants, by contrast, have proven their worth. They can add value. They're heroic doctors running emergency surgeries, nurses caring for the elderly, or teachers inspiring children. They're prize-winners in their field. They're business leaders, pouring money into tax reserves. They're successful, unthreatening, and very grateful.

In the retelling of the Ugandan Asian story of migration, the group has become typified as a success, both in terms of

243

integration and material results. From the millionaire busi-nessmen or presence on British high streets, to those sitting in the Houses of Parliament, the overarching tale is one of triumph. 'Few would have predicted such an outcome when the Ugandan Asians started arriving 50 years ago,' the *Economist* wrote. 'David Goodhart, a historian, has written that the East African Asians proved to be "the most success-ful non-European minority group in post-war Britain". It's hard to disagree.'[2] Other news reports talk of Ugandan Asians and their children having 'made good', being 'part of Britain's secret weapon for success' and of their 'remarkable story of triumph' in which 'penniless refugees are now Britain's most successful immigrant community.'[3] While the conceptualisation of Ugandan Asians as uniquely successful has taken on a life of its own, the idea is rooted in some real-ity. A recent academic study found that within forty years of their arrival in the UK, East African Asians 'have indeed done well', and were 'significantly over-represented among professional and managerial occupations.' This, the authors noted, was 'quite remarkable' given the disadvantages they came with, although they added that the group were 'rela-tively advantaged' in East Africa, with a propensity for entre-preneurism.[4] Nonetheless, over the four decades since the expulsion, the researchers showed East African Asians did as well, or better than the rest of the population, in terms of employment status and educational outcomes.

The genesis of Ugandan Asians as a model minority has become part of the collective imagination of much of the community, who retell stories in keeping with this positivity, leaving silences unspoken around more uncomfortable parts of their experiences. And success isn't just material, although the focus often ends up on the financial winners. As a Member of Parliament, Shailesh Vara, who was born in Uganda to

Gujarati parents, told parliament in an ode to the good migrant, it's also about appearing to be faultless citizens:

> Many, many success stories are recorded in the media, but we must not forget that not all those 28,000 people became millionaires: many simply got on with their everyday lives, in whatever trade or job they had, and became model citizens in their own way, doing their bit for the greater good of the country as a whole. It is important to record that. There can be no doubt that the community as a whole has punched above its weight in Britain – it has done more than its fair share for mainstream Britain.[5]

Back in the summer and autumn of 1972, there was huge confusion over how to label the Ugandan Asians. Were they refugees fleeing Idi Amin's rampage, or were they immigrants? The success arch arguably started being carved here, at the outset of the exodus, in the way the arrivals were first framed by the government as refugees. 'There's an uncertainty in public conversation around what box to put them in,' historian Becky Taylor tells me. This started to solidify first as the government made it clear UK passport holders would be able to come, despite the legislation that had restricted their right of entry and limited them to accessing Britain via the limited voucher system, and then as the Uganda Resettlement Board was set up. Added to this, the press started reporting more of the dangers being faced in Uganda, telling dramatic stories of families being attacked by soldiers as they fled to the airport, inspiring greater sympathy for the imminent arrivals. 'There's that idea that, okay, they're not immigrants, they're refugees,' says Taylor. 'And not only are they refugees, but they're good refugees. Crucially, they're middle class, they're educated, they're business people. They are "people like us".' The discussion had now moved beyond immigration to take in class and respectability. This was seen in the more sympathetic news reports that ran in tandem with scare stories about floods of arrivals, which showed middle-class Ugandan Asian women trying to settle their families, learn to adjust to life without servants and discuss how to get their children into the best grammar schools.[6] 'We see that foundation being laid from the point of arrival,' says Taylor. 'There's this idea that they've become the quintessential respectable refugee or immigrant group. That's a narrative that's continued and been sustained both within and outside the East African Asian population in Britain.'

This label of success is certainly one that many Ugandan Asians have taken up with enthusiasm. It's something artist Sunil Shah found when he worked on a commemorative project for the fortieth anniversary of the expulsion, a year in which Conservative politician Baroness Warsi described the Ugandan Asian story as 'one of this country's greatest success stories' and a 'lesson . . . about the successes of integration'.[7] Commemorating the expulsion made Sunil question what we decide is important to share versus what gets excluded when we retell our histories. 'Even in 2013 I was very critical about the way in which Ugandan Asians were using that history as a springboard for talking about success and material wealth,' Sunil tells me. 'We were interested in stories from everywhere. And there were some stories that I felt really don't get talked about, especially the racism towards Black Africans that the Asian community has, or how caste is implicated in that history.' Ugandan Asian histories are 'deeply political', he says, and his interests lay in exploring the legacies of colonialism, not 'trying to turn the history into a celebration of, "Here we are, we're all successful and various people have got into really high positions and earnt a lot of money."' While there is of course truth in the way many people worked hard and were entrepreneurial, Sunil wanted to tell more than this increasingly tired narrative. 'It's a whitewashing of a history, if everything is just represented as being rosy,' he says. 'Aspects of that are absolutely true, that should certainly be celebrated, but I feel it shouldn't just be about that. We should not be shy about talking about some of the other more problematic parts of our history. The nature of what you talk about doesn't have to be dumbed down, or desensitised.'

One of the many issues with typecasting a diverse group of people is that it obviously fails to take into consideration everyone's circumstances. The Ugandan Asian as the archetypal good immigrant based on their entrepreneurism ascribes one story to tens of thousands of people, overlooking the huge variety within the community. While many of the arrivals were middle class with business experience, and got readily to work, there were also students yet to embark on their professional lives, elderly relying on relatives for their care, people with illnesses and disabilities and many who didn't speak any English. People like my grandparents were educators, without any involvement in business, although by virtue of their profession, they arrived in both England and Australia as good immigrants. This would continue down the generations, as two of their children became doctors, not only a prized profession in South Asian households, but also one of the best for immigrants to be accepted for. As early as 1979, Ugandan Asians were being praised in the UK parliament for their entrepreneurism. Ugandan Asian shopkeepers in Harrow were 'better practisers of private enterprise than anyone I can think of, and most of them have started from nothing,' their Member of

Parliament said, and should be looked to as an example for entrepreneurial spirit.[8] 'The category of the willing entrepreneur is often the headline image we have of the Ugandan Asians,' says Taylor. 'From a historical point of view, that is problematic, because that kind of narrative flattens the diversity within a population. More broadly it speaks to an uncomfortable and problematic attitude within British society that we're only really willing to accept refugees if they're going to be useful to us. If the narrative is always around, "Good refugees are those who contribute", what about people who are unable to contribute because of vulnerabilities and characteristics, whether that's through having experienced torture, or being disabled, or traumatised, or whatever it is. There's this sense in which it speaks of Britain's complicated relationship with refugees and the limits to British tolerance and openness.'

As the conceptualisation of Ugandan Asians as a model minority has continued to bloom over the years, even people who were viscerally opposed to their arrival in the 1970s have realised that they might have been mistaken about this particular group of migrants. Writing in the *Daily Telegraph* in 2019, former Conservative politician Norman Tebbit conceded he had been wrong to call for Ugandan Asians to have 'gone back to India where their roots lay', rather than coming to the UK, 'where their arrival might increase racial tensions and where they would simply not fit in to our society and be a burden on our economy.' It took reading a memoir of the expulsion written by fellow House of Lords' member Lord Dolar Popat, *A British Subject*, for Tebbit to 'own up to my mistake'. Tellingly, he explains his reasoning, writing, 'Lord Popat and his fellow Ugandan Asians have been an asset to this country.'[9] They had, in short, changed from bad to good migrants. Lord Popat has been a vital, vocal voice for Ugandan Asians on a national stage, regularly tabling motions in the Lords Chamber on anniversary years, and ensuring the migration is not forgotten by new generations of politicians. Arriving in London in 1971 aged seventeen with £10 in cash, he went on to build an empire of hotels and care homes. The fortune he's acquired, estimated in 2019 to be over £120 million, is destined, he says, not for his children's inheritance, but for charity. Lord Popat is the ultimate Ugandan Asian success story, a phoenix rising from the ashes of poverty to sitting in the House of Lords, something he says would have been 'impossible anywhere else in the world'. Unsurprisingly for someone whose book is subtitled *How to Make It as an Immigrant in the Best Country in the World* and is described as a 'love letter to this amazing country', he takes an enthusiastic view towards Britain. But within that sits something perhaps more problematic, which often goes hand in hand with the concept of good immigrants. 'People talk Britain down and it upsets me, especially when the immigrant community do it,' he told *The Sunday Times*. 'I can understand the British criticising their own country – fine. But how dare you come here and talk so low of this place? If you don't like it, go back to where you were.'[10] The idea that to question anything about a country that offered you or the generation before sanctuary must be equated with showing unacceptable ingratitude is pervasive. Good immigrants don't talk back or question the status quo, they know their place.

Many people who've shared their stories with me are proud to be called a success story, something I initially found hard to understand. To me it feels so deeply dichotomous – if you're successful, or good, it means that someone else comparatively is not. I am equally uncomfortable with the idea that as a migrant you need to prove your worth before you are accepted. However, as I had more and more conversations about this, I started to understand the nuances within people's relationship with ideas of progress, as well as recognising the generational divide when it comes to feeling pride versus shame around the conceptualisation of success. As the next generation, I didn't have to experience what the first did, and so have a different relationship with this terminology. My perspective still stands, but it doesn't take into account the feelings of being a newly arrived forced migrant, when your identity has been stripped from you overnight, along with the things that made up part of it – your profession, your community, your home. Doing things for yourself and your children, and fast, was not only a matter of survival, but also a step towards taking back lost independence. To be praised retrospectively is a mark of recognition of what you went through. That Ugandan Asians are held up as a successful group in the UK is a point of pride to Lata, who started over in the west of England after her incredibly challenging start as an unaccompanied child in a resettlement camp and then navigating life in a children's home. 'It shows the determination of the first generation of Ugandan refugees,' she says. 'I am quite proud of that, because our pride and hard work has been recognised. We didn't rely on handouts, we didn't rely on anything. We just got on with it, did whatever jobs and lived in whatever accommodation you could afford. We thought, "Okay, this is the opportunity where we can better ourselves, rather than be stuck in a stagnant place," and we built our lives. I feel proud that the Ugandan refugees actually have become successful.'

Focusing on success is also a way to gloss over the difficulties faced and hide painful things people don't want to talk about, or maybe even remember. It's a trend that goes beyond the Ugandan Asian diaspora, says Taylor, and can be commonly seen within migration stories. 'Academics who work on immigration say that there's often a lot of silence around those experiences of migration and discrimination, and what you get are these trajectories of success,' she says. 'You don't want to say, "Yes, I've been a victim of discrimination and racism," you want to be able to look back on your life and go, "Things were difficult, but I've established myself and I'm successful." People contextualise it in a bigger narrative arc. We want to be seen as human beings on our own terms.' In these versions of their life story, people moved to the UK, found things difficult, but quickly established themselves, and their children and grandchildren have gone on to do wonderful things. Little is made of the continued ups and downs of life, the setbacks and sacrifices along the way, and the glass ceilings hit professionally and socially. 'It hides a lot of the racism and the discrimination that people experience,' says Taylor. 'And it hides the sheer hard work, effort and sacrifice.'

In living rooms and cafes, offices and events, at times I've heard the other side to the exceptionalism that is applied to East African Asians emerge in troubling attitudes towards migrants. Ideas of a good immigrant draw them-and-us distinctions among minorities. Within the framework of the East African success arc, it turns out there's plenty of space to look down on those who don't match up. 'There's this sense that, "We were the first migrants here, we're better than them,"' says Kavi. 'They've lost touch with who they were when they first arrived in a situation – there seems to be a disconnect in empathy for new migrants.' Perhaps part of buying into the idea that you are uniquely successful as a group involves viewing others as less than – if you could make it, anyone can, if they just tried a little harder.

Juxtaposing two contrasting groups is always going to create a false comparison, but particularly so given the unique nature of the Ugandan Asian migration. Compared to today's asylum seekers, Ugandan Asians were in many ways set up for success. That's not to say there weren't major challenges – the widespread discrimination and institutional racism, language barriers and challenges in the job market. But those who made use of the camp system were accommodated in an environment that was actively trying to find them work and housing, even if not everyone took the Resettlement Board up on these offerings. Many spoke English and had either had a British education, or exposure to some elements of exported British culture, from the Victorian architecture in Bombay to the BBC broadcasts in Kampala. Although there was scant support from the government outside of the camps, and Ugandan Asians faced poor wages and inflated rent, unlike many other forced migrants, they had access to the labour market allowing them to work straight away, because they came in with citizenship.[11] And the mass migration meant a relatively sizeable number travelled in a short space of time, allowing for social support between family, friends and acquaintances, social networks that have been shown to correlate with better chances of employment.[12]

East African Asians had been embedded within empire, invested in it with all the prejudices this entailed. 'Asian groups in East Africa very much ran interference between the British Empire and black subjects of Empire; they acted as a buffer – explicitly or implicitly,' says Priyamvada Gopal, professor of postcolonial studies at the University of Cambridge. At the expulsion, they arrived 'to Britain as grateful subjects of Empire to whom the mother country was giving shelter.'[13] Empire was built on the idea of white

supremacy, but in Uganda it was also built on Brown supremacy over Black. This internalised racism and anti-Blackness
within South Asian communities extended beyond Uganda
to their new environment too. A further way of understanding the judgement towards other migrants is through a scar-
city mindset. Being let into a country doesn't always offer a
deep sense of stability. Assimilating and blending in is often
advantageous, while associating with other migrants almost
marks you as an outsider again. Creating a hierarchy in these
circumstances isn't uncommon, says Taylor. 'You'll see a
migrant group going, "Well, things were difficult for us. But
we were respectable, and we worked hard. The problem is
these immigrants today, who are bogus asylum seekers,
they're not like us." It's a very established and comforting
narrative, and you can then articulate yourself as being an
insider and distance yourself from these outsiders.' A good
migrant doesn't want to get tarred by the brush of a bad
migrant. Pushing against stereotypes means you have to
work twice as hard as the next person from the outset, and
there's often a glass ceiling ahead. If you're faced with the
binary choice, to be seen as a bad migrant or a good migrant,
who wouldn't choose good?

When Queen Elizabeth II passed away, among the carpet of
floral tributes laid outside Buckingham Palace were some
more unusual offerings – small soft toy bears and plastic-
wrapped marmalade sandwiches. Paddington Bear had
become a figurehead of the nation's grief, to the point that
the Royal Parks had to request that people stop bringing
the toy tributes. Thanks to Michael Bond's 1986 book
Paddington at the Palace, the bear in his iconic blue raincoat
and red hat had a Royal connection. This was cemented in a
sketch with the Queen sitting down to afternoon tea with

Paddington as part of her Platinum Jubilee celebrations, which went viral with over 14.5 million views on YouTube.[14] Paddington, the bear with a love of marmalade sandwiches, had become the quintessential symbol of Britain, but in reality, he's an immigrant – and an illegal one at that. It's a motif immigration lawyer Colin Yeo explored eight years earlier when he reviewed the Paddington movie from a legal perspective. 'Paddington's story is that of the modern migrant,' he wrote. 'He is in many ways typical of my clients.' Stowing away to escape Peru, the bear arrives into the UK as an illegal entrant. Yeo charts the relevant legislation affecting him, from the criminal offence he's committed under the Immigration Act 1971 to the fact he wouldn't qualify for refugee status.[15] 'Paddington is a really useful emblem of migration and welcome and what it means to be British,' Yeo tells me. 'It seemed to really resonate. There's such a failure of meeting of minds on this, so something like Paddington, which is a universal reference point, is actually quite a useful advocacy tool.'

Britain today likes to think of itself as a warm and welcoming nation, but the reality is that Paddingtons don't settle in with kindly families who find them in train stations. They're detained and deported. An increasingly hostile climate towards immigrants has visions of sending asylum seekers to third countries rather than taking them in and paints refugees as a problem to be eliminated. But the UK is a country that has been made by immigration, both long before its empire but of course also after it. 'The treatment of migrants arriving in the UK has been problematic for quite a long time, so it's not that there were some glorious Halcyon Days,' Yeo tells me. 'But there weren't any immigration controls at all until the Aliens Act 1905. "Aliens" is a word we don't really use these days, but it's very important in the context of the history of immigration to understand that there were aliens and British subjects. And British subjects were everybody in the entire empire, then the Commonwealth – a huge number of people.' The Aliens Act was the first peacetime legislation to restrict entry into Britain and was targeted at restricting Jewish migration. It drew distinctions between good migrants who could pay their way and those who would be a burden.[16] Further legislation in 1914 required would-be British citizens to have a solid grasp of the English language and 'good character'.[17] The 1948 British Nationality Act codified British nationality for the colonies and former colonies, but the immigration curbs that followed in the 1960s and 1970s, halting East African Asian migration, signalled the start of a time period which would last until the 1990s when, Taylor says, 'migration became collapsed with the idea of immigration as a problem, and then mapped almost solely onto pigmentation.' A former minister would later admit that, despite a reluctance to say so at the time, the legislation of 1962 was introduced 'to restrict the influx of coloured immigrants'.[18]

A survey of newspaper coverage in twenty British papers over two years from 2010 found the word most commonly paired with 'asylum seeker' was 'failed'. While the UN 1951 Refugee Convention maintains that everyone has the right to seek asylum in another country, this idea is under threat from leaders who want to prevent people from doing so here.[19] Not-in-my-backyard on a national scale. Theresa May set the ball rolling in 2012 with her so-called 'hostile environment' immigration package – a term she proudly coined herself. 'The aim is to create here in Britain a really hostile environment for illegal migration,' she told the *Daily Telegraph*.[20] A witch hunt was launched against undocumented migrants, preventing them from accessing the NHS, from working, or renting property and turning doctors, landlords, police officers and teachers into immigration officers by proxy. Despite the Home Office itself conceding that the 'vast majority' of undocumented people had done nothing wrong, it pushed ahead with policies that would lead to innocent people being targeted. Five years after the hostile environment was introduced, it emerged that hundreds of members of the Windrush generation – British subjects who had arrived from Caribbean countries between 1948 and 1973 – had been wrongly detained and even deported. They'd been told to prove they had the right to be in Britain, but the landing cards that showed their arrival had been destroyed by the Home Office in 2010.[21] The Windrush scandal showed the devastating human toll of these kinds of policies. Author Nadine El-Enany has called British immigration law a continuation of the colonial power enacted in the former empire.[22]

'Immigration today is in a way what it's always been, which is a really stark dichotomy about what we talk about and what we don't, what we think we ought to be able to get from immigrants, and what we don't,' refugee and migration expert Zoe Gardner tells me. 'Currently, we have a duality. We have a huge focus on people arriving on small boats to the Kent coast and seeking asylum, and this being quite literally characterised as an invasion. And on the other side, we have the much less talked about other pathways to migration, which are very high, not spoken about and generally seen as positive.' Gardner regularly goes to bat with politicians, select committees and journalists, calmly detailing the same unwavering facts about asylum seekers, explaining how deterrence policies don't work as more lives are lost to European waters, and explaining the true motivations of why people travel to Britain, or indeed anywhere else other than home.* Formerly at the Joint Council for the Welfare of Immigrants and now the European Network on Statelessness, she's long been at the coalface when it comes to humanising the impact of Britain's migration policies.

Pitching one group of migrants against another, or a nationality or culture being deemed to be more or less problematic at different times, is a tale as old as time, she says. 'The evidence is that there will always be somebody that they can say is the problem.' Precisely who is the problem can change with the click of a finger. When the labelling of migrants as problematic is subjective, groups can fall out of favour or suddenly be redeemed. 'The ground,' writes Maya Goodfellow, 'is constantly shifting under people's feet.'[23] Back in the Edwardian era, German and French migrants were broadly classified as good, but Italians were viewed with suspicion and Chinese migrants were seen as dangerous cultural threats bearing opium, in the so-called 'Yellow Peril'. But the First World War immediately shifted opinion when it came to European migration, with Germans and Austrians now liable to internment.[24] More recently this has been neatly illustrated in the Brexit years. Brexit turned the migration narrative on its head. Once more, it wasn't just Brown and Black people that were the perpetual problem – it was European migrants too. The run-up to the referendum stoked fears of Eastern European labourers swamping the market, placing them as the ultimate threat above any other migrants. Seven years later, when Russia's war drove millions of Ukrainians from their country, in Britain, Eastern Europeans were presented differently to before. They were

---

* For much more on the devastation faced by migrants at sea, see Sally Hayden, *My Fourth Time We Drowned: Seeking Refuge on the World's Deadliest Migration Route*, Fourth Estate, 2022.

no longer culturally incompatible, but people like Britons, refugees to be rightfully welcomed into people's homes – but notably in ways Afghan and Syrian refugees hadn't been.

An obsession with reducing the numbers of migrants is at the centre of the recent decades of increasingly draconian immigration policy. But the fact that it's not really about numbers but about the 'right' kind of migrant couldn't be clearer, seen in the migratory schemes that are allowing much larger numbers of people to settle in the UK at the same time as tabloids scream about a crisis of people crossing the Mediterranean and the Channel on small boats. The wrong migrants are those so desperate to reach Britain, fleeing humanitarian disasters and civil wars, they risk their lives at sea crossing with people smugglers for overinflated costs in underinflated boats. Decades of Conservative politicians have used increasingly dehumanising language towards asylum seekers. Then Prime Minister David Cameron started us off with describing 'a swarm' of people coming across the Mediterranean during the European migrant crisis, and his foreign secretary Philip Hammond followed the next year by describing 'marauding' migrants in Calais and African refugees as undermining Europe's 'standard of living', words Amnesty International called 'shameful'.[25] In 2022, the day after migrants at an immigration centre were attacked by a terrorist who set off a firebomb, Home Secretary Suella Braverman said the south coast was facing an 'invasion' of migrants.[26] And yet Britain as a country does allow significant inward migration. Special visa schemes like those that around 160,000 Ukrainian refugees have used to enter the UK, along with a bespoke scheme for people from Hong Kong that over 144,000 people have used in two years, dwarf the numbers of asylum seekers trying to enter the country. There's a stark double standard at play, a question of good versus bad migrants.

When China cracked down on dissent in Hong Kong in 2020 and imposed its sweeping national security law to suppress pro-democracy protests, Britain decided to open the doors to its former colony. British National (Overseas) status, which was created when Hong Kong was handed back to Beijing in 1997, the true end of the British empire, already entitled holders to British passports. The new visa scheme now offered the opportunity to live, study and work in the UK for five years, as well as presenting a route to apply for citizenship. Like the Ugandan Asians, Hongkongers are a legacy of Britain's empire, and in this case, Britain has chosen to, as the minister for immigration said, 'uphold our moral and historic commitment to the people of Hong Kong.'[27] In the first year and a half, 130,000 people took advantage of the scheme – a significant migration, far eclipsing the one this book has focused on – but one that's hardly been talked about or even seen in the national consciousness.[28] Government funding to the tune of millions is covering skills training such as language classes, volunteering opportunities and support in job hunting, all extremely welcome moves, but which do make for a contrast with other migrants who are stuck in hotels and prevented from working.[29] The money spent here is much more than would be needed to provide even the basic dignity for the tens of thousands of migrants arriving by irregular means, adds Gardner. 'It's much more than finding the right policy that could work to reduce numbers,' she says. 'Because the numbers really, really don't matter. People have no idea what the numbers are.' In fact, UK net migration hit an all-time high in 2022. Of the 504,000 people that came in the year to June, asylum applications, including small boat arrivals, made up just 73,000, or less than fifteen per cent. The majority, 277,000, came as students, with 170,000 Ukrainians and 76,000 from

Hong Kong. 'It's entirely about narrative,' adds Gardner. 'We could double or triple the number of immigrants if we had a good narrative being spread about it.'[30]

When Rishi Sunak launched his bid to enter 10 Downing Street, he dedicated a third of his three-minute video to weaving an upwards trajectory of migration. Starting his leadership campaign to become prime minister of the UK with a broadcast, he leaned on his family's story of empire, while failing to mention half of it. Speaking over a montage of black and white photos and stirring piano music, he told how Britain offered his family new opportunities after they boarded a plane in the 1960s. 'Family is everything to me and my family gave me opportunities they could only dream of,' he said. 'But it was Britain, our country, that gave them, and millions like them, a chance of a better future.' In this heroic arc, where the UK offered his grandparents and mother sanctuary, there's no mention of how the same country had played a role in their migratory lives prior to arriving. In fact, we don't even hear what country his family was coming from.[31] Sunak's arrival at Number 10 was celebrated in South Asian quarters as the ultimate symbol of success for Indians, and East African Asians, even if an Oxford-educated, ex-Goldman Sachs billionaire was less of a break with Tory tradition than his ethnicity suggested. And he was curiously keen to position himself within the immigrant space, cherry-picking the parts to share while espousing anti-immigration policies. His parents Usha and Yashvit, from Tanzania and Kenya, had of course come to East Africa on the winds of empire. But the gaps in stories like this feed into the collective amnesia around empire today, something which stretches so far that it's often been forgotten how empire continues to impact migratory patterns today.

Two successive home secretaries who also have East African Asian backgrounds are part of cabinets that have been championed as the most diverse in British history. There's Suella Braverman, the former attorney-general, whose father arrived from Kenya in 1968, and before her, Priti Patel, whose parents migrated from Uganda in the 1960s ahead of Amin's actions. Both have pursued staunchly anti-immigration policies. Far from a softening of migratory policies from these quarters, there has been a rise in racist dog whistles and an impression that almost in spite of their colour, or gender, they will be tougher than anyone else, perhaps a tacit justification for a seat at the table. This pair's work includes taking such an uncompromising stance towards asylum seekers that they would see them relocated to Rwanda, to the chagrin of many who question how they can be so unsympathetic towards migrants when they have direct familial experience. How can a child of immigrants pull the ladder up behind them so triumphantly? Professor Kishan Devani, who describes himself as a son of Ugandan refugees, tweeted that he found her actions 'difficult and troubling', adding, 'If it wasn't for immigration both our families would not have been in the UK, living the lives we do. It is truly shocking.'[32]

It's an interesting quandary, because while it's galling to see a diverse cabinet pushing through legislation devastating towards ethnic minorities, it would be obviously wrong to put additional expectations on people of colour to act more charitably because of their background, or for us to hold them any more accountable than their white colleagues. Representational politics falls down if it presumes that a viewpoint will be shaped by someone's family history. The children of immigrants, and in this case, voluntary economic migrants, aren't required to act in the interests of other immigrants, and people like Patel are permitted their own views, not those one might assume from their appearance. The policies enacted by these home secretaries are in keeping with the Conservative Party they are members of, proving it's not only representation that matters, but institutional thinking and the racism intrinsic to this politics. Their identities are paraded as progress, the government leaning on the optics of diversity to allow their policies to go unchallenged, when in reality these individuals continue to uphold systems that oppress other minorities.

Musa Okwonga, whose parents also left Uganda in the Amin years, described how Patel's behaviour benefits her party. 'The racial gatekeeper is a crucial role because it allows a group of white people with racially regressive views to say: "Look at us, we have found a non-white person who agrees with us, our policies therefore do not have racially regressive effects." Racial gatekeepers are an interesting contradiction: they pride themselves on their rebellious streak, defying what people expect them to think, yet the positions which they take rigidly reinforce the racial status quo.'[33] There's an even more insidious side to this, when minority cabinet members weaponise their backgrounds as a shield to invalidate any possible criticism. When cheerfully announcing the end of free movement 'once and for all', Patel clearly laid out her feelings of being untouchable on these topics as a minority. 'Because, let me tell you something,' she smiled, 'this daughter of immigrants needs no lectures from the North London metropolitan liberal elite.'[34] Similarly, then Home Secretary Sajid Javid, the son of Pakistani Punjabi immigrants, told the former shadow home secretary that she didn't have a 'monopoly on anger' over the Windrush scandal, because he was a 'second-generation immigrant too'. That was true, but it's also true that Javid voted for the legislation that led to the scandal.[35] Both Conservatism and East African Asian migration have become linked with the tenets of individualism, the belief that anyone can be successful if they apply themselves. It's reflective of the attitudes of many South Asians within Uganda, where capitalism flourished. East African Asians like Sunak and Braverman, Yasmin Alibhai-Brown says, were 'attached to the empire and attachments of the empire,' finding a natural home in the Conservative Party.[36] They're not alone. More broadly, British Indians have been held up by the Conservatives since Margaret Thatcher's years as the good immigrant exemplars of what the free market can achieve. By 2010 British Indians were the most pro-Conservative ethnic minority after the Jewish community, and by 2017 the party got forty per cent of their vote.[37]

Focusing on representation as a binary overlooks the complexities of the racial spectrum and the divergent experiences within it. When we talk about them and us in terms of colour, it very often squashes people into white and non-white, a descriptor that jars with me, for making white the default and everything else something that doesn't fit the mould. Recent home secretaries have been 'deployed in the interests of anti-blackness', Gopal writes, which can be hidden when we only look at race in terms of white and not. 'Asians have had a very specific role in terms of the racial politics of empire. The deployment is historically old – this is something that the British white establishment has long done, to use Asians to run interference on behalf of white supremacy and racism frankly. So I don't see Patel or Braverman as breaking with empire – they're very much of a piece with a very old deployment.'[38] Where South Asians have become the 'good' people of colour, that often leaves Black people as the bad. While the political Blackness of the 1960s and 1970s played a vital role in combating racism, it is of its time, and we need to speak to each community or risk grossly misrepresenting people's experiences. The category BAME, Black, Asian and Minority Ethnic, has caused a similar problem, doing greatest disservice to the truth of Black Britons' lives. There are more than double the number of unemployed Black people than Indian, and while Asian women are twice as likely as white women to die during pregnancy, Black women remain the most at risk, five times more than white women.[39] Meanwhile Black people are nine times more likely to be stopped and searched than white people, and two thirds of Black people say they have experienced prejudice from healthcare staff.[40] A two-year research project concluded in 2023 that, 'Britain is not close to being a racially just society.'[41]

Fifty years after the Ugandan exodus, the government is overseeing some of the harshest immigration policies on record, from the attempted offshore processing in Rwanda of asylum seekers to the passing of the Nationality and Borders Act, which allows British people to be stripped of their citizenship without notice and asylum seekers to be criminalised depending on how they arrived in the country. This legislation codifies Windrush fears, which is that if you have any other country in your familial background, you could without warning be deported there – policies that overwhelmingly discriminate against people of colour. There are now also ambitions of a points-based immigration system, emulating the Australian model, which exemplifies the acceptance of good migrants only – those that are useful within a capitalistic framework. The Rwanda proposal has been broadly condemned by rights organisations and is one of the most extreme immigration policies in the world. When I started exploring Ugandan Asian history, I would never have guessed that the UK government would attempt to deport people to the country next to the one my family had originally fled from. Half a century after politicians proposed shipping East African Asians and other imperial hangovers offshore to the Falklands or the Solomon Islands, I was hearing politicians talk about sending migrants to East Africa. The circumstances differ, of course, between a specific group of British citizens, and asylum seekers more broadly, but there are undeniable parallels in the hostility of Britain's migratory approach then and now. On the most simplistic level, two different Conservative governments fifty years apart have wanted to abdicate responsibility of supporting people fleeing persecution and relocate people of colour on other countries' land.

What's more, many of those risking their lives to come to the UK, do so out of legacy ties borne out of empire. 'The first thing to say in terms of why people come to the UK is that of course most people don't,' says Gardner. The vast majority of people who are displaced never cross their country's border, after which most stay in adjoining countries. 'All the evidence shows us that people who choose to come to the UK come because of connections, whether that be language, history, family, people from their community having moved here. And it has a lot to do with our colonial history.' The imperial expanse introduced people across the world to Britain, something we're encouraged to celebrate in the Commonwealth but denigrate in people crossing our borders. 'Half the countries in the world have English as an official language and we have well-established, well-integrated communities from those countries who have been living here long term, so people know this is a country they can find people from their culture and be welcomed,' explains Gardner. 'We have a reputation for being safe and prosperous and those connections are not things you can change by putting in so-called policies. The only way to change that would be to change the fundamental nature of what the UK is, and its history.' There's a further legacy of empire that arguably drives migration too. While Britain built wealth out of the resources it took from colonies, in exchange it left behind systems of governance, including laws that discriminate. Uganda is one of the many countries around the world where homosexuality is illegal, a legacy of colonial rule. Some of those seeking sanctuary in the UK from anti-LGBTQ+ bills, head for the country that set these laws and viewpoints into place. 'These people are connected to the UK,' says Gardner. 'Our empire spanned the globe and people were British citizens for a really long time under that. And those connections are real – in terms of connections with people across borders, but also culturally, historically, linguistically. Those connections are the primary thing which drive migration flows.' People from former French and Belgian colonies are more likely to go to migrate to those countries too. Britain's former imperial expanse has just left a bigger legacy, one which continues to be felt in myriad ways today.

Chapter 11
Where Are You (Really) From?

But still
you
are permanent.
You who perfected the ratio.
Blood to sugar to money to bricks.
Each bougie building we flaunt
haunted by bones.

Vanessa Kisuule, 'Hollow'[1]

Some 4,000 miles from Kampala as the bird flies, lies another city set on seven hills. My university city of Bristol is a vibrant community fiercely proud of its creativity and independent spirit, and is celebrated for its multicultural calendar, including St Paul's Carnival, which was built up among the Windrush Caribbean migrants. The inner-city streets of St Paul's were once the only places Afro-Caribbean immigrant communities could find housing, amongst the undesirable bomb-damaged buildings. Ugandan Asians moved into these same parts of the city in the 1970s, in the spirit of migrants around the world responsible for repopulating run-down, deprived areas and turning them into living communities again. Today, those same gentrified streets play home to huge faces graffitied in the city's typical street art, showing Black icons who changed history here. Local artist Michelle Curtis' Seven Saints of St Paul's subverts the typical white-centric history to showcase Black Bristolians who fought for racial equality. Surrounded by bold colours and joyful patterns, faces fill the entire sides of buildings, bringing an alternate history to the fore. These include Owen Adolphus Henry, Audley Evans and Roy Hackett, pioneers of the Bristol Bus Boycott – the first Black-led campaign against a ban on people of colour working as bus drivers or conductors.[2] In just four months, the Bristol Omnibus Company was forced to end its colour bar. Raghbir Singh, a Punjabi Sikh, was hired as the city's first bus conductor of colour.[3]

But walk through some of the wealthiest parts of this city and the architecture takes on a different significance. These Georgian buildings celebrate history of a more sinister origin. Here the legacies of empire stand proud to this day, bought with tainted money borne of the slave trade, the streets laced with blood. *Blood to sugar to money to bricks*, as Bristol poet Vanessa Kisuule encapsulated it. Britain has its secrets when it comes to race, says journalist and author Afua Hirsch, even if we're taught not to see race. 'They lurk in the language, and the brickwork and the patterns of society, so that, for those who are silent or desperate enough to listen and search, clues gradually begin to reveal themselves.'[4] When I first moved to Bristol, while walking the streets my thoughts were mostly centred on the bars and dancefloors within the historic buildings, the vintage shops and music. It took me many more years to truly appreciate how my student experience had been shaped by the shadows of empire cast down from the city's architecture, down to the very buildings I lived in.

As I made my home in Bristol, I was following in the footsteps of the early Ugandan arrivals who came to the city forty years earlier. Seeking solidarity in one another, different groups banded together, forming tight-knit communities that endure to this day. While a Ugandan or East African Asian identity might no longer lead front and centre, the personal histories within families are celebrated down the generations. My conversations with people in Bristol echo a wider sentiment of duality: that you can look back and remember your origins while fully investing in the here and now when building a home. What's less clear is how much people see the continuity between the two, the thread of empire running through their experiences and outlook to this day.

Arriving into Bristol on the train, and walking towards the central harbour, you pass the imposing church of St Mary Redcliffe. In years gone by, its upkeep and enlargement came thanks to its wealthy congregation, who turned in healthy offerings of blood money during services. Parishioners included members of the Society of Merchant Venturers, who owned and invested in slave trade voyages. A particularly unsavoury celebration of slavery was said to have taken place here too. When abolitionist William Wilberforce's bill to ban the trade of slaves failed in parliament in 1771, the church bells rang out in celebration.[5] Many of the city's cobbled streets, pubs and prestigious homes take on a new light when viewed through the lens of the past. The Hatchet, a pub better known in my student days for sticky tables, metal music and cheap spirits, is Bristol's oldest inn going back as far as 1606 and would, in the era of slavery, have played host to business meetings between merchants, plantation owners and officials. The sugar processed in the city came with imperial origins and the goods created here were being directly exchanged for enslaved people.[6] In the upmarket suburb of Clifton, under the shadow of Brunel's Suspension Bridge, a number of private residences are used by Bristol University as student accommodation. I learnt

from friends living at Goldney Hall of its familial association with slavery, through the Goldney merchant dynasty,
but I remained painfully oblivious that I was myself living
within corridors once walked by slave-owners. The bright
white terraced houses making up Richmond Terrace were
once home to John James Vidal, who owned 173 slaves on
the Berkshire Hall plantation in Jamaica when he moved to
Bristol.[7]

When I graduated with my history degree, it was from
Wills Memorial Building, a tall neo-Gothic tower making up
one of the highest points of the Bristol skyline. Walking
awkwardly across the stage in the Great Hall, peeking out at
my parents tucked in the rafters among the clapping crowd,
I was unwittingly a part of something as historic as anything
I had studied during my degree. This striking 215-foot-high
building, evoking the style of Oxbridge colleges, has come
to be synonymous with the university, and was opened by
George V. But it is also a building steeped in the history of
the oppression of people of colour. Constructed in the early
twentieth century in honour of Henry Overton Wills III, the
first chancellor of the university, it was funded by the Wills
family – who made their fortune trading tobacco, during the
era of slave-produced tobacco on American plantations, and
whose company would later be merged to form Imperial
Tobacco.[8] The university has rejected a petition calling for
the name to be changed.[9] Other universities are also grap-
pling with their past, from considering reparative justice to
launching reviews into their colonial links.[10]

But this goes much deeper than individual landmark
buildings. In 2018, it was estimated that a staggering eighty-
five per cent of the wealth used to found Bristol University
depended on slave labour. And to this day, these funders
remain in pride of place on the university's crest, prestigious

families who each profited from colonialism given an ongoing legacy on every letterhead. The emblem shows a sun for the Wills family; a dolphin for the slave-trading Colston family, featuring Edward Colston, whose statue was pulled down by protestors in the summer of 2020 in front of global audiences online; and a horse for the Fry family, of Fry's Chocolates, who were responsible for thirty-nine per cent of all cocoa imports from the Caribbean and its slave plantations. Like so many things carrying a colonial legacy, it's not clear at first glance that these symbols are associated with slavery. They are, as the university's economic and social historian Dr Richard Stone says, hiding in plain sight.[11]

Imperial signposts like this do not exist in a vacuum for a person of colour today. For those either from or with relatives from a former colony, the British empire's legacy sits within just a few generations. In the case of Ugandan Asians, it's currently the same generation, or once removed. This is our very recent past, and its impact is still felt when you look directly at the colonial legacies around us, or the wide-ranging imperial nostalgia paired with a surprising lack of discussion of the realities of this period of time. Events like the Windrush scandal, historian Ian Sanjay Patel says, shows how 'this particular history is never far away' and remains subject to 'historical abridgements'.[12] As Sathnam Sanghera, journalist and author of *Empireland: How Imperialism Has Shaped Modern Britain*, said in a documentary exploring similar themes, 'For me as a child of immigrants from the Punjab, the British empire isn't just a few chapters in a history book. It's something very much alive and personal.'[13] For me, empire is both around and within me. Each of us has our own empire stories. It's a strange feeling to feel so critical of something that is also the reason why you exist.

When Ugandan Asians built new lives, many starting over with nothing and launching new careers far removed from how they had imagined their futures, in many ways Uganda was behind them. Some would never even speak of these years again, firmly locking up the past and throwing away the key. Others would allow the warm times to stay, closing off the hardships and traumas in lieu of retaining fond memories of their former home. Whichever way Uganda was carried with the exiled, it's perhaps been less obvious how the forces that shaped their lives in the country had filtered into people's sense of selves. When we think of something like the British empire as a monolithic and very physical experience, it excludes the psychological impact of growing up under its influence. Within my family these were very British upbringings, from the curriculums to the BBC broadcasts and the starched-white tennis stars. Royalty was revered, hymns were sung and aspirational English brands were coveted. But beyond these visible tips of icebergs lie the far greater impact of the worldview you gain from living within a hierarchical system that places you above others. The vast British empire is often thought of in abstract terms, or in purely geographic ones. It spanned five centuries and around a quarter of the world's land mass but amounted to more than just territory – as author Samir Puri writes, it was also a 'state of being and of mind'.[14] As well as leaving its marks on the streets and within institutions, empire is also embedded within culture, politics and perspectives. When it comes to the Ugandan Asian diaspora, or the next-generation identities of immigrants from former colonies, we can't easily remove empire from the equation. To come from colonialism makes for a complicated heritage, especially as a Ugandan Asian, when that heritage involves participation in settler-colonialism. Empire was the force at

the root of the exodus, but it was also more than circumstance. Colonialism was as much a mission of winning
hearts and minds as territory, with the former outlasting the
latter over the years.

This reminds us that the forces that have shaped East
African Asian politicians in parliament also apply to those
outside of politics. The legacy of growing up in a society
without a welfare state and where you sought to avoid paying
taxes, is a fundamentally capitalist perspective and is part of
what leads to notable numbers of East African Asians finding solace in Thatcherism and home in the Conservative
Party, says Yasmin Alibhai-Brown.[15] The impact of this
worldview is expressing itself today, as journalist Hardeep
Matharu argued when exploring how her parents, who
migrated from Kenya and India forty years earlier, went on
to vote for Brexit. This vote was 'in no small part, about
Empire for Commonwealth immigrants', she writes in the
Byline Times. Life under British rule was good to her father,
who describes a sense of loyalty to Britain, far stronger than
any allegiance to Europe. And that loyalty went both ways
– the UK owed its former colonies trade deals and immigration routes today, in exchange for its centuries of extraction.
That sense of a global Commonwealth family that was built
through the imperial years lives on.

While many recognise the damage done to countries like
India, colonisation created a 'patriotic allegiance in immigrants who see themselves as "British" – more British than
the British – rather than as migrants,' writes Matharu.[16] This
certainly tallies with my mother Betty's sense of self, which
I've often felt was exemplified by its Britishness. Sitting
together in a living room visibly illustrating the duality in
her life – where a row of carved wooden elephants march
silently atop a piano next to quintessentially English William

Morris curtains – I ask how she feels about her national identity. 'I feel that I'm English really, and I felt that in Uganda – maybe even more so, because there was more of a separation between people there,' she says. 'I definitely didn't feel Indian, or that because I was born in Africa, I was African.' My family were brought across borders by empire but made choices to move towards Britain because of the affiliation developed during their imperial lives. After living eighteen years in Uganda, my mother's arrival in England felt like a natural progression of a life that had already been twinned with the UK. 'I didn't realise how essential empire was to everything until recently,' she says, reflecting on the things she took for granted in her upbringing. 'It's why it's so interesting, because it impinges on everything. I can now see how there were two sides to everything we did in Uganda, but I didn't see it at the time, which is why we just thought we had a wonderful upbringing.' She's referring to the inequities in society, and the fact that it was routine and unquestioned for South Asians, as with white families, to have Black Ugandans working for them. 'I've always had a long story to explain to people,' she adds. 'I don't feel where you feel you come from has anything to do with where you are born, because it depends on how you are brought up within the place that you are born.' That sense of home means something different to all of us.

The sun breaking behind clouds above the limestone Twelve Apostles along Australia's Great Ocean Road cuts to images of those same rays being cast over the iconic Manhattan skyline, and then through the hazy morning skies over the Great Wall of China. Beaming young singers raise their choral voices in unison, singing, 'I still call Australia home'.[17] When I first saw Qantas' perennially popular ad campaign in

The Adamsons may have been the famous lion owners in Kenya, but Kausar and her husband Ishtiaq were doing it too, raising little Sheru by hand.

Sheru would grow into a handsome lion and outgrow the house, but never forgot his family.

A single, cherished photo is the only one Lata, pictured with her brother, has from her childhood in Jinja, before they were uprooted to Britain without their parents.

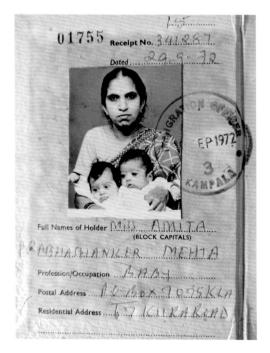

Amita Mehta was too young to have memories of Uganda, but has treasured her passport – notably stamped out in September 1972.

Arriving in Cambridge in late 1972 thanks to the support of the church and vicar Mark Ruston, pictured, my grandmother is seen decked out in a flamboyant fur coat that had been given to her.

Kavi's mother Sarla Pujara (right) celebrating her niece Vishva Murtha's (left) sixteenth birthday in the summer of 1970. This was her first in Leicester, having migrated from East Africa the previous winter, ahead of her husband who was winding down his business in Kenya.

For others who didn't have connections in the country, resettlement camps beckoned. Lunchtime at Stradishall in October 1972 saw Ugandan Asians queue up for peas and pasta.

The wind howled across the pebble beach on the west coast of England, a sharp departure from the Kenyan sands for the Majothi family when they arrived in late 1972.

Christmas 1972 was spent in a corrugated iron billet at Doniford camp for the Majothis, their extended family and friends.

Getting back to their shopkeeping roots on St Mark's Road, Bristol, Kassam and Fatma opened Sweet Mart in 1978.

The Majothi children, fifty years on from their arrival in the West Country. From left to right: Yunas Kassam, Abdul Gani Ismail, Hamida Sumar, Saleem Kassam Ismail and Rashid Kassam.

My parents Betty and Martin carving their way into married life in the summer of 1978. A silk sari with embroidery in gold thread from India, and cheese, pineapple and glacé cherry sticks from 1970s England.

My family would end up in Sydney – their fourth country and continent.

The most clichéd Australia photo in our album –
me making friends as a toddler.

Three generations of Ugandan Asians/Malayalis/Brits/Australians:
Betty, me and Rachel in the Sydney suburbs, replete with
bottlebrush tree.

When Kavi Pujara returned to Leicester, he started photographing the community in a work that would become *This Golden Mile*. His portraits showcase the multiplicity within British Asian households.

Holding a photo taken fifty years ago at my family's former home in Kampala in 2022, piecing together my past with my present.

1998 selling the Australian dream at home and abroad, I did call Australia home. Living in the Sydney suburbs, peals of laughter rang out from kookaburras on tree branches outside, and every evening a dark shadow of wings would descend over the bungalow's roof, as hundreds of fruit bats took their nightly migration to the city's parks in search of nocturnal feeds. Although I held multiple countries within my family tree, I didn't question the notion of home, and nor did others. During my childhood, my classrooms were full of different cultures, all of us fiercely and unquestionably Australian, but speaking of relatives in Europe or Asia, equally likely to be eating onigiri, Japanese rice triangles, for lunch, as sandwiches. But as I grew older, and moved to the UK, I found myself increasingly facing what Hirsch capitalised as The Question, the 'most persistent reminder of that sense of not belonging.' Four simple words. Where are you from? Actually, sometimes it's five, emphasis on the fourth. Where are you *really* from?

People have widely differing opinions on this question – it's a personal one – and the many people of different ages and backgrounds I've spoken to vary in their tolerance to it. For some, it's an affront, a provocation. It's something that marks them as different. For others, it isn't exclusionary or diminishing at all, but rather reflecting a relevant curiosity and interest, which can amount to an affirmation of their past, an opportunity to be better known. For Hirsch, 'being asked where you're from in your own country is a daily ritual of unsettling,' and, as a question saved for those who look different, something which ensures you regularly feel different. Although she's lived in five different countries as an adult, Hirsch says she's never been asked the question more than in the UK, where she *is* from.[18] For me, it's less about the question, than the tone. Because of those negative instances, when it's fired at you accusatively, I hold some challenges around being asked where I'm from. A seemingly innocuous question can feel like a fishhook in the stomach, jerking you to those conversations that were not innocuous, which turned into interrogations, or contained poorly veiled layers of judgement. Those are the times when it culminates in the grand finale of 'but where are you *really* from', which tells you to stop the charade and answer the question relating to your skin colour, which is all that is being seen of you in that moment. And yet my grandmother would happily ask people this question in corner shops and watching the conversation coming from the other side of the fence, not from the mouth of a white person, gave me a whole new perspective on its capacity to not exclude, but include. Having watched this in action, I realised how the recognition and community that came from this place was a stark contrast to the way many of these conversations had always made me feel. An irony of telling stories about immigration and identity is that I have become a prolific asker of The Question myself.

It's not an easy question to answer when you hail from multiple places. Where are you from sometimes asks me where I live now. Where are you from sometimes conjures up images of a jigsaw, the pieces coming from four corners of the earth. Where are you from sometimes asks me what I am, genetically, conjuring up images in my mind of those immigration officers in the White Australia days, making mental calculations of the percentage of acceptable blood in a hopeful applicant. For years, my default answer to the question was Australia – it's my birthplace, my real home and my heart. But this floors people, because I never looked the way people imagine an Australian to, nor do I sound like it, having lost my accent within the first year of school abroad where I swiftly and subconsciously realised that standing out as a twelve-year-old was a fate to be avoided at all costs. When that answer wasn't readily accepted, in my combative mode, I would counter that I was from England. That's also true – I've lived here, my father was English and I've got the passport to prove it. But still you'll find that's not it. Capitulating, I would say my mother was from India and be done with it, getting to the root of my Brown skin, the complexities of adding in Uganda not worth my while.

As a mixed-race person, this conversation sometimes takes on a further indignity, when, after having first been quizzed about my looks, I'm then dismissed as not looking Indian enough to warrant mentioning it. Once, after attempting to explain some racial nuances to a group of women through my own experiences, I was repaid with comments about how they never thought of me as anything other than white, more than slightly missing the mark and my point. Or when saying you're Indian yields further questioning about being a Hindu or speaking Hindi – neither of which apply – and without going into India's twenty-two official languages, hundreds of mother tongues, and multitudes of religions, you can feel like you've failed whatever test you didn't know you were sitting. With my family not one of the majority Indian groups in Uganda, I'm an outsider within an outsider group. When your origins aren't clear to people, sometimes you can be left over-explaining your existence. Nowadays, I'm less sensitive about telling people where I'm from. But it's still a long story, from four continents, two hemispheres, and multitudes of cultures. So the truncated version goes, I was born in Australia, and my mother is Indian. If someone is ready to buckle in for the geographic journey, they can hear the whole lot, taking in East Africa too.

The problem with seeking a singular answer to a question like this is that it places a national affiliation over all the other many facets of our identities, and also doesn't account for them shifting over time and circumstance. 'The reality is we're complex human beings. We've got all kinds of identities and they interchange with each other. They're multi-faceted. They end up evolving over time,' says Shezan Muhammedi, an adjunct research professor working on the history of migration at the University of Carleton, whose mother came to Canada from Uganda in 1972 with her family when she was nineteen. He had always been fascinated with his mother's story, Muhammedi says, and became curious about the wider resettlement experience in Canada. Exploring newcomer and next-generation identity has been a part of his exploration of the Canadian Ugandan Asian diaspora. 'The other thing that's really interesting is scholars have started to point out things like situational identities. So, depending on what context you're in, different identities come to the fore and others move to the background.'[19] I really relate to these concepts, as I can feel more attached to any one of my countries depending on who I'm with, and this has also varied at different points of my life. And my conversations have shown that there's no correlation between generation and identity. Some people who have never been to India or Uganda feel huge affinities with this part of their background, becoming more embedded with Indian traditions than people in India itself, while others think very little of anywhere other than where they reside.

Still, the questioning of your right to belong somewhere can feel systemic, and it's illustrated neatly in an event involving none other than the King of England. Four years before taking on the crown, Prince Charles himself posed The Question to a Brown woman in an exchange so uncomfortable she wrote an open letter published in the *Guardian* under the title, 'Dear Prince Charles, do you think my brown skin makes me unBritish?', which shortly after went viral. Meeting the royal at a Commonwealth event in London, journalist and author Anita Sethi shook his hand and talked about her mother's birth in Guyana. She detailed the exchange as follows. ' "And where are you from?" asked the Prince. "Manchester, UK," I said. "Well, you don't look like it!" he said, and laughed. He was then ushered on to the next person.'[*][20] This is the establishment in action, with the same colonial views of yesteryear.

My DNA test results are in. I've never been particularly interested in doing a test, having a pretty strong knowledge of where both of my parents come from and feeling a sense of belonging in countries not captured in my genetics. But I'm spending a lot of time thinking about identity and belonging, so I take up a Black Friday discount offer and am soon running the cotton wool around the inside of my cheek, more times than they ask, making sure there's no part of me lost in their findings. When I get the email that my results are ready, it's late at night. I'm entirely sure there aren't any surprises or scandals coming, but just in case, I decide I'll look in the morning. And when I do, it does something strange to me. There's nothing really out of the ordinary – I've got India on my mum's side, and Western Europe on my dad's. But there's something surprisingly affirming to see these parts of a map lit up. And to discover the nuance within these regions. Mostly, I'm from Southern India, as I expect. But there's also Northern India there too. Something about seeing this connects me to the country and my experiences in

* For more of her thoughts on navigating race in Britain, see Anita Sethi, *I Belong Here: A Journey Along the Backbone of Britain*, Bloosmbury Publishing, 2021.

that part of it even more. When I tracked the tourist trail across the Golden Triangle, gazing at the pearly iridescence of the Taj Mahal and joining the colourful melee of Holi festival in Jaipur, I never knew that some relations, however distant, had once been rooted there. Meanwhile along with my dad's staunchly English DNA, there's Germanic Europe. Perhaps that's why I always preferred learning German to French.

Multi-national and diasporic identity is something artist Sunil Shah has explored in his work critically examining his relationship with Uganda and his family's journey. Just three years old when the family left in 1972, looking over photographs and Cine films at family gatherings was one of the ways Sunil got to know his parents' past. 'My father used to talk very affectionately about that life in Uganda, because it was so different to life in the UK,' he tells me over a video call. 'The photographs became a way of accessing that past, especially as most Asians that came over weren't able to bring much with them other than a suitcase full of valuables. So, the photographs became a very poignant connection to that past.' They also became a way for him to interact with this past. 'I think there was always a kind of question of how the second and third generation Asian diaspora would address certain aspects of their history. How do we talk about the past, and what happened and why we're here? And what kind of information gets passed on?' His project *Uganda Stories* paired family and found photographs or objects with extracts from conversations with his father and uncles to form a documentary art project based on family testimony. Sunil described it as both a 'subjective journey to recollect the past' and an exploration of documentary photography to 'reassemble fragments of a history that can never be fully realised.'[21] The work ranges from black and white family photos and images bought on eBay through to a striking antelope head contained in a black plastic wrap. 'I was particularly interested in found images, and the documentary nature of how pictures tell stories, but also how they hide things,' he says. Photographs can create blind spots in cultural memory, especially with historical events like the expulsion, when only certain things are deemed worthy to photograph. 'Couple that with the fact that most people's photographic albums are commemorations, especially within Asian communities during the colonial era – a photograph was a very important document as a reminder to people who were back home or in other parts of the world of how things were progressing, whether things were going well or not.'

When it comes to the way he personally relates to his Ugandan past, his feelings have changed over the years. 'Growing up in the UK in the 1970s in a white working-class market town, there was a lot of racism, especially that my parents would have had to deal with.' In Banbury, Oxfordshire, they were far removed from an Indian community. 'There was just my dad and my uncle, a Hindu Punjabi family, some Pakistani families and then maybe two or three Black families, and that was the sum total in the whole town.' While he feels that they never experienced the kind of racism you hear of in cities like Leicester or Bradford, 'I grew up being made aware that I was different, and that we weren't English.' When they watched cricket, his family supported the West Indies, Pakistan, or India – notably failing Norman Tebbit's 1990 'cricket test', where sport met identity politics. The Conservative politician famously tested the loyalty of immigrants by asking, 'When England play India, which team do Britons of Indian or Afro-Caribbean origin, who were born and grew up here, support or should support?'

The implication being that supporting India amounted to high treason, in daring to choose their old country over their new benevolent one, while of course overlooking the capacity of people to contain multiple identities and affiliations. 'Now it's different,' Sunil says. 'But when we were kids, certainly, probably up until our teens, we were very much like, "We're not English". I felt like there was always this aspect of us that was politically Black. There was this solidarity between us and anyone that was not white in the 1970s and 1980s.' Being politically Black at this point referred to a way of relating to the same struggle, South Asians and Black Britons facing racism together. In the preceding decades, articles, reports and surveys had often grouped anyone of colour together under the singular label of Black. Despite being different groups with distinct experiences, racism placed them side-by-side. As actor Riz Ahmed wrote in an essay on race, 'As children in the 1980s, when my brother and I were stopped near our home by a skinhead who decided to put a knife to my brother's throat, we were black.'[22]

Things started shifting in the late 1980s and 1990s, Sunil says, as New Labour and diversity policies came in, and for him, racism became quieter. 'When I was in my teens, when I was trying to find myself, whatever that means, I didn't see myself as English and I didn't see myself as Indian,' he tells me. 'I certainly thought of myself as being some kind of hybrid person, who was born in Africa, grew up in England and was of Indian heritage. You no longer feel like you fit in anywhere, really. But because I've done quite a lot of thinking around identity and identity politics, I'm very much of the belief now that there's a sort of double consciousness that arrives when you're straddling different cultures. So, when people ask me now, I say I am a bit of everything. There's a bit of me that is still politically Black, there's a part of me that is most definitely Indian, and then probably eighty per cent of my life is lived like an English person.' Sunil doesn't subscribe strongly to fixed identities and embraces the multitudes within his own. 'I actually like that possibility that we have aspects of us that are globally spread,' he says. 'I think that also sometimes being in the diaspora does connect you more to your life. For most people, security comes with some form of national identity. There are some people that wouldn't be comfortable saying, "Oh, I'm a nomad, I don't belong anywhere." I take joy in saying that.'

Someone else who has been getting in touch with their nomadic roots is Aneesha Khimani Green, the daughter of little Noori, the ten-year-old who made it through military checkpoints with family gold stuffed under her dress. Ever since she'd first heard stories in her childhood of her mum's pet parrot and monkey alongside her dogs and cats, the tropical idyll of Uganda had been on Aneesha's mind. 'I don't remember the first time I heard the story, I just grew up with it and I'd always wanted to go,' she tells me, as I chat with her and her mother together. 'Despite the political situation, or bad things people would say about Uganda, it was always about the natural beauty in my eyes.' After Noori and her parents landed in the UK, they spent a year in the West Malling and Greenham Common camps, before being placed in Swindon. Running away from home and into marriage took Noori to Harrogate, North Yorkshire, where Aneesha grew up surrounded by the town's Georgian and Victorian architecture. 'There wasn't much diversity then, so I felt like I never fitted in,' Aneesha, now thirty-four, remembers. 'I was bullied for how I looked.' Her plans to travel to Uganda took a back seat when her university experimentation turned into eight years of drug abuse. But her travel ambitions never left her. 'It wasn't a good time in my life, but even during that time, Uganda was a distant dream in my head. I knew one day I'd be in Uganda.' When Aneesha and her mother travelled to India in 2017, she had a lightbulb moment around her multi-continental identity. 'It was amazing,' she smiles. 'I felt like I understood Nanima [grandmother] so much more. I just loved it. And connecting with my roots, because I've never felt connected to England or British culture, even though I was born there. It's a really weird feeling. That was when I learned the term diaspora, and I was like, "Ah, I'm part of this. I actually have other homes." When I visited those places, so much more about myself made sense.' I can relate to the feeling of being in situ with your past, as I too had felt a sense of dislocation that was met with an odd, bones-deep connection within moments of first landing in India.

Aneesha's long-awaited journey to Uganda finally came in 2020, and the small matter of a global pandemic wouldn't stop her. 'I just had to go,' she says. Bedded down in an Airbnb, growing vegetables in the garden and making fresh juices from fruit from the market, she felt a growing sense of something she had always felt was missing. 'I feel like Uganda is my first home and India is my second home,' Aneesha says, from the town of Fort Portal where her relatives packed up fifty years ago. 'This issue of home has been a real thing for me. I've had this recurring feeling of homelessness for a long time, perhaps since my parents got divorced. I feel like I'm finally reconnecting with my home.' Aneesha felt such an innate connection to the country her mother was born in, but which she'd never been to until her thirties, that she's decided to make a permanent move. I ask her mother what she thinks of her daughter's affinity with her home country, the pull that skipped down the generations. 'I'm very happy for her, because she's following her path. I think it's absolutely brilliant.' Noori wouldn't move back herself, but now she's faced her nerves and returned on her first trip, she's sure that she too wants to spend much more time in Africa. Her daughter's abstract dreams built on snatches of stories have evolved into very real ones – of bringing her motorbike to Uganda and riding across the whole country, learning some of the seventy-odd local languages, getting a patch of land to start a permaculture farm and wellness retreat connected to nature, and getting her Ugandan citizenship, using her grandfather's old papers. 'I just know that this is where I need to be,' she says. 'It's where I feel I can settle and have my life, and it feels amazing actually. It's been a beautiful journey.'

For many children of empire, their journeys of discovery are self-directed, searching for answers to questions that have long shadowed them, but very rarely come up in education or in public spaces. Barely taught in schools or discussed widely, the public discussion of empire generally amounts to celebration of the abolition of slavery, without mention of who initiated the slave trade, or imperial nostalgia centred around the building of railways in India and the force for good arguments that insist that the empire spread English, education, democracy and civil values.[23] This cultural amnesia encourages a lack of awareness and understanding of this enormous part of history, and leaves those of us with roots within empire cut off from a part of us. The predominant response across the board when I tell people about the Ugandan Asian story is, 'I wish I knew more about this.' Because while the almost Biblical tale of exodus is epic on its own, it's also the story of the British empire and multi-culturalism today. As such, this isn't a niche topic – it's about all of us. The legacy of colonialism and the ongoing shifting sands of immigration affect everyone, every day and the reckoning with Britain's imperial history and how it relates to people's identity is fresh and live. And yet there is staggeringly little taught about this in schools, or even displayed in museums. London has monuments to its empire in the reams of artefacts looted during colonialism, from the contested Elgin marbles to the Benin bronzes housed in the aptly-named British Museum, and yet there is still no museum dedicated to examining empire itself. Magnificent ships like the *Cutty Sark* in London, HMS *Victory* in Portsmouth and Brunel's SS *Great Britain* in Bristol stand proudly as monuments to the past, but curiously, not a single slave ship has been preserved.[24]

Across the UK, signs of empire shine out at you if you look closely, down to the colonial statues carved into the building of the Foreign and Commonwealth Office, and Wembley Stadium's former iteration as the Empire Stadium, built for the 1924 Empire Exhibition that drew in millions of visitors.[25] But while statues seem to have taken over the entire decolonisation debate, imperial artefacts hide in the corners of our literature, art, and, most importantly, our institutions. The Royal Family, that very greatest of British institutions, is intimately linked to the empire – and the slave trade. As organisations have at long last admitted a need to address the injustices of the past and admit what sections of their wealth were generated by enslaved people, the monarchy has remained silent. Never complain, never explain. The royal connection with slavery goes back centuries, with Queen Elizabeth I supporting the slaving expeditions of one of Britain's first slave traders in the sixteenth century, John Hawkins. Under King Charles II, the Crown continued to pour money into the African slave trade, from financing slave ships to offering the Royal Navy's services in protecting voyages. Queen Victoria adopted the title Empress of India in 1877, ruling over the subjugation and enslavement of people of colour.[26] 'Coloured immigrants or foreigners' were banned from serving in clerical roles in the royal household until at least the late 1960s, although they were permitted to work as domestic staff, and equality legislation that makes it illegal to refuse to employ someone based on their race or ethnicity is one of the many laws the Crown is exempt from.[27] As the wealth generated by and jewels stolen from colonial subjects sits within the Royal coffers, and is displayed at coronations, in the post-colonial world, the royals have kept up their links to empire through Empire 2.0 – the Commonwealth. Today the Commonwealth is presented as a global family, a warm embrace showing unity, rather than as a collection of former colonies invaded by Britain. It requires a kind of 'double-think', says Sanghera, to understand how 'countries all want to celebrate being part of a shared language, when they gained it by being invaded and subjugated.'[28]

There also remains an honours system in the UK where celebrated people are annually awarded CBEs, OBEs and MBEs, respectively Commander of, Officer of or Member of the Most Excellent Order of the British Empire. Many turn them down on this basis, including spoken word artist George the Poet, who is of Ugandan background. Describing himself as a 'student, admirer and friend of Britain', he said he was prevented from accepting due to the 'colonial trauma inflicted on the children of Africa, entrenched across our geopolitical and macroeconomic realities.' He added, 'The gesture is deeply appreciated, the wording is not. It will remain unacceptable to me until Britain takes institutional measures to address the intergenerational disruption brought to millions as a result of her colonial exploits.'[29] Poet Benjamin Zephaniah also said 'no way' to an OBE, due to being 'profoundly anti-empire', along with director Ken Loach, who amongst other things took issue with it having 'the name of the British Empire, which is a monument of exploitation and conquest.'[30]

And discussing these topics as a Brown person can make you the target of hate – as Sanghera, has spoken of. 'There's still a lingering sense that people like me should be grateful for all that empire has done,' he says.[31] Particular outrage at any critical examination of this past comes from the 'sins of the parent are not the sins of the children' contingent, who insist we must stop judging the past by today's standards. As Nusrat Ahmed, a co-curator of the new South Asia Gallery at Manchester Museum, says, 'It has been hard for us British-born members of the diaspora to connect to our South Asian backgrounds. This is a place I would bring my child and say, "This is your heritage." If you saw yourself in a museum, you'd go back – why wouldn't you?'[32] Uncovering these parts of the past often comes to people later in life, because on the curriculum, the imperial years are something of a black hole in Britain.

Learning about empire is politicised. There's a reason I can recite the names of Henry VIII's wives, and cite the battles of the First World War, but never learnt how far the tentacles of empire stretched or how they continued to wind through the UK today. From Margaret Thatcher through to Michael Gove, politicians have turned their noses up at attempts to introduce anti-racist learning or critical analysis of the imperial years.[33] History curriculums for secondary school students should teach 'how Britain has influenced and been influenced by the wider world' and 'the diversity of societies', but research has shown that the actual numbers of children learning about empire are astonishingly low. While migration, belonging and empire can be taught to fourteen- to sixteen-year-olds in history and English classes, the Runnymede Trust found its uptake depended on what modules schools chose, and teachers wanted more support to teach these subjects sensitively and effectively. Of the students that choose to take history at GCSE level in the first place, only around four per cent study the 'Migration to Britain' unit, which covers some parts of empire.[34] Initiatives like Black History Month and South Asian Heritage Month seek to enrich learning with diversity and colour, in the hope that people of all backgrounds can see themselves in their country, but there is certainly a tokenistic slant to stories appearing for one month only, before again retreating to the shadows. The impact of this lack of learning can be felt right through the systems that govern us. One of the recommendations of an independent review into the Windrush scandal was for Home Office staff to learn about Britain's colonial history.[35] But even if we did learn about empire, we would reach a brick wall. The truth is, we will never know the full truth of decolonisation, thanks to a concerted cover up during the end of empire.

In December 2022, Dutch prime minister Mark Rutte formally apologised for his country's role in 250 years of slavery, saying that centuries of oppression and exploitation were reflected to this day in racist stereotypes, discriminatory patterns of exclusion and social inequality. 'To break those patterns, we also have to face up to the past, openly and honestly.'[36] Australia introduced National Sorry Day in 1998, the same year the prime minister finally issued an apology on behalf of the government and Australian people to Aboriginal communities. There are growing calls for recognition of the sins of the father, including paying reparations to countries plundered by colonialism. But there remains silence from the UK. However, in 2013 William Hague, the then foreign secretary, apologised to Kenya for Britain's colonial-era violent suppression of the Mau Mau rebellion. He expressed 'sincere regret' as he announced payments of £2,600 each to 5,200 claimants in a case that had been launched four years earlier by Kenyans tortured at the hands of the colonial administration in the 1950s. It was the first case of its kind against the British empire. It's doubtful an apology like this would have happened without the extraordinary legal case.[*37] But the case had uncovered something extraordinary too. During legal proceedings, the Foreign Office was forced to reveal the existence of a secret cache of colonial-era documents it was illegally keeping classified beyond the thirty-year limit. These revealed there had been a wholesale purge of colonial government records in an undertaking codenamed Operation Legacy. As colonies were handed over at independence, bonfires burnt hundreds of thousands of pages of documents, while others were to be weighed down and buried at sea. Files that would embarrass the government, police, military or public servants, betray intelligence sources, show religious or racial bias, or be used 'unethically' by a forthcoming government were all ripe for destruction. In some cases, it was a mad rush to the finish line to destroy the evidence in time, with some officials warning they feared 'celebrating Independence Day with smoke'. As these vital historical records literally went up in flames outside colonial offices around the world, they left huge gaps in the archives. 'What that means is that it is completely impossible to write a truly accurate history of the British empire, and anything written before Operation Legacy was revealed is certainly incomplete,' writes Akala in *Natives*.[38]

---

* For more, see Caroline Elkins, *Imperial Reckoning: The Untold Story of Britain's Gulag in Kenya*, Holt McDougal, 2005.

The cost of empire has remained largely out of sight and out of mind. As Salman Rushdie famously wrote in his stuttering character in *The Satanic Verses*, the 'trouble with the Engenglish is that their hiss hiss history happened overseas, so they dodo don't know what it means.'[39] Perhaps this goes some way to understanding the startling results of an oft-cited poll from 2014 in which fifty-nine per cent of people said the British empire was 'something to be proud of'. That was compared to just nineteen per cent who described themselves as 'ashamed of' the empire in the YouGov research. A third of those polled also said they would like it if Britain still had an empire.[40] More recently, a survey in 2020 compared attitudes towards former empires in eight countries including Britain, France, Spain and the Netherlands. While the Dutch topped the poll as the country proudest of its former empire, with half saying yes, Britons came second at thirty-two per cent. While pollsters commented that the dominant emotion towards empire seemed to be indifference, notably, a third of people believed Britain's colonies were better off for being colonised. Interestingly, this data could also be drawn down by Brexit referendum voting preferences. This showed that half of Leave voters felt empire was more something to be proud of, compared with twenty per cent of Remain voters. And half of Leave voters felt the former colonies were better off for having been in the British empire, against twenty-two per cent of Remainers.[41]

The problem, writes historian and broadcaster David Olusoga, is not that national feelings about the British empire are too positive or negative, but that 'we know too little of the actual history to make a sound judgment.'[42] It's incredibly difficult to get your head around something of this scale compared with more easily bookended historical eras, even before you consider the lack of teaching around it.

The silence around empire, essentially amounts to silence around how so many people ended up living in the UK, a root cause of today's racial diversity. The idea of Black and Brown people as interlopers, uninvited, with no previous link to Britain, is pervasive, and, as Sanghera says, 'the defining political narrative of my lifetime.'[43] Groups like Ugandan Asians have somehow been reimagined as migrants, rather than children of empire, with a long and generational history connecting us to Britain.[44] The way post-war migrants are conjoined to the empire that came before them was perhaps best laid out in Sri Lankan British novelist and director of the Institute of Race Relations A. Sivanandan's well-known saying, 'We are here because you were there'. Finding home can be a journey of a lifetime, particularly when you've been forced from yours. Perhaps it's not always a physical place, but a feeling, or a person. For diaspora, 'where are you from' asks many more questions of us than its few words belie. For Ugandan Asians, the short answer could simply be, in a word – empire.

Chapter 12
Fifty Years

We are all migrants through time.
                                      Mohsin Hamid, *Exit West*[1]

The glass cabinets are filled with keepsakes, precious items invoking memories of a long-lost life. A leather-lined transistor radio and an embroidered white table cover, a paraffin lamp and a driving licence. Two ties, one embroidered with tiny crested cranes, the national bird of Uganda, the other with a small gold elephant. A wedding sari, a red and white silk panetar, embellished with gold thread and tassels. These were some of the treasured items chosen for the journey from Uganda to the UK. Perhaps most poignantly is Madhu Mistry's colourful contribution, which is captioned, 'Dad brought some Ugandan money with him in case we wanted to go back.'

I'm walking around an exhibition of Ugandan Asian history at Leicester Museum, and it's the first time I'm seeing this displayed in a formal museum setting. There's something surprisingly moving about seeing something of my story standing proudly on the walls. I've always loved history, and I've visited museums around the world, soaking in each country's tales. But something about this compact exhibition, which fills just one large room, has provoked a totally new feeling within me. I suppose it's being seen, having your family story reflected back to you as history. Just as there is no dedicated empire museum, there is also a lack of sites showing these kinds of stories even as exhibits. This is my history, and seeing it displayed like the histories I've seen elsewhere lends the stories I've heard and told during my life a sense of legitimacy I didn't realise I'd been lacking. The Ugandan Asian story is here, from reproduced pages of the *Uganda Argus* through to Idi Amin pontificating from a screen on the wall, uttering words I know well, in which he pronounces that the South Asians must leave. It's here in the black and white images showing the shuttered shops after the expulsion and a busy auction selling off Ugandan Asian-owned cars, in the depictions of race protests in Britain and of Leicester as a city rebuilt by immigrants. *Rebuilding Lives – 50 Years of Ugandan Asians in Leicester* curated by Navrang Arts naturally offers a simplified version of this vast migratory story, which reflects that common motivational upwards trajectory, but it's Ugandan Asian history on the walls of a museum, and today that feels powerful.

A large model tree ahead of me has luggage labels hanging down from its branches alongside its leaves, which have been marked with the names of those who travelled to the UK. Memory tags about people's lives. Beneath it, there's a map of Uganda, speckled with stick-on red dots. Where did your family come from, it asks, next to sheets of stickers, waiting to be picked up and imbibed with meaning. It's unlike me to engage in any interactivity in a museum, where I usually read and watch and quietly process, leaving the buttons and games for the kids. But I'm drawn to this display, which is something I feel I can really be a part of. Below the main map of Uganda there's a smaller one of the continent. People have added place markers to this too, from Sudan to Togo, with clusters of dots in Morocco and Nigeria. In the right-hand corner of the Ugandan map I notice a zoomed-in section of central Kampala. This is the part for me. Tracing the outline of the streets under my finger, I cross from Nakasero out to Kololo, my eyes searching for the familiar. I'm certain the map will give out before I find my target. But then, there it is, the last marked street on the edge of the map. I gently peel off a sticker and press it onto the corner of the road where my family used to live. Just a few months earlier I had been driving along these same roads, nerves building in the pit of my stomach as I rounded the curve that would reveal my mother's old house. The route wasn't totally new to me, as, like many in the diaspora, I'd walked these streets from thousands of miles away, familiarising myself with the terrain online. My mother and I had combed Google Street View over the years, looking for what she remembered of her childhood home. I was now moving out of the digital world into the real one, but I hadn't summoned up the courage to knock on the door just yet.

Flying into Entebbe, as my ears popped to mark the start of the descent, I had gazed keenly out of the window. I normally choose the aisle seat, preserving freedom over views, but for this journey there was only one seat to be in. The last time I'd come to Uganda I had landed at night, without the chance of an airborne view. Dropping below the clouds, the islands of Lake Victoria came into view, and I was reminded of those who have told me this was their last memory of Uganda, flying up towards the clouds and taking a last look at the pockmarked water. Soon after, with a bump and a squeal of brakes, we'd touched down. It was a packed flight from Addis Ababa, and as I sat by the window, I looked out as the first passengers disembarked and stood waiting for their companions. Women with headscarves and flowing skirts and robes, each with small bags on their arms or by their feet, formed shapes on the runway somehow evocative of the black and white photos of the exodus I have spent so much time looking at. Tears pricked my eyes, a surprising and sudden wave of emotion stirred by the years spent in a deep exploration of this past. The sun was setting in ripples of orange and pink as I stepped down the stairs and onto Ugandan soil. By the time I'd made it out of the airport with my battered bag, a local SIM card and a deeply unflattering photo on the Ugandan visa pasted in my passport, night had fallen. The long road from Entebbe to Kampala was clouded with darkness, the lights glimmering on the hills revealing the undulations otherwise hidden from sight. Traffic sped along, the warm night air flowing in through the open window, along with the sounds of street noise and roadside chatter. As we arrived into the outskirts of Kampala, we hit unusual traffic for the hour, causing the motorbike taxis that swarm the streets to rev their engines aggressively around the car, mounting the pavement, trying in vain to get around the blockade. Soon, the reason for the hold-up became clear in the cavalcade of cars rushing past on the other side of the road. We were stopped for the president, in just the same way as my last journey into Kampala, my life feeling momentarily stitched together with a snapshot in my mind from fifteen years earlier. I laughed at the synchronicity. It seems I am always given a presidential greeting in Uganda.

When Ugandan Asians talk about their past, one question inevitably comes up in conversation, asked by one person or the other. Have you been back? Would you go back? Unlike the returnees who chose to make new lives in the country they always felt was theirs, many of those who left Uganda in 1972 have never been back. It's a hugely emotive prospect, returning to the land you were exiled from, equal parts enticing and daunting. For some, the very thought fills them with terror, memories of their final fearsome moments leaving the country enough to put anyone off a return. The mere sight of a military post or armed solider in camouflage could trigger memories suppressed for years. Others hold onto the happiest of childhood memories of their equatorial lives and are unwilling to risk shattering their rose-tinted spectacles. They fear things just wouldn't be the same now, which, of course, thanks to the passage of time, they aren't. But there's a third group, travellers who have returned for visits. They have no interest in moving back, their lives are firmly set up elsewhere now, but there's still a connection there. One trip might be enough, to explore the old haunts and look back on what might have been. Or returning to East Africa might be the start of a beautiful relationship with somewhere that is no longer home but fills a space in your heart.

Kausar spent two decades living next door to Uganda in Kenya, but never crossed the border. She wanted to visit Kampala, but her husband warned her of impending disappointment. What was left for her there now anyway? Why go back when you had already seen the whole country? It took until they moved to the UK before a trip to Uganda was finally on the cards. While going to a wedding in Kenya, Kausar added on a week in Kampala. A young immigration officer was waiting to examine her passport. 'When he saw my passport, of course, it says I was born in Kampala,' she tells me. 'He looked at me twice, and my husband said, "Why are you looking, she was born here," and he said, "Yes, welcome my sister." I was so happy that he said that to me, welcome my sister. A female officer said, "I don't understand, why have you only come here for a week? Our country is so beautiful. I'm going to give you a visa for six months." And we said that we've seen the whole country, because we lived there. It was lovely, it was like we never left, because they were so friendly with us and welcomed us like that with open arms. They were so happy saying, "You've come back to see your country." Of course, things had changed. But our feelings were the same. We felt that was home for us.'

Return trips can also mean facing the thornier parts of the past. One day Kausar, her sister and brother took themselves on the nostalgia tour to see their old house and schools. When their taxi driver pulled over to get petrol, a local man on a bike caught sight of them and stared. Beeping his horn, focused on Kausar's increasingly unnerved sister, he said, 'Mama, I know you.' Then he started crying. 'We asked him, "Why are you crying?" And he said, "Because she's not believing me, I know this woman."' In stilted English, he explained how he was the only one of his family who survived the years after the expulsion, having escaped to a village with his neighbours. 'He said, "When I'm looking at this woman, I think I used to go to her house." I asked him where the house was, and he literally described our house,' says Kausar. 'My sister looks a lot like my mother and he didn't have the conception of how many years had passed by.' The chance pullover due to a low tank of fuel had led the family straight back to 1972, as their companion told them about his memories of their popular twin brothers, well known in the area as the best footballers, swimmers and climbers. 'He told us, "So many people were shot. You Asians went away, but we were the ones who suffered more than anybody else."' With some deliberately targeted for working for South Asians, and others caught up in violence elsewhere through Amin's regime and then the years of civil war, Uganda's stories did not end in 1972.

Some of the people I've spoken with who haven't returned to Uganda, have instead formed a close connection with another country in their family history. Lata hasn't made it back to Jinja yet, although like me she has traced the path on

Street View, scrolling up and down the streets she used to run as a child. But a holiday in 2000 to India changed everything. 'I just fell in love with it,' she tells me. 'My husband asked me what it was about it, and I said, "I feel like I'm at home". He said, "But you've never lived in India". No one was staring at me, no one was judging me, which believe me is a big deal when I've lived what I have. People are really friendly and no one gives me a second glance.' Lata and her husband, Tony, had such a connection on their first trip that they decided to buy a place here, and now Goa has become a second home. Having another base has also allowed Lata to honour a promise she made to herself when she arrived in the UK with her two brothers, having been torn from her parents in Kampala. 'One thing I said to myself on the plane steps when I was eleven was I would never die in this country,' she says. 'Standing on the top of the steps, I think it had been so traumatic leaving my parents, and looking down at the ground, where there was a light snow, thinking, "What is this, I didn't want to come here," I told myself, I will not die here.'

Back in Uganda, as I made my way around the country, I felt something of a cliché returnee. Having coincidentally travelled in the fiftieth year since the expulsion, it was clear that Uganda was full of people on vision quests. Group visits were planned, and a number of us from the next generation returned, wanting to uncover our roots in the country, and document our interactions with the past. Author Radhika Sanghani had wanted to go to Uganda since hearing her first childhood stories, but her parents didn't want to. 'For years, I've been waiting for them to change their minds, but this year, I realised I didn't have to wait anymore; I could go alone,' she wrote in the *i* newspaper. She too told of immigration officers welcoming her, saying, 'You're Ugandan', and of retracing her family's steps in Jinja. 'I have never lived in Uganda, but it's still a part of my history, my life and my story,' she wrote. 'I was rewriting my family history, letting go of my parents' past to create my own present.'[2] Journalist Reha Kansara's grandfather had been a store manager working for the Madhvanis on their sugar estate. The family had at first lived on site in Kakira, before moving to Jinja, opposite the airport where her mother would run to shake Idi Amin's hand when his plane landed. Seeing the family home was a 'really surreal and special moment', Reha said, allowing her to find the 'missing piece of the puzzle' by walking in the spaces her grandmother, whom she never met, had inhabited.[3] Even those who do not return permanently have an ongoing relationship, whether they spend time there or not. As travel writer Meera Dattani, who first visited Uganda in 1989, eighteen years after her mother had left, says, 'I love to return. Because though Uganda was never my home, it's where all our stories are.'[4]

On this trip, as well as exploring the capital, I drive west to a game park, riding on horseback past Ankole cattle roaming amidst herds of zebras, kicking the dusty soil up with their hooves, and a baby hippo shooting water out of the small waterhole left amid the parched landscape. And heading east to Iganga, I find Kassam and Fatma Majothi's former shop on the main road, holding up pictures from the past sent to me by one of his sons to match against the buildings in front of me. Not all of his children have returned, although some have taken their own pilgrimages to Iganga. For Abdul, visiting Uganda merely served to show what he'd built elsewhere in the years since their sudden departure. 'I travel a lot all over the world,' he tells me. 'And as soon as I'm on a plane, I sit down and I think I'm coming back to Bristol. It is home for me. I'm not a refugee now.'

One afternoon in my hotel room in a Jinja side street, an American voice floats in through the open window. 'My mother used to live in this house,' I hear, raised with the inflection of someone trying to convey meaning through increasing decibels. 'She left in 1972.' Sticking my head past the curtains and around the security bars, I see a middle-aged South Asian woman gesticulating on the street, standing by a car with an open door. We really are everywhere these days. I stamp my feet into some shoes, locate my key with its needlessly large wooden keyring, and dash outside, but by the time I round the corner, she's gone. In Kampala I pass the schools my mother and her siblings studied in, and those my grandparents taught in, getting into a huge tumble of traffic at one of the latter, which is in the middle of one of the city's busiest markets, a hum of wheels moving, plates spinning and produce selling. In Kololo I drive slowly around the streets, gazing hungrily at the sights around me, trying not to look suspicious to the armed guards of the many embassies I'm passing. I do another pass by the house, but I don't stop.

There was always going to be a question of how to process this time. Big anniversaries draw attention and fifty years since the expulsion was no different, with events, exhibitions, reunions and interviews planned. But what exactly was this anniversary doing? Was it a celebration, as it sometimes seemed to be, and if so, of what? You could hardly celebrate the expulsion itself, a forced migration with the associated trauma. Unless perhaps you took the view of one Leicester businessman, and the many said to have done the same, who displayed a photo of Amin in his home surrounded with flowers. An ode to Amin thanking him for throwing the South Asians out, giving them a pass to Britain and the new lives they loved. Or was it a celebration of that eternal redemptive story, good triumphing over evil? The anniversary couldn't really be a commiseration, because despite the emotional upheaval and lifelong impact of being wrenched across the globe, this wasn't a devastation of the same scale as genocides or wars. Perhaps it would be a commemoration, simply marking the occasion, the passage of time and the lessons learned. Remembering, a key word in the memorialisation landscape, was often repeated. These histories remained within living memory, but not for all that much longer for the older generation. They needed to be heard before people moved onto the next life, taking their memories with them.

For the British government, the anniversary would turn out to absolutely be a celebration – of themselves. Amin's expulsion date offered an opportunity to reinstate themselves in a starring role both historically and contemporaneously. Boris Johnson, prime minister at the time, boasted that, 'the whole country can be proud of the way the UK welcomed people fleeing Idi Amin's Uganda,' before making the frankly audacious statement that, 'This country is overwhelmingly generous to people fleeing in fear of their lives and will continue to be so.'[5] No one could rationally describe today's official immigration stance, in the same month that the government pressed ahead with deportation plans for asylum seekers, as 'overwhelmingly generous'. Reframing the Ugandan Asian migration to try and rehabilitate present policy shows the way history is weaponised. The expulsion is used to shore up the image of Britain as a welcoming nation, part of the 'proud history' of welcome trotted out by the Home Office whenever they are questioned.[6] One might argue that a person who previously wrote that colonialism in Uganda should never have ended, and dismissed Britain's role in slavery, should not have been handed the microphone on this particular topic. 'The continent may be a blot, but it is not a blot upon our conscience,' Johnson wrote about a trip to Uganda while editor of the *Spectator* magazine. 'The problem is not that we were once in charge, but that we are not in charge anymore.' It wasn't 'convincing' to him that Africa's problems forty years on could still involve legacies of colonialism, as he reframed Britain's arrival in Uganda into an emancipation. Suggesting the best way to boost the economy would be to holiday at Murchison Falls, he wrote, 'The best fate for Africa would be if the old colonial powers, or their citizens, scrambled once again in her direction; on the understanding that this time they will not be asked to feel guilty.'[7]

Along with the anticipated self-congratulation among the leadership, the commemoration brought with it the ever-present partner of the good immigrant – gratitude. This was exemplified in the words of the Ugandan-born chair of the British Asian Trust Lord Gadhia, who said, 'The 50th anniversary of the arrival of Ugandan Asians is a moment to express our community's eternal gratitude to all those who supported us in our hour of need.'[8] Not speaking exclusively politically, but also to the many volunteers who worked in the resettlement camps and doubtless deserve praise, it was still yet another reminder of a debt owed by Ugandan Asians. There's a conflict that sits in the hearts of many of the 1972 generation, as the devastation and rootlessness of losing home is paired with an understanding that the expulsion brought unforeseen opportunities. Many appreciate that their lives just wouldn't be the same if they'd stayed in Uganda. The freedoms afforded to them were far greater, especially for women able to earn their own money, marry outside of family arrangements, or express their true sexuality. Even the prejudice Lata faced during her relocation shaped the trajectory of the rest of her life, drawing her to work in social care to help other vulnerable women of colour. Gratitude comes up again and again both in Ugandan Asian oral histories and in the conversations I have had with people.

There's of course nothing wrong with being grateful for support in settling, which made the world of difference during a deeply traumatic time. But the gratitude is often directed at the government, not the army of volunteers, and goes hand in hand with a tendency not to critique the country that offered sanctuary. Some of this stems from a feeling that Britain did the Ugandan Asians a favour in taking them in. 'You do feel you must be grateful because of this tremendous thing that has happened for you, so you tend to think you can't criticise anything,' my mother Betty reflects. 'And it's human nature to be grateful. But you need to remember that the government did this out of obligation, not charity. It was their responsibility, so you don't need to feel grateful for it. And really you have as much of a right to say how you feel, because you're a citizen.' The feeling of Ugandan Asians being given the gift of a new life goes hand in hand with Indian cultural norms not to complain, she says. 'So you don't. But you're not complaining, you're just sticking up for your rights.' As Mohamed Keshavjee, who left Kenya shortly after the exodus, tells me, 'I don't think it's to say, we don't say thank you to people who opened the doors. But we need to understand how much the door was open.'

From a wider perspective, it feeds into the idea that immigrants, and their children, should remain forever grateful above and beyond the norm. Musa Okwonga has written about his experiences growing up Black in Britain, after his parents came to the UK as refugees from Amin's regime. In his essay, 'Ungrateful Country', he says it was 'always a case of making sure I was grateful'. He explains, 'As I got older, I began to notice more and more that the very moment immigrants were seen as contributing anything less than wholesomely to the national effort, they were viewed with contempt. It was as if, even though we had been born here, we were still seen as guests, our social acceptance only conditional upon our very best behaviour.'[9] When it comes to exploring the truth of the Ugandan Asian history, this tendency has muted certain challenging elements, and encouraged the victim narrative, in which Britain is the saviour and neither hold any responsibility for what occurred. When Edward Heath, the prime minister at the time of Amin's edict, wrote his memoirs of his political life, he certainly reflected this position. 'Uganda was still a part of the Commonwealth and we therefore had a moral duty to accept these unfortunate people,' he wrote:

> In an attempt to ease some of the burden, we contacted 50 other countries . . . We did what any civilised nation would do, by taking the greater share of the emigrants, some 25,000 people. I have never regretted this, for the Ugandan Asians have brought a wealth of endeavour, enterprise and natural talent to these shores.[10]

Another common story in the community tells of the homes that have not only Amin's photo on display on the mantelpiece, but also Heath's. This double gratitude says – thanks for throwing us out, and thanks for taking us in.

So how will we come to remember the expulsion and the years that followed? The government's global efforts had succeeded in resettling around half of Uganda's Asian population elsewhere. The Ugandan Asians who came to the UK in the exodus totalled upwards of 28,000, a number presented as a potentially catastrophic disrupting force on British society, but which was really a drop in the ocean. And within today's migratory patterns, it's even smaller. In 1972 around 200,000 people migrated to the UK in total, the others greeted without fanfare. When compared with the 200,000 Poles resettled after the Second World War or the 20,000 Hungarians who fled the Soviet crackdown in 1956, the commotion made over Ugandan Asians then, and the continued discussion now, shows the colourism behind the branding of it as a major migration. The Ugandan Asian episode remains a showpiece for immigration because the arrivals were not white.[11] However, when taken as a whole, the wider East African Asian migration was more significant. The 1972 arrivals were part of the larger East African movement from the late 1960s, which cumulatively made for a larger diasporic community. Over the nine years up until spring 1974, over 100,000 East African Asians had come to Britain – one of the largest groups of post-war migrants to Britain.[12]

The narration of the exodus usually starts on 4 August 1972. Amin's order is seen as a bolt from the blue, without precedent, reasoning or warning. While it's true that such a sudden move was unexpected, there had been clear signs leading up to it both within Uganda and in Britain. This was a time of liberation from the colonial powers and the South Asians were standing on the fault line. And the challenges didn't stop when people lifted off from Entebbe. A holistic understanding of this recent past requires us to explore the layers of complexity in a global forced migration like this, from the legal precedents to the historic colonial input and the environments in which people found themselves settling in. 'We saw an earthquake 7.8 on the Richter scale, with the aftershocks going right through the world of former British colonial settlements through to Indian minorities until today,' says lawyer Mohamed. 'A migration does not happen overnight, it's a problem that has been brewing for some time, I think any education programme must try and capture those dimensions as well. I don't personally think the fiftieth commemorative process was very embracing in that sense.'

One of the large oral history projects in the UK moved past the expulsion itself by focusing on the resettlement experience. Its original remit was to focus on the camp volunteers, not the Ugandan Asians themselves, but thankfully this was broadened to include the voices of the exiled, not just the Britons who welcomed them. While interviews covered the last frenetic days in Uganda, they gave a rich picture of life in the resettlement scheme and beyond. There was, at times, a familiar theme to it though. 'We wanted to make it a good news story of celebration,' Alan Critchley, the son of one of the resettlement board's pioneers, who was a part of the *British Ugandan Asians at 50* project, tells me. The funding of the project meant it couldn't be political, he says, but they hoped the government could still learn from their stories. 'It is part of the heritage that really does illustrate the diversity of the country. Some people hadn't talked about it, and it's a way of getting that story in the open. But also, for me, it's an illustration of a time when Britain was welcoming to a diverse community.' He adds, 'One of the things that we have been criticised for is that we've concentrated on the successful people who came. And it wasn't a success for everybody, it was difficult. We have been celebrating on the 50th anniversary and the success of it. But not to forget that it was a difficult episode for a lot of people.'

Trauma and dissonance often feel far removed from the conversation, beyond the theft of belongings at the airport. And yet many carry the burdens of their forced expulsion with them, from the people who live with few possessions, never fully trusting in their safety to settle, to those who go the other way, holding onto more than usual, because they once lost everything they owned. Those who live with the trauma of the violence they experienced or witnessed. And those who lost social bonds as they were split up across the world, or who have spent their lives struggling to match their cultural identity within environments that don't recognise them for who they are. 'The sense of trauma and dislocation is something that's not talked about within the Ugandan Asian experience,' Fiyaz Mughal, the director of Faith Matters and oral history project *From East to West: The History of Ugandan Asians*, has said. He was just a baby when he and his family were expelled, but feels the impact of 1972 today in a sense of dislocation. 'What's drastically missing in this whole arena . . . is the fact that actually there has been an emotional trauma that is carried by refugees.'[13] The singular stories within memorialisation also often become an opportunity to 'curate images of a technocratic, western-oriented and achievement-oriented community,' says Karim H. Karim of Carleton University, a communal self-image from which the 'socio-economically marginalised are absent.'[14] It's also too easy to slip into 'hand clapping and back patting' types of stories, says Mohamed. 'I understand people want to celebrate and be happy. Everybody's hearing about who turned up at Entebbe and how they got to Stradishall and were given great hospitality through cakes they baked and jerseys they knitted, all that. That's good. But we need deeper analysis into the nature of minority dynamics at the end of empire in colonial states.'

Yet there remains much to be gained from retelling the same stories. Britain institutionally comes off as the hero of the story, rather than the instigator, and on a societal level, prejudice gets deflected by the positivity of volunteerism. The exiled can rest on a cushion of victimhood and cover their traumatic memories with the warm glow of success, shielding themselves and others from the fact that they, consciously or subconsciously, played an active and embracing role in the colonial structures in Uganda. Still, across the recent outpouring of material concerned with Ugandan Asian history, you can find the diversity of viewpoints needed. From the walls of museums to travelling exhibitions, plays tackling the wealth divides and anti-Blackness with Ugandan Asian society, panel discussions bringing together Ugandan Asians of varied backgrounds, oral history projects challenging ideas of next-generation identity and podcasts speaking to the geographic, cultural and religious diversity of this migration – there is no single story.

I was sitting in an office at the back of an appliance showroom in Kampala's Wankoko district when I realised just how small the world can be. Over a Ugandan lunch of matooke, groundnut sauce and fish stew, Bharat Chandrana was filling me in about his move back to Kampala in the years after the expulsion. After making a life in Britain, he returned to Uganda with his wife, having been granted a government engineering contract. 'Her attraction to come here was that her parents were in Kenya, and my attraction was that I was from here,' he says. On one of his first days back, Bharat walked up the road from the Fairway Hotel, and immediately bumped into a friendly face from school. 'Imagine, I'm coming back after so many years, and the first person you can meet can be a classmate,' he says. His family hadn't had the money to send him to study in an Indian school, which meant he'd gone to local schools. When he returned, it turned out he knew most of the cabinet, who had been his classmates. 'In a way, you feel at home, because you knew the people who ran the country.' After growing up in Kabale, in the west of the country, where his father bought cotton from ginneries in Uganda and Tanzania, he had come to Kampala briefly to attend a different school. His teacher encouraged him to continue his education in England, but Bharat knew he couldn't afford it. As it happened, the teacher's mother was based in Cambridge, and he offered to arrange for her to put him up. Bharat moved there ahead of the exodus.

We'd been connected through someone I'd met in Kampala, and knew nothing about each other, so when I heard the word Cambridge, my ears pricked up – after all, it's where my family moved, so I knew the streets he was describing well. I mentioned that my grandparents left their teaching jobs and went to Cambridge too, and his attention focused. 'What was their name?' he asked. Giving it, I couldn't believe the reply. 'I knew her,' Bharat said. 'She was headmistress at Nakivubo and I bumped into her in Cambridge.' Thumbing through my envelope of black and white photos I had brought with me, I handed a fading print of my grandparents across the wooden desk. Bharat nodded in recognition as we laughed at the incredible coincidence. He had studied at Nakivubo Primary School for just one year, during which time he remembered my grandmother as a tiny but fierce presence. So much so that when he spotted her on the street in Cambridge, saying, 'Mrs Mathen, I know you,' he was filled with fear at her invitation to come around for a meal. There's something very funny about a grown man remembering your diminutive grandmother with nerves, even if I knew the spirit he spoke of. He joined my grandparents for dinner at their terraced house, a short walk from where he was staying. 'We met a couple of times, and then they moved to Australia and that was the end of that until I see you, the granddaughter of my headmistress, walking into my office,' he laughed.

A few days after our serendipitous meeting I found myself back in Kololo, this time standing outside my family's house, a grey concrete bungalow, now surrounded by a small office and the bones of a half-constructed tower looming behind it. The place was now rented out to two businesses and I'd been chatting to the men who worked at the estate agents to try and get in touch with the owner. But the message had got lost in translation, and I'd had a phone call that had made my stomach flip. 'I've spoken with the landlady and she has asked us not to let you on the property again, and if you're trying to reclaim it . . .' Panic washed over me, along with a wave of understanding. What must it look like to a Ugandan if a person who looks Indian arrives out of nowhere, says she used to live somewhere, and starts asking questions? Some people are still in property disputes now, all these years after it was made possible to reclaim formerly South Asian-owned properties. I was looking for connection, and I'd ended up making someone fear for their land and livelihood. And if any of my relatives hoped to visit in the future, I'd jeopardised any semblance of a happy reunion by getting us all blacklisted. I had to make it right. Insisting that I wanted to do nothing of the sort – my grandparents had never even owned the house, as it had been provided as part of their teaching contracts – I tried desperately to meet the landlady. By now I was staying on the other side of Kampala, and driving back and forth to Kololo involved taking on the city's most chaotic of roads, where roadworks meet impenetrable traffic jams, with huge articulated lorries jostling for space with dozens of Kampala's 200,000-plus boda boda moto-taxis. I was running out of time to fix this before my trip ended, emboldened by adrenaline to forge through the inter-sections more assertively than ever.

On my last day in town, I turned off the Lugogo Bypass and onto a quieter residential road, slowing my pace as I drove past the neat hedges and palm-tree-lined tall fences bordering the road. Pulling over by a grey double gate, I parked, grabbed my envelope of photos and headed inside past the security guard who by now knew my face well. Turning left I found the tenant I'd been speaking with and sitting down on a wooden chair in his small office, I ran through it all again. After a moment, he handed me his phone with the owner's number on the screen. Punching the numbers into my own phone, I dialled, my heart in my throat, braced for the worst. As the most welcoming voice came on at the other end, I let myself exhale, and jumped straight in with the fact that I had zero claim on her home and was just a curious visitor. She said she'd heard I had some old photographs of the house and would love to see them. WhatsApping her some photos, I waited for her to speak to her husband. My phone pinged. She was on her way. Half an hour later, Irene walked in, a slight and smiling woman, here with joy and hugs and everything I had hoped that meeting the people connected to this house from my past could be. She rang her husband and put him on speak-erphone, and we worked out that his parents had bought the house from the government a decade after my grandparents left, and it had been in the same family ever since. He'd grown up playing in this garden, just like my mother had. Poring over my old photos, we saw that some of the trees my grandfather had planted fifty years ago were still standing. I could see the sloped lawn where my mother had practised handstands, and the driveway where their VW had been parked. I was just in time, Irene said, because when they continued work on their apartment block, they were going to knock down the house. Taking photos together in the sun, my fears of the past few days drifted off on the wind.

While I was waiting for Irene to arrive, I'd been chatting with the tenant. He'd started asking me more questions, and asked, 'So your family used to live here?' I nodded. 'So, you have come to your village,' he laughed. 'You've come to your ancestral home.' And that's when I realised why all of this had mattered so much. This was a piece of my past and I wanted it to feel right. As author Zadie Smith said, 'It is very hard to live and to live well and in an undamaged way without having a history . . . And for diaspora people it's a more complicated journey back.'[15] I hope everyone who wants to can find their village.

Acknowledgements

Like so many writers, I've always wanted to write a book. But I didn't think it would be this one. For years I didn't believe that a story that was so much a part of me was one I could tell, or one anyone wanted to hear. I'm indebted to everyone who helped change my mind, from the writers before me, carving paths I could follow when discussing race and identity, to the many wonderful people in my life who showed interest in the jumbled ideas that would become *The Exiled*. This book is a sum of its parts, of which I am only a small one.

My biggest thanks go to everyone who spoke to me for this book, many more than would end up fitting into these finite pages. Every conversation informed my understanding of this piece of the past. Thank you for your generosity and openness in sharing your stories and trusting me with them. It has been the privilege of my life to have you open up such personal memories for me and find connection in our shared heritage.

The academics and journalists sharing minority voices and marginalised histories allowed me to add nuance and depth to my conversations, as did all those who have collected vital Ugandan Asian testimonies. Thank you for document-ing and scrutinising these under-explored histories. I'm particularly grateful to the many organisations who have digitised files and made history more accessible across borders – from the National Archives and the India Overseas

Trust, to the National Archives of Australia, the University of Carleton's Uganda Collection and Derek Peterson's Oder Commission reports. Special thanks to StoryTrails for giving me space to focus on Ugandan Asian narratives, and to the ingenious archivists at the British Film Institute for the gems you unearthed. And Hanif, you went out of your way for me and made a chapter of this book possible. Thank you to everyone who welcomed me in Uganda, to Irene and Robert for your kindness, and those who contributed to this book anonymously.

To the team at Coronet, and Hodder more widely, I'm so lucky to have had you bring my first book into the world. Thanks to my agent Broo Doherty for first seeing the potential in my idea, and Joelle Owusu-Sekyere for picking up the baton. I'm extremely grateful to Harriet Poland for taking the editorial reins and guiding me with such heartfelt encouragement – what every writer dreams of! – Tom Atkins for managing this project with the perfect mix of deadlines and generous flexibility, and Alyssa Ollivier-Tabukashvili for bringing such sensitivity and expertise to the copy-edit, among everyone else in the team who has brought this book into being.

Once upon a time, I thought of book-writing as a solitary activity – I couldn't have been more wrong. Where would I be without the inimitable Penguin WriteNow class of 2020? Never has joining a group WhatsApp proved to be such a good decision! Thank you all for the inspiration, solidarity, encouragement and friendship. Petra, Alison, Manuela and Christopher – we may not have read all that much, but you're still the best writers' group. Preeti, Daisy, Freya, Elli – I wouldn't have done this without you. Thanks also to the HarperCollins Author Academy for having me in your inaugural intake, which gave me the framework and motivation

Acknowledgements

to finish the proposal for this book, Spread the Word and Scribe UK for the encouragement to pursue this idea, Jericho Writers for longlisting this work during their Summer Festival of Writing, and for Writing on the Wall's excellent programming. I'm beyond grateful to everyone who read early versions of this work, including Molly Slight and Cash Carraway.

To my long-suffering friends who have supported my writing quietly and loudly over the years, I cannot thank you enough. Lauren, Laura, Bronwen, Leila, Alex, Emma, Freddie, Michelle, Tess, Rubin, Barney, Kate, Johnny, Jeff, Dan, Claire, Ty, Morter, Naomi and many more – I'm the luckiest girl going to have all of you in my life. Karl, you were my political sounding board and you wrote Chapter 10 together with me in my heart. Mhairi, you breathed belief and life into me and my writing, and this is your book too.

To R, you changed everything. Thank you for believing in me, especially when I didn't, and taking on this book with me. To my family, eternal thanks for allowing me to tell parts of the mosaic of our lives. Mum, you've been my lifelong inspiration long before I learnt about the twists and turns of your journey. Thanks for letting me probe into your past and for fielding impromptu interrogations so graciously. To Dad, you're the other half of my story and have been gone from it for far too long. I wish you could have seen me write a book, but at least you saved us arguing about politics. To my grandparents, thanks for starting this adventure, sharing your love of the world with me and for writing your love story down.

Photo credits

Pages 1–3: all © author's collection
Page 4: both © Majothi family collection
Page 5: (top) © Mohamed Amin Collection; (bottom) © Marion Kaplan/Alamy Stock Photo
Page 6: both © Mohamed Amin Collection
Page 7: (top) © Keystone Press/Alamy Stock Photo; (bottom) P. Felix/Daily Express/Hulton Archive/Getty Images
Page 8: © P. Felix/Daily Express/Hulton Archive/Getty Images
Page 9: both © Kausar Chaudary
Page 10: (top) © Lata Walter; (bottom) © Amita Mehta
Page 11: (top) © author's collection; (middle) © Pujara Family Archive 2023; (bottom) © Keystone/Hulton Archive/Getty Images
Page 12: both © Majothi family collection
Page. 13: (top) © Majothi family collection; (bottom) © Tom Skipp/British Film Institute/StoryTrails
Pages 14 & 15: all © author's collection
Page 16: (top left and right) © Kavi Pujara 2022, from *This Golden Mile* (Setanta Books, 2022); (bottom) © author's collection

Resources

The Exiled touches on everything from multinational racial identities and intersectionality to post-colonial politics and contemporary immigration policy – all of which can be explored in much more depth. Here are some of the many books, memoirs, podcasts and interviews exploring these topics.

UGANDAN ASIAN ARCHIVES AND ORAL HISTORIES

AFFCAD UK, 50 Ugandan Asian Stories, https://affcaduk.org/ugandan-refugees-1972-uk/.

British Ugandan Asians at 50, https://www.bua50.org/transcripts/.

Faith Matters, *From East to West, The History of Ugandan Asians*, https://www.ugandanasians.com/

Gujarati Yatra: Journey of a People, *Oral History*, https://www.gujaratiyatra.com/oralhistory.

Vali Jamal, *Ugandan Asians: Then and Now, Here and There, We Contributed, We Contribute*, forthcoming.

Yasmin Jamal, *Ugandan Asian Migration: Forced to Flee*, https://podcasters.spotify.com/pod/show/forced-to-flee-refugees/.

Shezan Muhammedi, *Gifts from Amin: Ugandan Asian Refugees in Canada*, (Manitoba: University of Manitoba Press, 2022).

Refugee Council Archive, University of East London, http://www.livingrefugeearchive.org/

Jake Rodrigues & Susan Rodrigues, *Paradise Won and Paradise Lost: 50 Years after the Asian Expulsion from Uganda* (Morrisville: Lulu Press, Inc., 2022).

The India Overseas Trust, *Asians from Uganda*, http://www.asiansfromuganda.org.uk/index.php.

The National Archives, *Ugandan Asians 50th Anniversary Event: online display documents*, https://www.nationalarchives.gov.uk/

education/outreach/projects/migration-histories/marking-the-50th-anniversary-of-the-arrival-of-ugandan-asians-in-britain-2022/ugandan-asians-50th-anniversary-event-online-display-documents/.

The National Archives, *Ugandan Asians 40 years on*, https://www.nationalarchives.gov.uk/education/outreach/projects/migration-histories/ugandan-asians-40-years-on/.

The Ugandan Asian Archive Oral History Project, Carleton University Library, 2017, https://carleton.ca/uganda-collection/.

Dolar Vasani, Expulsion @ 50, YouTube, https://www.youtube.com/@expulsion50/videos.

Ashak Nathwani, *50 Year Journey: Australians from Uganda – Tales of Trials, Tribulations & Triumphs* (Self-published, 2022).

UGANDAN ASIAN FICTION AND MEMOIR

Yasmin Alibhai-Brown, *No Place Like Home* (London: Virago Press, 1995).

Tasneem Jamal, *Where the Air is Sweet* (New York: Harper Perennial, 2018).

Manubhai Madhvani and Giles Foden, *Tide of Fortune: A Family Tale* (Manubhai Madhvani Bermuda Trusts, 2009).

Mahmood Mamdani, *From Citizen to Refugee: Uganda Asians Come to Britain* (Nairobi: Pambazuka Press, 1973).

Shenaaz Nanji, *Child of Dandelions* (Honesdale: Front Street Inc., 2008).

Neema Shah, *Kololo Hill* (London: Picador, 2021).

Hafsa Zayyan, *We Are All Birds of Uganda* (London: Merky Books, 2021).

UGANDA – NON-FICTION

Alicia C. Decker, *In Idi Amin's Shadow, Women, Gender and Militarism in Uganda* (Ohio: Ohio University Press, 2014).

Henry Kyemba, *A State of Blood* (New York: Ace Books, 1977).

Mark Leopold, *Idi Amin – The Story of Africa's Icon of Evil* (London: Yale Books, 2021).

Phares Mutibwa, *Uganda Since Independence: A Story of Unfulfilled Hopes* (Trenton: Africa World Press, 1992).

Richard J. Reid, *A History of Modern Uganda* (Cambridge: Cambridge University Press, 2017).

Resources

Andrew Rice, *The Teeth May Smile but the Heart Does Not Forget: Murder and Memory in Uganda* (London: Picador, 2009).

UGANDA – FICTION

Giles Foden, *The Last King of Scotland* (London: Vintage, 1999).

Arthur Gakwandi, *Kosiya Kifefe* (Kenya: East African Educational Publishers, 1997).

Moses Isegawa, *Abyssinian Chronicles: A Novel* (London: Vintage, 2001).

Goretti Kyomuhendo, *Waiting: A Novel of Uganda's Hidden War* (New York: The Feminist Press at CUNY, 2007).

Jennifer Nansubuga Macumbi, *Kintu* (London: OneWorld Publications, 2014).

Nick Makoha, *Kingdom of Gravity* (London: Peepal Tree Press, 2017).

Mary Karooro Okurut, *The Invisible Weevil* (Uganda: Femrite Publications, 1998).

RACE AND IDENTITY

Gurnek Bains, Bryony Heard and Kylie Bains, *England Our England: Stories of the Black and Asian Migrant Pioneers* (London: Profile, 2020).

Preeti Dhillon, *The Shoulders We Stand On* (London: Dialogue Books, 2023).

Afua Hirsch, *Brit(ish): On Race, Identity and Belonging* (London: Vintage, 2018).

Shushella Nasta, *Asian Britain: A Photographic History* (London: The Westbourne Press, 2014).

David Olusoga, *Black and British: A Forgotten History* (London: Pan Macmillan, 2016).

Kavi Pujara, *This Golden Mile* (London: Setanta Books, 2022).

Nikesh Shukla ed., *The Good Immigrant* (London: Unbound, 2016).

MIGRATION

Jordanna Bailkin, *Unsettled: Refugee Camps and the Making of Multicultural Britain* (Oxford: Oxford University Press, 2018).

Maya Goodfellow, *Hostile Environment: How Immigrants Became Scapegoats* (London: Verso, 2019).

Sally Hayden, *My Fourth Time We Drowned: Seeking Refuge on the World's Deadliest Migration Route* (London: Fourth Estate, 2022).

Becky Taylor, *Refugees in Twentieth-Century Britain: A History* (Cambridge: CUP, 2021).

Robert Winder, *Bloody Foreigners: The Story of Immigration to Britain* (Boston: Little, Brown, 2004).

EMPIRE AND POST-COLONIALISM

Akala, *Natives: Race and Class in the Ruins of Empire* (London: Two Roads, 2019).

Caroline Elkins, *Imperial Reckoning: The Untold Story of Britain's Gulag in Kenya* (New York: Holt McDougal, 2005).

Mahmood Mamdani, *Citizen and Subject: Contemporary Africa and the Legacy of Late Colonialism* (Princeton: Princeton University Press, 1996).

Ian Sanjay Patel, *We're Here Because You Were There: Immigration and the End of Empire*, (London: Verso, 2021).

Santham Sanghera, *Empireland: How Imperialism Has Shaped Modern Britain* (London: Viking, 2021).

Notes

Epigraph

1 Kazuo Ishiguro, 'My Twentieth-Century Evening – and Other Small Breakthroughs', Nobel Lecture, Swedish Academy, Stockholm, May 7, 2017. https://www.nobelprize.org/prizes/literature/2017/ishiguro/lecture/.

Prologue

1 Rainer Maria Rilke, *Rilke's Book of Hours: Love Poems to God*, trans. Anita Barrows and Joanna Macy, (New York: Riverhead Books, 1997), 88.

Introduction – A General's Dream

1 Ronald Bell, MP, '1972: Asians given 90 days to leave Uganda', Speech in Conservative Monday Club Immigration Committee, BBC, 1972. http://news.bbc.co.uk/onthisday/hi/dates/stories/august/7/newsid_2492000/2492333.stm.

2 David Cameron in Dolar Popat, *A British Subject: How to Make It as an Immigrant in the Best Country in the World*, (London: Biteback Publishing, 2019), foreword.

3 Christopher Munnion, 'The African who kicked out the Asians, who said Hitler was right, who has made his country a state sinister', *The New York Times*, November 12, 1972, https://www.nytimes.com/1972/11/12/archives/if-idi-amin-of-uganda-is-a-madman-hes-a-ruthless-and-cunning-one.html.

4 'The Future of the Asians in Uganda', *Uganda Argus*, August 5,

1972, 1; Patrick Keatley, 'Britain could face influx of 80,000 Asians', The Guardian, 5 August 1972, https://www.theguardian.com/ theguardian/1972/aug/05/fromthearchive. 1971 Statistical Abstract (Entebbe: Government Printer, 1971) in Mittelman, *Ideology and Politics in Uganda*, 228, in Shezan Muhammedi, 'Gifts From Amin': The Resettlement, Integration, and Identities of Ugandan Asian Refugees in Canada', (The University of Western Ontario, 2017), 89. Amin declared there was no place in Uganda for the 'over 80,000 Asians holding British passports who are sabotaging Uganda's economy and encouraging corruption'. This figure was likely based on the 1969 census numbers of 74,308 South Asians in Uganda, but didn't take into account the fact that more than 25,000 of them were Ugandan citizens. The 80,000 number was immediately contested by the British government, who themselves put numbers at half that amount.

5 'Ugandan Asians advert 'foolish', says Leicester councillor', *BBC News*, August 8, 2012, https://www.bbc.co.uk/news/uk-england-leicestershire-19165216.

6 'Britain's £2,000 "carrot" to deter Ugandan Asians', *Daily Telegraph*, January 1, 2003, https://www.telegraph.co.uk/news/uknews/1417591 /Britains-2000-carrot-to-deter-Ugandan-Asians.html.

7 'Ethnic group, England and Wales: Census 2021', *Office for National Statistics*, November 29, 2022, https://www.ons.gov.uk/ peoplepopulationandcommunity/culturalidentity/ethnicity/bulle-tins/ethnicgroupenglandandwales/census2021.

8 Nikesh Shukla ed., *The Good Immigrant*, (London: Unbound, 2016).

9 For details of archives and oral history projects consulted, and recommended, see the additional resources section.

10 Taushif Kara, host, 'Don't call yourselves Asian! Uganda's Indians and the problem of naming', Asian Studies Centre University of Oxford (podcast), June 27, 2022, https://podcasts.ox.ac.uk/dont-call-yourselves-asian-ugandas-indians-and-problem-naming.

11 Parminder Bhachu, *Twice Migrants: East African Sikh Settlers in Britain*, (London: Tavistock Publications, 1985).

Chapter One – Where the Sun Never Sets

1 Boris Johnson, 'Africa is a mess, but we can't blame colonialism', *Spectator*, February 2, 2002, republished July 14, 2016, https://www.spectator.co.uk/article/the-boris-archive-africa-is-a-mess-but-we-can-t-blame-colonialism.

2 Thunchaththu Ramanujan Ezhuthachan, *The Keralolpathi: The Origin of Malabar.*

3 Angus Maddison, *The World Economy: A Millennial Perspective*, (OECD Publishing, 2001), 97, 241.

4 Shashi Tharoor, *Inglorious Empire: What the British Did to India*, (London: Hurst, 2017), 196.

5 Anthony Farrington, *Trading Places: The East India Company and Asia 1600–1834*, (London: The British Library, 2002), 42.

6 Radhika Mongia, *Indian Migration and Empire: A Colonial Genealogy of the Modern State*, (Durham: Duke University Press Books, 2018), 24-5.

7 Radhika Mongia, *Indian Migration and Empire*; Michael Taylor, *The Interest: How the British Establishment Resisted the Abolition of Slavery*, (London: Bodley Head, 2020), 297.

8 Ian Sanjay Patel, *We're Here Because You Were There: Immigration and the End of Empire*, (London: Verso, 2021), 25.

9 Debjani Bhattacharyya, Review of Radhika Viyas Mongia, Indian Migration and Empire: A Colonial Genealogy of the Modern State. H-Diplo, H-Net Reviews, June, 2019, https://networks.h-net.org/node/28443/reviews/4225401/bhattacharyya-mongia-indian-migration-and-empire-colonial-genealogy; Radhika Mongia, *Indian Migration and Empire*, 2.

10 Richard J. Reid, *A History of Modern Uganda*, (Cambridge: Cambridge University Press, 2017), 19-23.

11 Richard J. Reid, *A History of Modern Uganda*, 1.

12 Richard J. Reid, *A History of Modern Uganda*, 2.

13 'Britain, 1953: so long ago, so far away', *Guardian*, June 1, 2003, https://www.theguardian.com/politics/2003/jun/01/monarchy.uk.

14 'BI's fleet spanning 116 years', *Biship*, http://www.biship.com/ships.htm.

15 Ian Sanjay Patel, *We're Here Because You Were There*, 33.

16 Ian Sanjay Patel, *We're Here Because You Were There*, 33.

17 'Forbes lists 10 richest Ugandans', *Daily Monitor*, August 27, 2018, https://www.monitor.co.ug/uganda/news/national/forbes-lists-10-richest-ugandans-1775120; 'Ugandan Asians: The making of Ruparelia Group', *Daily Monitor*, October 3, 2012, https://www.monitor.co.ug/uganda/lifestyle/reviews-profiles/ugandan-asians-the-making-of-ruparelia-group-1527008.

18 Michel Adam, 'From the Trading-Post Indians to the Indian-Africans', *Indian Africa: Minorities of Indian-Pakistani Origin in Eastern Africa*, ed. Michel Adam, (Nairobi: Mkuki na Nyota Publishers, 2016), 6.

19 Ruth Evans, 'Kenya's Asian heritage on display', *BBC News*, May 24, 2000, http://news.bbc.co.uk/1/hi/world/africa/762515.stm; Sophie Vohra and William Law, 'Beyond the 'Lunatic Line': Ugandan Asians and British Railways', *Railway Museum blog*, August 4, 2022, https://blog.railwaymuseum.org.uk/beyond-the-lunatic-line/.

20 Harold Stephen Morris, *The Indians in Uganda*, (London: Weidenfeld & Nicolson, 1968), 11; Vali Jamal, 'Asians in Uganda, 1880–1972: Inequality and Expulsion', *The Economic History Review*, New Series, Vol. 29, No. 4 (Nov. 1976), 602–604.

21 Saima Nasar, Lecturer in the History of Africa and its Diasporas, University of Bristol, speaking at 'From Expulsion to Settlement: The Ugandan Asian Story', at Leicester Museum & Art Gallery, October 29, 2022.

22 'An Oral History with Anwer Omar', *The Ugandan Asian Archive Oral History Project*, Carleton University Library, 2017, https://carleton.ca/uganda-collection/wp-content/uploads/Anwer_Omar_Transcript.pdf.

23 Mukesh Kumar, 'Indian Immigration in Uganda: Trends and Patterns,' *Proceedings of the Indian History Congress 67*, (2006–7): 936–42, https://www.jstor.org/stable/44148012.

24 'An Oral History with Bashir Lalani', *The Ugandan Asian Archive Oral History Project*, Carleton University Library, 2016, https://carleton.ca/uganda-collection/wp-content/uploads/Bashir_Lalani_Transcript.pdf.

25 Mukesh Kumar, 'Indians in Post-war Uganda, 1948–62,' *Proceedings*

of the Indian History Congress 72, Part II (2011), 1096, https://www.jstor.org/stable/44145722.

26 Mukesh Kumar, 'Indians in Post-war Uganda, 1948–62', 1098, https://www.jstor.org/stable/44145722. European migrants rose from 3,448 to 10,866, and South Asians from 35,215 to 71,933.

27 Kehinde Andrews, *The New Age of Empire: How Racism and Colonialism Still Rule the World*, (London: Allen Lane, 2021).

Chapter Two – The City of Seven Hills

1 Kiran Desai, *The Inheritance of Loss*, (London: Open Road, 2007), 122.

2 'Why the name: Kampala?', *Afro Legends*, March 17, 2015, https://afrolegends.com/2015/03/17/why-the-name-kampala/.

3 Yasmin Alibhai-Brown, *The Settler's Cookbook: A Memoir of Love, Migration and Food*, (London: Granta Books, 2010), 127.

4 Sara Cosemans, 'Undesirable British East African Asians. Nationality, Statelessness, and Refugeehood after Empire', *Immigrants & Minorities* 40, no.2 (2021): 210–239, 2.

5 Derek Humphry and Michael Ward, *Passports and Politics*, (London: Penguin Books, 1974), 12.

6 Mahmood Mamdani, 'The Asian Question: Mahmood Mamdani writes about the expulsion from Uganda', *London Review of Books* 44, no.19 (6 October 2022), https://www.lrb.co.uk/the-paper/v44/n19/mahmood-mamdani/the-asian-question.

7 Mahmood Mamdani, *From Citizen to Refugee: Uganda Asians Come to Britain*, (Nairobi: Pambazuka Press, 1973), 15.

8 Harold Stephen Morris, *The Indians in Uganda: Caste and sect in a plural society*, (London: Weidenfeld & Nicolson, 1968), 17.

9 Sara Cosemans, 'Undesirable British East African Asians', 2.

10 Saima Nasar, at 'From Expulsion to Settlement: The Ugandan Asian Story'.

11 'Madhvani History', *Quasar Electricity*, https://www.quasarelectricity.com/madhvani-history/; 'Between a rock and a distant, unknown place: Origin of the Madhvani empire', *Daily Monitor*, May 20, 2012, https://www.monitor.co.ug/uganda/special-reports/

uganda-50/between-a-rock-and-a-distant-unknown-place-origin-of-the-madhvani-empire-1516878; Thomas Patrick Melady, *Uganda: The Asian Exiles*, (New York: Orbis Books, 1978), 58–9, in Max Russel, 'Enduring Empire: A Case Study of the Ugandan Asian Diaspora', (MA diss., University of Bologna, 2021), 36–7; Derek Humphry and Michael Ward, *Passports and Politics*, 12.

12 Mahmood Mamdani, 'The Asian Question'; Mahadev Desai, 'Tide of Fortune: A Family Tale', review of *Tide of Fortune: A Family Tale* by Manubhai Madhvani, *Atlanta Dunia*, https://www.atlanta-dunia.com/dunia/Features/F166.htm.

13 'About Kakira's Founder: Muljibhai Prabhudas Madhvani', *Kakira Sugar*, https://www.kakirasugar.com/?q=content/our-history.

14 Saima Nasar, at 'From Expulsion to Settlement: The Ugandan Asian Story'; William G. Kuepper, G. Lynne Lackey, E. Nelson Swinerton, *Ugandan Asians in Great Britain: Forced Migration and Social Absorption*, (London: Croom Helm, 1975), 27.

15 'About Kakira's Founder'.

16 William G. Kuepper, *Ugandan Asians in Great Britain*, 29.

17 Thomas Sowell, *Migrations and Cultures: A World View*, (New York: Basic Books, 1996), 317–23. Full figures – 5,227 Asian retail traders had an annual turnover of £28.4 million, amounting to £5,433 per trader, compared with a turnover of £10.6 million for 11,634 African traders, at just £911 per trader.

18 'Why Ugandan Asians were expelled by Idi Amin and how they ended up in UK', *ITV News Central*, December 9, 2022, https://www.itv.com/news/central/2022-07-17/how-brutality-in-uganda-forced-tens-of-thousands-of-asians-from-home.

19 William G. Kuepper, *Ugandan Asians in Great Britain*, 29; 'Chronologies: Uganda Timeline', *Uganda Collection*, Carleton University, https://carleton.ca/uganda-collection/chronology/.

20 Yasmin Alibhai-Brown, *The Settler's Cookbook*, 104.

21 British Connection, 1972, https://www2.bfi.org.uk/films-tv-people/4ce2b8d4cac16.

22 Anneeth Kaur Hundle, '1970s Uganda: Past, Present, Future,' *Journal of Asian and African Studies* 53, no.3 (2018): 455–75, 462.

23 Valerie Marett, *Immigrants Settling in the City*, (Leicester: Leicester University Press, 1989), 18.

24 Mahmood Mamdani, 'The Asian Question'.

25 Neha Shah, 'How did British Indians become so prominent in the Conservative party?', *Guardian*, February 27, 2020, https://www.theguardian.com/commentisfree/2020/feb/27/how-did-british-indians-become-so-prominent-in-the-conservative-party.

26 Harold Macmillan, 'The Wind of Change' Speech, Houses of the Parliament of the Union of South Africa, Cape Town, 3 February 1960. https://web-archives.univ-pau.fr/english/TD2doc1.pdf; '1960: Macmillan speaks of 'wind of change' in Africa', *BBC On This Day*, February 2, 1960, http://news.bbc.co.uk/onthisday/hi/dates/stories/february/3/newsid_2714000/2714525.stm.

27 'Africa After Independence', *The School of Life*, https://www.theschooloflife.com/article/africa-after-independence/.

28 'Prince Edward the Duke of Kent Speaks at Uganda Independence 1962', *The Nile Journal*, https://nilejournal.net/culture/society/duke-of-kent%27s-speech-at-uganda-independence-1962.

29 'Uganda Wins Independence', British Pathé, *Pathe News*, 1962, https://www.youtube.com/watch?v=ylDMrkHrWcg

30 Yasmin Alibhai-Brown, *The Settler's Cookbook*, 105.

Chapter Three – The Writing on the Wall

1 Paul Theroux, 'Hating the Asians', *Transition* 33 (1967), 61.

2 Alicia C. Decker, *In Idi Amin's Shadow, Women, Gender and Militarism in Uganda*, (Ohio: Ohio University Press, 2014), 37.

3 Andrew Rice, *The Teeth May Smile but the Heart Does Not Forget: Murder and Memory in Uganda*, (London: Picador, 2009), 92.

4 '1971: Idi Amin ousts Uganda president', *BBC On This Day*, http://news.bbc.co.uk/onthisday/hi/dates/stories/january/25/newsid_2506000/2506423.stm.

5 Mark Leopold, *Idi Amin: The Story of Africa's Icon of Evil*, (London: Yale Books, 2021), 180–2. Andrew Rice, *The Teeth May Smile*, 89–90.

6 '1971: A dictator comes to power', *BBC On This Day*, http://news.bbc.co.uk/onthisday/hi/witness/january/25/newsid_3404000/3404157.stm.

7 Robert Siedle's personal diary in Edward Siedle, *A Tree Has Fallen*

In Africa: The Journey to Find My Father's Murderers, 2022, unpublished, 18. Andrew Rice, *The Teeth May Smile*, 92.

8 Colm O'Regan, 'The rise of inflated job titles', *BBC News*, July 17, 2012, https://www.bbc.co.uk/news/magazine-18855099.

9 George Alagiah, *A Passage to Africa*, (Boston: Little, Brown, 2001), 190.

10 '1971: Idi Amin Dada takes over as president of Uganda through a military coup', *Uganda Today*, May 6, 2017, https://www.youtube.com/watch?v=8OLisR6YUpY; George Alagiah, *A Passage to Africa*, 190.

11 Richard Slater to FCO, 3 February 1971, FCO 31/1024 in Yasmin Alibhai-Brown, *The Settler's Cookbook*, 253.

12 Mark Curtis, *Unpeople: Britain's Secret Human Rights Abuses*, (New York: Vintage, 2004), 245–8.

13 George Alagiah, *A Passage to Africa*, 190.

14 Sara Cosemans, 'Undesirable British East African Asians', 5, 7.

15 Mahmood Mamdani, 'The Asian Question'.

16 Sara Cosemans, 'Undesirable British East African Asians', 8. CUKCs or BPPs had until the second anniversary of Uganda's independence to register for citizenship and had to prove at least five years' continuous residency.

17 Klaus Neumann, '"Our own interests must come first": Australia's response to the expulsion of Asians from Uganda', *History Australia* 3, no.1 (2006), 10.2.

18 'Ugandan Asians: The Reckoning', *BBC Radio 4*, September 14, 2022, https://www.bbc.co.uk/sounds/play/m001bykk.

19 Ian Sanjay Patel, *We're Here Because You Were There*, 10.

20 Sara Cosemans, 'Undesirable British East African Asians', 2.

21 Maya Goodfellow, *Hostile Environment: How Immigrants Became Scapegoats*, (London: Verso, 2019), 63.

22 Ian Sanjay Patel, *We're Here Because You Were There*, 192. While citizenship for people of African descent was automatic after Kenya's independence, everyone else, including East African Asians, had to apply. They had two years to do so, but had become citizens of the United Kingdom and Colonies under the terms of the 1948 British Nationality Act, so they retained this if they didn't gain Kenyan citizenship.

23 *Conservative Party Archives (CPA), Bodleian Library, Oxford, CRD 2/16/4*, 'Memorandum by Patrick Cosgrave for Edward Heath', 19 Mar. 1970 in Randall Hansen, *Citizenship and Immigration in Postwar Britain*, (Oxford: Oxford University Press, 2000), 154; Ian Sanjay Patel, *We're Here Because You Were There*, 212.

24 Nadine El-Enany, *(B)ordering Britain: Law, Race and Empire*, (Manchester: Manchester University Press, 2020), 103; Maya Goodfellow, *Hostile Environment*, 73.

25 Labour MP Charles Pannell quoted in Nadine El-Enany, *(B)ordering Britain*, 103.

26 India, J. Freeman, Report to the Secretary of State for Commonwealth Affairs, H. Bowden – The 'Asian Exodus' from Kenya, July 4, 1968. FCO 50/134/12 *The National Archives* in Sara Cosemans, 'The politics of dispersal: Turning Ugandan colonial subjects into post-colonial refugees (1967–76)', *Migration Studies* 6, no.1 (March 2018), 101.

27 Nadine El-Enany, *(B)ordering Britain*, 108.

28 Randall Hansen, *Citizenship and Immigration*, 153.

29 Ian Sanjay Patel, *We're Here Because You Were There*, 225 in Mahmood Mamdani, 'The Asian Question'. Citizens of former colonies from African to the Caribbean and Asia had held an automatic right of entry into Britain – now 1.5 million non-white British citizens (Citizens of the United Kingdom and Colonies) had lost that right.

30 Nadine El-Enany, *(B)ordering Britain*, 103.

31 Enoch Powell's 'Rivers of Blood' speech, https://anth1001.files.wordpress.com/2014/04/enoch-powell_speech.pdf

32 Nadine El-Enany, *(B)ordering Britain*, 104.

33 Yasmin Alibhai-Brown, *The Settler's Cookbook*, 254.

34 Alicia C. Decker, *In Idi Amin's Shadow*, 25–36.

35 Andrew Rice, *The Teeth May Smile*, 10. 'Idi Amin Being Interviewed For UPITN by Reporter Jon Snow', *AP Archive*, July 21, 2015, https://www.youtube.com/watch?v=GwHJK5zyoK0.

36 Anneeth Kaur Hundle, '1970s Uganda', 456. The narratives people weaved about Amin overlooked the reality of his rule, says Hundle. 'Amin, as a historical subject and discursive site, and the field of scholarship that was produced around him, tended to overpower

The Exiled

the "truths" and social realities of this era of military dictatorship in Uganda.'

37 Mark Leopold, *Idi Amin: The Story of Africa's Icon of Evil*, (London: Yale University Press, 2020), 303.

38 Mark Leopold, *Idi Amin*, 268.

39 Richard Vokes, 'Photographies in Africa in the digital age', *Africa* 89, no.2, (2019): 207–24, https://www.cambridge.org/core/journals/africa/article/photographies-in-africa-in-the-digital-age/73E3F4CF06CB5A2D9BC433938713D70D.

40 Derek Peterson and Richard Vokes, *The Unseen Archives of Idi Amin*, (London: Prestel, 2021).

41 Alicia C. Decker, *In Idi Amin's Shadow*, 3.

42 Anneeth Kaur Hundle, '1970s Uganda', 457–9.

43 Mahmood Mamdani, 'The Asian Question'.

44 Bernard Ryan, professor of migration law at the University of Leicester, at 'From Expulsion to Settlement: The Ugandan Asian Story', at Leicester Museum & Art Gallery, October 29, 2022; Yumiko Hamai, '"Imperial Burden" or "Jews of Africa"?: An Analysis of Political and Media Discourse in the Ugandan Asian Crisis (1972)', *Twentieth Century British History* 22, no.3 (2011), 418.

45 Milton Obote, *The Common Man's Charter*, (Entebbe, 1970), 37 –8, in Mark Leopold, *Idi Amin*, 165.

46 Yumiko Hamai, 'Imperial Burden', 418.

47 Sara Cosemans, 'Undesirable British East African Asians', 16. Ian Sanjay Patel, *We're Here Because You Were There*, 247.

48 Andrew Rice, *The Teeth May Smile*, 27.

49 Robert Siedle's personal diary in Edward Siedle, *A Tree Has Fallen In Africa,* 18; Alicia C. Decker, *In Idi Amin's Shadow*, 57. Faustin Mugabe, 'How Bataringaya risked to arrest Amin', *Daily Monitor*, March 12, 2016, https://web.archive.org/web/20190110042400/https://www.monitor.co.ug/News/National/Bataringaya-risked-arrest-Amin/688334-3113094-5lfp9j/index.html.

50 Alicia C. Decker, *In Idi Amin's Shadow*, 38; George Alagiah, *A Passage to Africa*, 190–1.

51 Robert Siedle's personal diary in Edward Siedle, *A Tree Has Fallen In Africa*, 19.

52 Alicia C. Decker, *In Idi Amin's Shadow*, 1.

53 John Martin, 'Looking Back at the 1971 Uganda Coup', Wilson Center Sources and Methods, April 19, 2021, https://www.wilson-center.org/blog-post/looking-back-1971-uganda-coup.

54 *How to Become a Tyrant: Reign Through Terror*, Netflix, 2021, https://www.netflix.com/gb/title/80989772.

55 Yasmin Alibhai-Brown, *The Settler's Cookbook*, 246.

56 Kim Wall, 'Ghost Stories: Idi Amin's Torture Chambers', *Harper's Magazine*, December 27, 2016, https://harpers.org/2016/12/ghost-stories/.

57 'Uganda reburies Lake Victoria's Rwanda genocide victims', *BBC News*, June 25, 2010, https://www.bbc.com/news/10417150.

58 George Alagiah, *A Passage to Africa*, 190–1.

59 Alicia C. Decker, *In Idi Amin's Shadow*, 126.

60 Henry Kyemba, *A State of Blood: The Inside Story of Idi Amin*, (London: Paddington Press, 1977), 119–20.

61 Alicia C. Decker, *In Idi Amin's Shadow*, 142.

62 Christina Lamb, *Our Bodies, Their Battlefield: What War Does to Women*, (London: HarperCollins, 2020), intro.

63 Yasmin Alibhai-Brown, *The Settler's Cookbook*, 251–2. Names were written on people's doors so tribes could be easily identified; Mark Leopold, *Idi Amin*, 46. As well as growing up under colonialism, Amin had also experienced prejudice by virtue of his background. He was part of the Kakwa tribe, from Uganda's West Nile region, a group seen by the dominant parts of Ugandan society, the Baganda and other southern groups, as inferior. Once he held absolute power, he wielded it against those he felt had previously wronged him.

64 Colin Grimes speaking at 'Finding Home: The Ugandan Exodus, 50 Years On', Leicester Curve Theatre, August 4, 2022, https://www.youtube.com/watch?v=LNijbUMyQtA.

65 Invitation to the Queen, National Archives, FCO 57/401, 10 January 1972, https://www.nationalarchives.gov.uk/education/outreach/projects/migration-histories/marking-the-50th-anniversary-of-the-arrival-of-ugandan-asians-in-britain-2022/ugandan-asians-50th-anniversary-event-online-display-documents/invitation-to-the-queen/. In early 1972 Amin would invite Queen Elizabeth II to join Uganda's celebrations for the country's tenth anniversary of

independence. She politely declined, and later that year, before the anniversary, Amin would announce the Ugandan Asian expulsion.

66 Derek Peterson, professor of history and African studies at the University of Michigan, in *How to Become a Tyrant: Reign Through Terror*.

67 John Martin, 'Looking Back at the 1971 Uganda Coup', Wilson Center Sources and Methods, April 19, 2021, https://www.wilson-center.org/blog-post/looking-back-1971-uganda-coup. In a secret, now declassified memo, the national security advisor said, 'Two American citizens apparently were recently killed by Amin's undisciplined troops, and it is inappropriate for you to agree to receive him while that matter is still in flux.'; Memorandum From the President's Assistant for National Security Affairs (Kissinger) to President Nixon, Foreign Relations of the United States, 1969–1976, Volume V, United Nations, 1969–1972, Office of the Historian, Washington, undated, https://history.state.gov/historicaldocuments/frus1969-76v05/d37.

68 Derek Peterson and Richard Stokes, *The Unseen Archives of Idi Amin*, 128–35; *How to Become a Tyrant: Reign Through Terror*.

Chapter Four – Ninety Days

1 Nick Makoha, 'At Gunpoint', *Proletarian Poetry*, September 12, 2017, https://proletarianpoetry.com/2017/09/12/at-gunpoint-by-nick-makoha/.

2 'Uganda says no room for 40,000 Asians with British passports', *The Times*, August 5, 1972, 1.

3 Mahmood Mamdani, *From Citizen to Refugee*, 13, 17.

4 Idi Amin, 'Message to the Nation, 12/13 August 1972' in Martin Minogue and Judith Molloy eds., *African Aims and Attitudes: Selected Documents*, (Cambridge: Cambridge University Press, 1974), 368; 'General Idi Amin Announces His Intention To Expel South Asians From Uganda | Kampala | August 1972', *Adeyinka Makinde*, June 15, 2021, https://www.youtube.com/watch?v=nD0CTrUlNI4; 'RR7233 UGANDA EXPELS ITS ASIANS', *AP Archive*, May 29, 2022, https://www.youtube.com/watch?v=efHU6WtPX4s.

5 Ian Sanjay Patel, *We're Here Because You Were There*, 247.

6 Ian Sanjay Patel, *We're Here Because You Were There*, 195.

7 Becky Taylor, 'Good Citizens? Ugandan Asians, Volunteers and "Race" Relations in 1970s Britain', *History Workshop Journal 85*, (Spring 2018): 120–41, https://doi.org/10.1093/hwj/dbx055.

8 Duncan Sandys speaking in Parliament, 15 November 1967, 'Volume 754: debated on Wednesday 15 November 1967', *Hansard*, UK Parliament, https://hansard.parliament.uk/Commons/1967-11-15/debates/51b1846a-f76e-48ee-b7b6-909dd185df22/ (ActsContinuedTillEndOfDecember1968).

9 Sara Cosemans, 'Undesirable British East African Asians', 12.

10 Peter Evans, 'Six Countries Offer to Take Asians', *The Times*, September 7, 1972, 2.

11 Ian Sanjay Patel, *We're Here Because You Were There*, 262.

12 FCO to Downing Street, 29 August 2002, PREM15/1259 Confidential Letter from Anthony Acland, Foreign & Commonwealth Office, to Lord Tom Bridges of the Prime Minister's Office at 10 Downing Street, briefing on offers of help from other governments, http://www.asiansfromuganda.org.uk/images/13.gif.

13 Klaus Neumann, 'Our own interests must come first', 10.6. William G. Kuepper, *Ugandan Asians in Great Britain*, 52; FCO to FCO, December 13, 1972, FCO80/26 Draft note by the Secretary of State for Foreign and Commonwealth Affairs about the possibility of settling East African Asians on an island in the 'dependent territories'. http://www.asiansfromuganda.org.uk/images/21.gif FCO to FCO, 28 December, 1972, FCO80/26 Secret Letter from E. J. Emery of the Pacific Dependent Territories Department of the FCO to Mr. J.D.B. Shaw of the Gibraltar & General Department also of the FCO, dealing with the possibility of moving the Asians to the Solomon Islands, http://www.asiansfromuganda.org.uk/images/24.gif; Alan Travis, 'Ministers hunted for island to house Asians', *Guardian*, January 1, 2003, https://www.theguardian.com/uk/2003/jan/01/past.politics; 'UK 'did not want Ugandan Asians"', *BBC News*, January 1, 2003, http://news.bbc.co.uk/1/hi/uk/2619049.stm.

14 'Britain's £2,000 'carrot' to deter Ugandan Asians', *Daily Telegraph*, January 1, 2003, https://www.telegraph.co.uk/news/uknews/1417591/Britains-2000-carrot-to-deter-Ugandan-Asians.html; Ian Sanjay Patel, *We're Here Because You Were There*, 257.

15 Robert Winder, *Bloody Foreigners: The Story of Immigration to Britain*, (Boston: Little, Brown, 2004), 381.

16 Yumiko Hamai, 'Imperial Burden', 418; Derek Humphry and Michael Ward, *Passports and Politics*, 42.

17 William G. Kuepper, G. Lynne Lackey and E. Nelson Swinerton, 'Ugandan Asian Refugees: Resettlement Centre to Community', *Community Development Journal* 11, no.3 (October 1976), 199.

18 Ian Sanjay Patel, *We're Here Because You Were There*, 250.

19 Sara Cosemans, 'The politics of dispersal', 108; Robert Winder, *Bloody Foreigners*, 381.

20 'Uganda Asians', The London Television Service, FCO, archived by the British Film Institute, https://player.bfi.org.uk/free/film/watch-uganda-asians-1972-online.

21 Lizzie Dearden, 'Suella Braverman says it is her "dream" and "obsession" to see a flight take asylum seekers to Rwanda', *Independent*, October 5, 2022, https://www.independent.co.uk/news/uk/politics/suella-braverman-rwanda-dream-obsession-b2195296.html.

22 Trevor Grundy, *Daily Telegraph*, August 2, 2002 in Yasmin Alibhai-Brown, *The Settler's Cookbook*, 279.

23 Mahmood Mamdani, *From Citizen to Refugee*, 25.

24 Mahmood Mamdani, *From Citizen to Refugee*, 18; Hasu H. Patel, 'General Amin and the Indian Exodus from Uganda,' *Issue: A Journal of Opinion*, 1972, 18; Nicholas Van Hear, *New Diasporas: The Mass Exodus, Dispersal and Regrouping of Migrant Communities* (London: University College London Press Limited, 1998), 71, and Tony Kushner and Katharine Knox, *Refugees in an Age of Genocide: Global, National, and Local Perspectives during the Twentieth Century* (New York: Frank Cass, 1999), 267, in Shezan Muhammedi, 'Gifts From Amin': The Resettlement, Integration, and Identities of Ugandan Asian Refugees in Canada', (The University of Western Ontario, 2017), 2017, 89. A census in 1969 had given the Ugandan Asian population at around 74,000 but some scholars believe over 20,000 left the country between then and the expulsion decree. Notable numbers of Ugandan Asians were unaccounted for within these migratory patterns, but a minimum 50,000-strong population was expelled in 1972.

25 Interview with Richard Jackson, December 14, 2022.

26 Ashak Nathwani, Uganda Diaries: British Ugandans at 50 (Series 4, Part 4 of 10), https://www.youtube.com/watch?v=t_vJ0Q_UnKI; 'Chronology: Uganda Timeline', *Uganda Collection*, Carleton University, https://carleton.ca/uganda-collection/chronology/.

27 Michael A. Hiltzik, 'Powerful Dynasty: All in the Family Feud Rips Uganda', *Los Angeles Times*, April 4, 1989, https://www.latimes.com/archives/la-xpm-1989-04-04-mn-943-story.html. '"Legend has it that Amin tried to marry into the Madhvanis by proposing to the widowed Meena. Asked about it today, she smiles mysteriously and says, "Some people said it was so".'

28 Anneeth Kaur Hundle, '1970s Uganda', 464. 'He's Nuts', *Sunday Mirror*, September 3, 1972.

29 Jan Jelmert Jørgensen, *Uganda: A Modern History*, (London: Croom Helm, 1981), 288. https://archive.org/details/ugandamodernhist00jrge/page/288/mode/2up.

30 Derek Peterson and Richard Vokes, *The Unseen Archives of Idi Amin*, (Munich: Prestel, 2021), 55.

31 Christopher Munnion, 'The African who kicked out the Asians'.

32 Mahmood Mamdani, 'The Asian Question'.

33 Ian Sanjay Patel, *We're Here Because You Were There*, 261; Derek Humphry and Michael Ward, *Passports and Politics*, 46.

34 Michael Knipe, '"Not a Single Ugandan Shilling" to Leave, Airport Notice Says', *The Times*, September 1, 1972, 2.

35 Calculated by the Bank of England's inflation calculator, https://www.bankofengland.co.uk/monetary-policy/inflation/inflation-calculator.

36 Yasmin Alibhai-Brown, *The Settler's Cookbook*, 284.

37 'Oral History with Mayur Seta', *Ugandan Journeys Stradishall*, Series 1, Part 5, British Ugandan Asians at 50, https://www.bua50.org/project/mayur-seta/; 'Oral History with John Pughe', *Ugandan Journeys Tonfanau*, Series 2, Part 9, British Ugandan Asians at 50, https://www.bua50.org/project/john-pughe/; 'Oral History with Brian Watson', *Ugandan Journeys Tonfanau*, Series 2, Part 13, British Ugandan Asians at 50, https://www.bua50.org/project/brian-watson/; Yasmin Alibhai-Brown, *The Settler's Cookbook*, 284. On Yasmin Alibhai-Brown's journey to the UK, she met a woman on the plane who had baked fifty-five diamonds and some gold into battered mashed potato snacks.

38 'Oral History with Jatin Shah, *Ugandan Diaries*, Series 4, Part 3, British Ugandan Asians at 50, https://www.bua50.org/project/jatin -shah/.

39 'Asian Age', *Asians From Uganda*, September 1, 1997, http://www. asiansfromuganda.org.uk/asian_age.php.

40 Extract from Giles Foden and Manubhai Madhvani, *Tide of Fortune: A Family Tale*, (Manubhai Madhvani Bermuda Trusts, 2009) in 'First night in jail as Fate changes', *Economic Times*, 11 December 2009, https://economictimes.indiatimes.com/first-night-in-jail-as-fate-changes/articleshow/5324775.cms.

41 'A Very British History: Ugandan Asians', Series 1, *BBC 4*, December 2018, https://www.bbc.co.uk/programmes/b0btrrzm.

42 'A Very British History: Ugandan Asians', Series 1, *BBC 4*, December 2018, https://www.bbc.co.uk/programmes/b0btrrzm.

43 *World in Action, See For Yourself*, Granada, 1972 archived by the British Film Institute, https://player.bfi.org.uk/free/film/watch-see-for-yourself-1972-online.

44 Dominic Sandbrook, *State of Emergency: The Way We Were: Britain, 1970–1974*, (London: Allen Lane, 2010), 263.

45 Bernard Ryan speaking at 'From Expulsion to Settlement: The Ugandan Asian Story', Leicester Museum & Art Gallery, October 29, 2022.

46 Sara Cosemans, 'Undesirable British East African Asians', 18–19. 'Special Report: How They Did It, Office of the United Nations High Commissioner for Refugees in Asians From Uganda', http:// www.asiansfromuganda.org.uk/how_they_did_it.php.

47 'Special Report: How They Did It'. On 23 October, the Executive Secretary of the UN Economic Commission for Africa, and the Regional Representative of the United Nations High Commissioner for Refugees in New York, arrived in Kampala. They joined Winston Prattley, Resident Representative of the United Nations Development Programme, who was made responsible for running an emergency evacuation.

48 'Special Report: How They Did It'.

49 Kampala to FCO, 6 November 1972, FCO 68/430, 1–4. Confidential Telex No. 2197 from John Hennings, Acting British High Commissioner in Uganda to the Foreign & Commonwealth Office reporting on a meeting with Amin and colleagues.

Notes

Chapter Five – Stradishall to Somerset

1. Mahmood Mamdani, *From Citizen to Refugee*, 67.
2. 'Oral History with Mayur Seta', *Ugandan Journeys Stradishall*, Series 1, Part 5, British Ugandan Asians at 50, https://www.bua50.org/project/mayur-seta/.
3. 'Oral History with Mahendra Dabhi', *Ugandan Journeys Heathfield*, Series 3, Part 10, British Ugandan Asians at 50 https://www.bua50.org/project/mahendra-dabhi/.
4. '1972: Expelled Ugandans arrive in UK', *BBC On This Day*, September 18, 1972, http://news.bbc.co.uk/onthisday/hi/dates/stories/september/18/newsid_2522000/2522627.stm.
5. 'Uganda Asians, Volume 335: debated on Thursday 14 September 1972', *Hansard*, UK Parliament, September 14, 1972, https://hansard.parliament.uk/Lords/1972-09-14/debates/2ce7ab79-d4cd-4a48-9fd3-e5e24506acc8/UgandaAsians.
6. Kampala to FCO, 14 September 1972, FCO 50/404, 190 in Ian Sanjay Patel, *We're Here Because You Were There*, 261.
7. 'UGANDA (ASIANS), HC Deb 18 October 1972 vol 843 cc261–75', *Hansard*, UK Parliament, October 18, 1972, https://api.parliament.uk/historic-hansard/commons/1972/oct/18/uganda-asians#S5CV0843P0_19721018_HOC_200.
8. Valerie Marett, *Immigrants Settling in the City*, (Leicester: Leicester University Press, 1989), 70.
9. 'Former RAF station may house Asians', *The Times*, September 2, 1972, 1; William G. Kuepper, *Ugandan Asians in Great Britain*, 62.
10. 'Oral History with Alan Cordy', *Ugandan Journeys Stradishall*, Series 1, Part 8, British Ugandan Asians at 50, https://www.bua50.org/project/alan-cordy/.
11. Derek Humphry and Michael Ward, *Passports and Politics*, 61.
12. 'Ugandan Asians at Houndstone Camp', *Westward Television*, 1972, archived by the British Film Institute, https://player.bfi.org.uk/free/film/watch-ugandan-asians-at-houndstone-camp-1972-online.
13. Jordanna Bailkin, *Unsettled: Refugee Camps and the Making of Multicultural Britain*, (Oxford: Oxford University Press, 2018), 1.
14. 'Uganda Resettlement Board, Final Report', *Asians From Uganda*,

341

April 1974, http://www.asiansfromuganda.org.uk/uganda_resettle-ment_board.php.

15 BFI British Connection, *This Week*, Thames Television, 1972.

16 *Economist*, August 19, 1972 in William G. Kuepper, *Ugandan Asians in Great Britain*, 61–2.

17 Jordanna Bailkin, *Unsettled*, 11.

18 'Ugandan Asians, Volume 855: debated on Friday 4 May 1973', *Hansard*, UK Parliament, May 4, 1973, https://hansard.parliament.uk/Commons/1973-05-04/debates/5d846e27-2cac-41fa-8b2c-0a798bae263d/UgandanAsians.

19 'UGANDA ASIANS, HL Deb 14 September 1972 vol 335 cc487 –507', *Hansard*, UK Parliament, September 14, 1972, https://api.parliament.uk/historic-hansard/lords/1972/sep/14/uganda-asians.

20 'Ugandan Asians, Volume 855: debated on Friday 4 May 1973'.

21 Becky Taylor, 'Good Citizens? Ugandan Asians, Volunteers and 'Race' Relations in 1970s Britain', *History Workshop Journal* 85 (Spring 2018), 3.

22 Becky Taylor, 'Good Citizens?', 3.

23 Becky Taylor, 'Fleeing Idi Amin', *BBC History Magazine*, January 24, 2019, https://www.pressreader.com/uk/bbc-history-magazine/20190124/281590946728207; Sandra Bawick, 'From grief and fear to over here: On 6 August 1972 Idi Amin pronounced his expulsion order and 30,000 embattled Ugandan Asians headed for Britain. What did they find here and what have they made of it?', *The Independent*, July 31, 1992, https://www.independent.co.uk/lifestyle/from-grief-and-fear-to-over-here-on-6-august-1972-idi-amin-pronounced-his-expulsion-order-and-30-000-embattled-ugandan-asians-headed-for-britain-what-did-they-find-here-and-what-have-they-made-of-it-sandra-barwick-1537251.html.

24 'Oral History with Nancy Edwards', *Ugandan Journeys Stradishall*, Series 1, Part 12, British Ugandan Asians at 50, https://www.bua50.org/project/professor-nancy-edwards/.

25 'Oral History with Deborah Sheridan', *Ugandan Journeys Stradishall*, Series 1, Part 2, British Ugandan Asians at 50, https://www.bua50.org/project/deborah-sheridan/.

26 'Oral History with Jane Preece', *Ugandan Journeys Heathfield*,

Series 3, Part 2, British Ugandan Asians at 50, https://www.bua50. org/project/jane-preece/; 'Oral History with Sarah Richards', *Ugandan Journeys Heathfield*, Series 3, Part 4, British Ugandan Asians at 50, https://www.bua50.org/project/sarah-richards/.

27 'Oral History with Nancy Edwards', *Ugandan Journeys Stradishall*, Series 1, Part 12, British Ugandan Asians at 50, https://www.bua50. org/project/professor-nancy-edwards/; 'Oral History with Vanisha Sparks', *Ugandan Journeys Stradishall*, Series 1, Part 7, British Ugandan Asians at 50, https://www.bua50.org/project/vanisha-sparks/; 'Oral History with Brian Watson', *Ugandan Journeys Tonfanau*, Series 2, Part 13, British Ugandan Asians at 50, https://www.bua50.org/project/brian-watson/.

28 William G. Kuepper, *Ugandan Asians in Great Britain*, 79.

29 'Uganda Resettlement Board, Final Report', *Asians From Uganda*, April 1974, http://www.asiansfromuganda.org.uk/uganda_resettlement_board.php.

30 Derek Humphry and Michael Ward, *Passports and Politics*, 63.

31 Madge Dresser and Peter Fleming, *Bristol: Ethnic Minorities and the City 1000–2001*, (Chichester: Phillimore & Co., 2008), 190.

32 Derek Humphry and Michael Ward, *Passports and Politics*, 63.

33 *Daily Telegraph*, November 11, 1972 in Jordanna Bailkin, *Unsettled*, 83.

34 Jordanna Bailkin, *Unsettled*, 83.

35 'Oral History with Mayur Seta', *Ugandan Journeys Stradishall*, Series 1, Part 5, British Ugandan Asians at 50, https://www.bua50. org/project/mayur-seta/.

36 Jordanna Bailkin, *Unsettled*, 78.

37 Derek Humphry and Michael Ward, *Passports and Politics*, 59–60.

38 Lord Chancellor Lord Hailsham of Saint Marylebone, speaking to Parliament in 'UGANDA ASIANS, HL Deb 14 September 1972 vol 335 cc487–507', *Hansard*, UK Parliament, September 14, 1972, https://api.parliament.uk/historic-hansard/lords/1972/sep/14/uganda-asians.

39 Sandra Bawick, 'From grief and fear'.

40 'Ugandan Asians, Volume 855: debated on Friday 4 May 1973', *Hansard*, UK Parliament, 4 May 1973, https://hansard.parliament. uk/Commons/1973-05-04/debates/5d846e27-2cac-41fa-8b2c-0a798bae263d/UgandanAsians.

41 'Uganda Resettlement Board, Final Report'.

42 'Ugandan Asians, Volume 855: debated on Friday 4 May 1973'.

Chapter Six – White Australia to Amish Country

1 Kahlil Gibran, *The Farewell*, https://poets.org/poem/farewell-2 .

2 'World Migration Report 2022', *The International Organization for Migration* (IOM), UN Migration, https://worldmigrationreport.iom.int/wmr-2022-interactive/.

3 'Glossary on Migration, International Migration Law', *The International Organization for Migration* (IOM), UN Migration, https://publications.iom.int/system/files/pdf/iml_34_glossary.pdf; 'Diaspora for Development', *The International Organization for Migration* (IOM), United Kingdom, https://unitedkingdom.iom.int/diaspora-development.

4 'Diasporas', *Migration Data Portal*, June 9, 2020, https://www.migrationdataportal.org/themes/diasporas. The definition of 'diasporas' includes not only first-generation migrants, but their children born abroad, as long as they maintain some link to their parent's home country. 'These links – whether cultural, linguistic, historical, religious or affective – are what distinguish diaspora groups from other communities.'

5 *World in Action, See For Yourself*, Granada, 1972, archived by the British Film Institute, https://player.bfi.org.uk/free/film/watch-see-for-yourself-1972-online.

6 Sara Cosemans, 'Undesirable British East African Asians', 12.

7 Ian Sanjay Patel, *We're Here Because You Were There*, 270.

8 Sara Cosemans, 'The politics of dispersal', 102.

9 Sara Cosemans, 'Undesirable British East African Asians', 20. 'Ugandan Asians Volume 554: debated on Thursday 6 December 2012', *Hansard*, UK Parliament, 6 December 2012, https://hansard.parliament.uk/commons/2012-12-06/debates/12120640000001/UgandanAsians.

10 'British Laud Canada on Offer to Asians: 'Thank you, Pierre'', *Globe and Mail*, August 26, 1972, 1, in Shezan Muhammedi, 'Gifts From Amin: The Resettlement, Integration, and Identities of Ugandan Asian Refugees in Canada', *The University of Western Ontario*, 2017, 123.

11 'Chronology: Uganda Timeline', *Uganda Collection*, Carleton University, https://carleton.ca/uganda-collection/chronology/.

12 Interview with Mike Molloy, former ambassador of Canada to Jordan and second-in-command of the Canadian team sent to Kampala in 1972, in 'Building the Ugandan Asian Archive – A Portrait Series', Fateema Sayani, ed., *Carleton University Magazine*, https://express.adobe.com/page/iaRKG/.

13 The Canadian Immigration Historical Society in Roger St Vincent, *Seven Crested Cranes: Asian Exodus from Uganda: The Role of Canada's Mission to Kampala*, 40th Anniversary Edition, Canadian Immigration Historical Society, 1993, https://carleton.ca/uganda-collection/related-material-library-and-archives-canada/.

14 John Geddes, 'A Holy Man with an Eye for Connections', *Maclean's Magazine*, October 27, 2010, in Shezan Muhammedi, 'Gifts From Amin': 122–3.

15 Karim H. Karim of Carleton University speaking at the 'Beyond Resettlement: Exploring the History of the Ugandan Asian Community in Exile' conference, Carleton University, 14–16 November 2022.

16 'Chronology: Uganda Timeline'; 'The Longue-Pointe Log Book', *Uganda Collection*, Carleton University, https://carleton.ca/uganda-collection/longue-pointe-log-book/; 'Mapping the Resettlement', *Uganda Collection*, Carleton University, https://carleton.ca/uganda-collection/mapping-the-resettlement/.

17 'The Ugandan Asian Refugees in Canada', *Uganda Collection*, Carleton University, https://carleton.ca/uganda-collection/the-ugandan-asian-refugees-in-canada/

18 'Uganda Resettlement Board, Final Report'.

19 'Canada: Why the country wants to bring in 1.5m immigrants by 2025', *BBC News*, November 22, 2022, https://www.bbc.co.uk/news/world-us-canada-63643912.

20 Sara Cosemans, 'Undesirable British East African Asians', 22.

21 Office of the UNHCR, 'How They Did It', in Zane Lalani, ed., *Ugandan Asian Expulsion: 90 Days and Beyond through the Eyes of the International Press*, (Indiana: Indiana University Press, 1997), 164; 'How They Did It', *Asians From Uganda*, http://www.asiansfromuganda.org.uk/how_they_did_it.php

22 Malik Merchant, 'Uganda Asian Exodus: Laila Datoo's Exclusive Collection of Photos of Prince Sadruddin Aga Khan's Visit to a Refugee Camp in Italy in January 1973', *Barakah*, November 7, 2020, https://barakah.com/2020/11/07/uganda-asian-exodus-1972-photos-from-laila-datoos-collection-of-prince-sadruddin-aga-khans-visit-to-a-refugee-camp-in-italy/.

23 Sara Cosemans, 'The politics of dispersal', 110.

24 British Connection, *This Week*, December 1972. https://www.dropbox.com/s/f0kcegmgk76p8kj/2737S_BFI_756857_British%20Connection_1972_HLS%20Video_m55554.mp4?dl=0; 'Synd 17-11-72 Uganda Asians Refugee Camp, Traiskirchen', *AP Archive*, July 24, 2015, https://www.youtube.com/watch?v=MH8i7em1Yk8.

25 Chessyre, 'Future of Uganda's Exiles Poses Problem for Countries Who Gave Them Refuge,' in Zane Lalani, ed., *Ugandan Asian Expulsion*, 148.

26 'The Fakirani Family', *Uganda Collection*, Carleton University, https://carleton.ca/uganda-collection/about-us/the-fakirani-family/

27 'REFUGEES: A Home for Ugandans', *TIME*, November 13, 1972, https://content.time.com/time/subscriber/article/0,33009,910440,00.html

28 'REFUGEES: A Home for Ugandans'.

29 Sara Cosemans, 'The politics of dispersal', 102.

30 Office of the UNHCR, 'How They Did It', in Zane Lalani, ed., *Ugandan Asian Expulsion*, 164.

31 Sara Cosemans, 'The politics of dispersal', 20. Ian Sanjay Patel, *We're Here Because You Were There*, 270.

32 'Wedding guests fly in from Australia', *Cambridge Evening News*, August 29, 1978.

33 Interview with William McMahon, October 9, 1972, in *Department of External Affairs to Australian High Commission Nairobi*, 17 October 1972, NAA: A5758, 201/4/9/IUPART2 in Klaus Neumann, *Across the Seas: Australia's Response to Refugees, A History*, (New Zealand: Black Inc., 2015), 215.

34 'Defining Moments: White Australia Policy', *National Museum Australia*, https://www.nma.gov.au/defining-moments/resources/white-australia-policy.

35 'Defining Moments: White Australia Policy'.

36 Lorena Allam and Nick Evershed, 'The Killing Times: The Massacres of Aboriginal People Australia Must Confront', *Guardian*, March 3, 2019, https://www.theguardian.com/australia-news/2019/mar/04/the-killing-times-the-massacres-of-aboriginal-people-australia-must-confront.

37 'Dictation Test Passages Used in 1925', *National Archives of Australia*, A1, 1935/704, https://www.naa.gov.au/learn/learning-resources/learning-resource-themes/society-and-culture/migration-and-multiculturalism/dictation-test-passages-used-1925.

38 'FJ Quinlan, Assistant Secretary, Home and Territories Department and Collector of Customs, Western Australia, Directions for Applying the Dictation Test From the Home and Territories Department', *National Archives of Australia*, 1927, PP6/1, 1927/H/427, https://www.naa.gov.au/learn/learning-resources/learning-resource-themes/society-and-culture/migration-and-multiculturalism/directions-applying-dictation-test-home-and-territories-department.

39 'Cartoon of Members of Parliament Doing a Dictation Test, Argus newspaper', *National Archives of Australia*, 1936, M1617, 39, https://www.naa.gov.au/learn/learning-resources/learning-resource-themes/society-and-culture/migration-and-multiculturalism/cartoon-members-parliament-doing-dictation-test; 'Defining Moments: White Australia Policy'.

40 Arthur Nutt, 'Department of Immigration, Conditions for the Acceptance of Migrants of Mixed Heritage', *National Archives of Australia*, 1950, A446, 1970/95021, https://www.naa.gov.au/learn/learning-resources/learning-resource-themes/society-and-culture/migration-and-multiculturalism/conditions-acceptance-migrants-mixed-heritage; 'EJ Bunting and Department of Immigration, Circumstances When Non-white Migrants May Be Accepted – Minister's Powers,' *National Archives of Australia*, 1964, A446, 1970/95021, https://www.naa.gov.au/learn/learning-resources/learning-resource-themes/society-and-culture/migration-and-multiculturalism/circumstances-when-non-white-migrants-may-be-accepted-ministers-powers; 'MR Casson and Department of Immigration, Decisions on Immigration Applications Made on the Basis of Appearance', *National Archives of Australia*, 1963, A446,

1963/41459, https://www.naa.gov.au/learn/learning-resources/
learning-resource-themes/society-and-culture/migration-and-
multiculturalism/decisions-immigration-applications-made-basis
-appearance.

41 'Defining Moments: White Australia Policy'.

42 'Defining Moments: End of the White Australia Policy', *National Museum Australia*, https://www.nma.gov.au/defining-moments/
resources/end-of-white-australia-policy.

43 'Department of External Affairs and Prime Minister's Department,
Conditions for Entry of Non-Europeans to Australia – Restricted
Communication to all Consular Posts', *National Archives of Australia*,
1967, A1209, 1966/7143, https://www.naa.gov.au/learn/learning-
resources/learning-resource-themes/society-and-culture/migration-
and-multiculturalism/conditions-entry-non-europeans-australia-
restricted-communication-all-consular-posts; Klaus Neumann, ' "Our
own interests must come first", 10.4.

44 Klaus Neumann, ' "Our own interests must come first" ', 10.5

45 'Ugandan Diaries: Ashak Nathwani', Series 4, Part 4 of 10, British
Ugandan Asians at 50, https://www.youtube.com/watch?v=t_vJ0Q
_UnKI

46 Klaus Neumann, ' "Our own interests must come first" ', 10.5–6.

47 Klaus Neumann, ' "Our own interests must come first" ', 10.9.

Chapter Seven – Little Indias

1 Ijeoma Umebinyuo, 'Diaspora Blues', *Questions for Ada*, 2015.

2 Kavi Pujara, 'This Golden Mile', 2022, https://www.kavipujara.
com/projects.

3 Valerie Marett, *Immigrants Settling in the City*, (Leicester: Leicester
University Press, 1989), 2; 'Side by side', British Identity and Society,
Guardian, January 1, 2001, https://www.theguardian.com/uk/2001/
jan/01/britishidentity.features11.

4 Professor Gurharpal Singh speaking at 'From Expulsion to
Settlement: The Ugandan Asian Story', at Leicester Museum & Art
Gallery, October 29, 2022.

5 Valerie Marett, *Immigrants Settling*, 53.

6 Peter Soulsby speaking on a panel at 'Finding Home: The Ugandan

Exodus, 50 Years On', at Leicester Curve Theatre, August 4, 2022, https://www.youtube.com/watch?v=eqRYXiei3KA

7 'Britain Has Always Welcomed Refugees', Letters page, *Leicester Mercury*, August 23, 1972, 4.

8 Valerie Marett, *Immigrants Settling*, 56.

9 'Whitehall Told: No More – Leicester is Full Up', *Leicester Mercury*, August 31, 1972, 1.

10 Leicester Council for Community Relations in Valerie Marett, *Immigrants Settling*, 2.

11 Mahmood Mamdani, *From Citizen to Refugee*, 55.

12 'Ugandan Asians in Leicester', *ATV Today*, 1972, archived by the British Film Institute, https://player.bfi.org.uk/free/film/watch-ugandan-asians-in-leicester-1972-online.

13 Valerie Marett, *Immigrants Settling*, 53,3.

14 'Oral history from Imperial Tobacco workers', Histories, *The Strike at Imperial Typewriters*, https://strikeatimperial.net/histories/.

15 Rachel Yemm, *Immigration, Race, and Local Media in the Midlands: 1960–1985*, (Lincoln: University of Lincoln, March 2018), 225.

16 'About', *The Strike at Imperial Typewriters*, https://strikeatimperial.net/about/; Rachel Yemm, *Immigration, Race, and Local Media*, 225–6.

17 'Oral history from Imperial Tobacco workers'.

18 'Oral history from Imperial Tobacco workers.'

19 'About', *The Strike at Imperial Typewriters*.

20 Rachel Yemm, *Immigration, Race, and Local Media*, 193.

21 Rachel Yemm, *Immigration, Race, and Local Media*, 198.

22 Andy Beckett, *When the Lights Went Out: Britain in the Seventies*, (London: Faber & Faber, 2010), 367.

23 Derek Humphry and Michael Ward, *Passports and Politics*, 57. For more on Ugandan Asian community development in London red zones, see Chapter 6, 'Wandsworth: A Host Community', in William G. Kuepper, *Ugandan Asians in Great Britain*, 85–98.

24 'The Grunwick Dispute', *Striking Women*, https://www.striking-women.org/module/striking-out/grunwick-dispute.

25 Kavi Pujara, 'Leicester, Jan 2010', Instagram, https://www.insta-gram.com/p/B-M4gicnk7x/?hl=en.

26 Manzoor Moghal interviewed in interactive display at the 'Rebuilding Lives: 50 Years of Ugandan Asians in Leicester', *Leicester Museums*, https://www.leicestermuseums.org/Rebuilding Lives, https://www.leicestermuseums.org/news/rebuilding-lives-exhibition-360-viewer/; 'Uganda 50: How three families fled Idi Amin's terror for the UK, settling in Leicester', *ITV Central*, July 20, 2022, https://www.itv.com/news/central/2022-07-20/uganda-50-how-three-families-fled-idi-amins-terror-settling-in-leicester.

27 'Race Relations Board', Public Information Filler, 1968, archived by the British Film Institute, https://player.bfi.org.uk/free/film/watch-race-relations-board-1969-online.

28 'The Referee', Public Information Filler, 1976, archived by the British Film Institute, https://player.bfi.org.uk/free/film/watch-the-referee-1976-online.

29 Pramilla Dattani, interviewed in interactive display at the 'Rebuilding Lives: 50 Years of Ugandan Asians in Leicester', *Leicester Museums,* https://www.leicestermuseums.org/RebuildingLives, https://www.leicestermuseums.org/news/rebuilding-lives-exhibition-360-viewer/

30 'Ugandan Asians in Leicester', *ATV Today*, 1972, archived by the British Film Institute, https://player.bfi.org.uk/free/film/watch-ugandan-asians-in-leicester-1972-online.

31 Valerie Marett, *Immigrants Settling*, 53, 1–2.

32 William G. Kuepper, *Ugandan Asians in Great Britain*, 74.

33 'Oral History with Chandrika Keshavlal Joshi', *Ugandan Journeys Tonfanau*, Series 2, Part 10, British Ugandan Asians at 50, https://www.bua50.org/project/chandrika-keshavlal-joshi/.

34 Gurnek Bains, Bryony Heard and Kylie Bains, *England Our England: Stories of the Black and Asian Migrant Pioneers*, (London: Profile Editions, 2020), 79.

35 'Side by side', British Identity and Society, *Guardian*, January 1, 2001, https://www.theguardian.com/uk/2001/jan/01/britishidentity.features11.

36 Leicester Council for Community Relations in Valerie Marett, *Immigrants Settling*, 2.

37 Derek Humphry and Michael Ward, *Sunday Times*, June 10, 1973 in William G. Kuepper, *Ugandan Asians in Great Britain*, 83; Derek Humphry and Michael Ward, *Passports and Politics*, 148–9, 175.

The journalists, who covered the resettlement process in depth, deemed the Uganda Resettlement Board to be a 'government show-piece for public relations reasons', which allowed the government to report, ahead of elections, that they had successfully set up an organisation that had done its job and 'there was no cause to think that race was a serious problem under a strong government'.

38 Rina Valeny, '"From Pariah to Paragon?"': The Social Mobility of Ugandan Asian Refugees in Britain', University of Wales, 1998, 93 in Max Russel, 'Enduring Empire', 136.

39 '50 years on from the arrival of the Ugandan Asians', *Economist*, August 18, 2022, https://www.economist.com/britain/2022/08/18/50-years-on-from-the-arrival-of-the-ugandan-asians.

40 Valerie Marett, *Immigrants Settling*, 53, 3.

41 Shonal Gokani lived fifteen in a two-bedroom house and Jyoti Teli's family ran two shifts at home to fit everyone in. Interviewed in interactive display at the 'Rebuilding Lives: 50 Years of Ugandan Asians in Leicester', *Leicester Museums*, https://www.leicestermuseums.org/RebuildingLives, https://www.leicestermuseums.org/news/rebuilding-lives-exhibition-360-viewer/

41 Navtej Johal & Katie Thompson, 'Leicester one of first cities in UK with no ethnic group majority – data', *BBC News*, November 29, 2022, https://www.bbc.co.uk/news/uk-england-leicestershire-63743309; 'Ethnic group, national identity, language, and religion: Census 2021 in England and Wales', *Office for National Statistics*, https://www.ons.gov.uk/releases/ethnicgroupnationalidentitylanguageandreligioncensus2021inenglandandwales.

42 Interviewed in interactive display at 'Rebuilding Lives: 50 Years of Ugandan Asians in Leicester', *Leicester Museums,* https://www.leicestermuseums.org/RebuildingLives, https://www.leicestermuseums.org/news/rebuilding-lives-exhibition-360-viewer/

43 Gurnek Bains, Bryony Heard and Kylie Bains, *England Our England*, 155.

44 Interviewed in interactive display at 'Rebuilding Lives: 50 Years of Ugandan Asians in Leicester', *Leicester Museums,* https://www.leicestermuseums.org/RebuildingLives, https://www.leicestermuseums.org/news/rebuilding-lives-exhibition-360-viewer/; 'Natraj Cinema', *Cinema Treasures*, http ://cinematreasures.org/theaters/47293.

45 Navtej Johal & Katie Thompson, 'Leicester one of first cities in UK with no ethnic group majority – data', *BBC News*, November 29, 2022, https://www.bbc.co.uk/news/uk-england-leicestershire-63743309; 'Ethnic group, national identity, language, and religion: Census 2021 in England and Wales', *Office for National Statistics*, https://www.ons.gov.uk/releases/ethnicgroupnationalidentitylanguageand religioncensus2021inenglandandwales.

Chapter Eight – Hope on the High Street

1 Yasmin Alibhai-Brown, *The Settler's Cookbook*, 9.
2 Rozina Visram, *Asians in Britain: 400 Years of History*, (London: Pluto Press, 2002), 1–2.
3 Neha Shah, 'How did British Indians become so prominent in the Conservative party?'
4 Susheila Nasta, *Asian Britain: A Photographic History*, (London: The Westbourne Press, 2013), 165.
5 Babita Sharma, *The Corner Shop: Shopkeepers, the Sharmas and the Making of Modern Britain*, (London: Two Roads, 2019), 28.
6 'Service with a smile back in Britain', *Daily Mail*, February 11, 1976. Bhavini Shah, 'South Asian History Month Special – Marking 50 Years of the Contributions of Ugandan South Asians in the UK', *BAME in Property*, August 1, 2022, https://www.bameinproperty.com/new-blog/south-asian-heritage-month-special-marking-50-years-of-the-contributions-of-ugandan-south-asians-in-the-uk.
7 Babita Sharma, 'Counter Culture: My Life Growing Up in a Corner Shop', *Guardian*, May 19, 2019, https://www.theguardian.com/society/2019/may/19/counter-culture-my-life-growing-up-in-a-corner-shop-babita-sharma. Between 1956 and 1960, the number of general stores fell by 56.2%.
8 Mirza Shehnaz, '50 Years on from the arrival of Ugandan Asians', *Business Lend*, August 18, 2022, https://www.businesslend.com/news/50-years-on-from-the-arrival-of-the-ugandan-asians/; Jaffer Kapasi, *Gujarati Yatra: Journey of a People*, UEL Archives and Collections, https://www.gujaratiyatra.com/oralhistory; '50 years on from the arrival of the Ugandan Asians', *Economist*, August 18,

2022, https://www.economist.com/britain/2022/08/18/50-years-on-from-the-arrival-of-the-ugandan-asians.

9 'They Fled With Nothing But Built a New Empire', *Guardian*, August 11, 2002, https://www.theguardian.com/uk/2002/aug/11/race.world.

10 Yasmin Alibhai-Brown, *The Settler's Cookbook*; Robert Madoi, 'The culinary influence of Asians', *Daily Monitor*, November 23, 2022, https://www.monitor.co.ug/uganda/special-reports/the-culinary-influence-of-asians-4029610.

11 Meera Sodha, 'From Uganda to Lincolnshire: a mother's recipe for success', *Guardian*, July 5, 2014, https://www.theguardian.com/lifeandstyle/2014/jul/05/mothers-recipe-success-indian-uganda-meera-sodha; Meera Sodha, 'Matoke', *Meera Sodha*, https://meerasodha.com/recipes/matoke/.

12 'Bristol Illustrated', 1988, in Bristol Central Library archive.

13 'Family Fears in a Cold New World', *Bristol Evening Post*, October 11, 1976, in Bristol Central Library archive.

14 Madge Dresser and Peter Fleming, *Bristol: Ethnic Minorities*, 140, 144, 147.

15 'Refugees from a reign of terror', *Bristol Evening Post*, February 14, 1979, in Bristol Central Library archive.

16 Madge Dresser and Peter Fleming, *Bristol: Ethnic Minorities*, 192–3.

17 'Ugandan Asians', *BBC Inside Out: West*, January 6, 2003, https://www.bbc.co.uk/insideout/west/series2/ugandan_asians.shtml; Videos, *The Hindu Temple Bristol*, http://www.hindutemplebristol.co.uk/videoslist.php?#MIDDLE; Madge Dresser and Peter Fleming, *Bristol: Ethnic Minorities*, 193.

18 Paul Brown, 'Family-run Asian shops disappear', *Guardian*, January 5, 2022, https://www.theguardian.com/uk/2002/jan/05/socialsciences.britishidentity.

19 Babita Sharma, *The Corner Shop*, 28.

20 David Cameron in Dolar Popat, *A British Subject*, foreword.

21 Paul Lashmar, Arlen Harris, 'Who Wants to Be a Millionaire?', *Independent*, March 1, 1997, https://www.independent.co.uk/life-style/who-wants-to-be-a-millionaire-1270338.html; Saima Nasar, 'When Uganda Expelled Its Asian Population in 1972, Britain Tried to Exclude Them', *New Lines Magazine*, August 12, 2022, https://newlinesmag.

com/essays/when-uganda-expelled-its-asian-population-in-1972-brit-ain-tried-to-exclude-them/; Yasmin Alibhai-Brown, 'Uganda's Asians Were Also Sinners', December 17, 2017, https://www.thetimes.co.uk/article/ugandas-asians-were-also-sinners-gfc98rtt6.

22 '50 years on from the arrival of the Ugandan Asians', *Economist*.

23 Yasmin Alibhai-Brown 'Flight of the Ugandan Asians', *Saga*, September 7, 2022, https://www.saga.co.uk/magazine/entertain-ment/real-lives/flight-of-ugandan-asians.

24 Michael H. Freeman, 'Asian Enterprise in Leicester', *Special Collections*, University of Leicester, 1984, https://specialcollections. le.ac.uk/digital/collection/p16445coll2/id/4427; 'Celebrating the Contributions of Ugandan Indians Arriving in the UK in the Early 1970s', *BAME in Property*, August 4, 2020, https://www.bamein-property.com/new-blog/celebrating-the-contributions-of-ugandan-indians-arriving-in-the-uk-in-the-early-1970s.

25 Robert Winder, *Bloody Foreigners*, 382.

26 'South Asians', World Directory of Minorities and Indigenous Peoples, *Minority Rights Group*, https://minorityrights.org/minorities/south-asians/; Eleanor Rosalind, 'Black Was the Colour of our Fight: Black Power in Britain, 1955–1976', University of Sheffield, 2008, 221.

27 Paul Brown, 'Family-run Asian shops disappear', *Guardian*, January 5, 2022, https://www.theguardian.com/uk/2002/jan/05/socialsciences.britishidentity.

28 Babita Sharma, 'Counter Culture: My Life Growing Up in a Corner Shop', *Guardian*, May 19, 2019, https://www.theguardian.com/society/2019/may/19/counter-culture-my-life-growing-up-in-a-corner-shop-babita-sharma.

29 'Open All Hours and Other Stories', *The National Trust*, https://web.archive.org/web/20220707113821/https://www.nationaltrust.org.uk/features/open-all-hours-and-other-stories.

30 Babita Sharma, *The Corner Shop*, 45–6.

31 Babita Sharma, *The Corner Shop*, 44.

32 Babita Sharma, *The Corner Shop*, 39.

33 Sana Noor Haq, 'How South Asian Corner Shop Culture Helped the UK Survive Covid-19', *Gal-Dem*, August 2, 2020, https://gal-dem.com/how-south-asian-corner-shop-culture-helped-the-uk-survive-covid-19/.

34 'Open All Hours and Other Stories', *The National Trust*, https://
web.archive.org/web/20220707113821/https://www.nationaltrust.
org.uk/features/open-all-hours-and-other-stories.

35 *Gary Younge's Facts That Matter*, Season 1, Episode 1, February 19,
2023, https://shows.acast.com/unedited-pilot-season-2023/episodes
/63f20c83d9d2740012dbc787.

36 Bronwen Weatherby, 'Bristol's Grand Iftar Ramadan Celebration
will be UK's Biggest Street Party with 3,000 People Expected',
Bristol Post, June 5, 2018, https://www.bristolpost.co.uk/news/bris-
tol-news/bristols-grand-iftar-ramadan-celebration-1640707;
Alexander Turner, 'Thousands Attend Bristol's Grand Iftar – in
pictures', *Guardian*, May 31, 2019, https://www.theguardian.com/
world/gallery/2019/may/31/grand-bristol-iftar-in-pictures.

Chapter Nine – The Returnees

1 Salman Rushdie, *The Satanic Verses*, (New York: Random House,
2011), 205.

2 Richard M. Kavuma, 'Revisiting the life of Fairway hotel owner
Bandali Jaffer', *Observer*, January 9, 2015, https://observer.ug/news
-headlines/35850--revisiting-the-life-of-fairway-hotel-owner-
bandali-jaffer; 'Fifty years after expulsion, Asians are thriving again
in Uganda', *Economist*, November 17, 2022, https://www.econo-
mist.com/middle-east-and-africa/2022/11/17/fifty-years-after-
expulsion-asians-are-thriving-again-in-uganda.

3 Anneeth Kaur Hundle, '1970s Uganda', 467–8; Anneeth Kaur
Hundle, 'Exceptions to the expulsion: violence, security and
community among Ugandan Asians, 1972–79', *Journal of Eastern
African Studies* 7, no.1 (2013): 174–5.

4 'Fifty years after expulsion, Asians are thriving again in Uganda',
Economist.

5 Richard Vokes, 'Photographies in Africa in the Digital Age', Africa,
89(2), 2019, p207–24. https://www.cambridge.org/core/journals/
africa/article/photographies-in-africa-in-the-digital-age/
73E3F4CF06CB5A2D9BC433938713D70D

6 'Fifty years after expulsion, Asians are thriving again in Uganda',
Economist.

7 'Idi Amin Declares Himself "Conqueror of the British Empire"', *Adeyinka Makinde*, August 15, 2020, https://www.youtube.com/watch?v=oRKyOoutPbQ. Idi Amin Dada speaking at the summit of the Organisation of African Unity in Khartoum, Sudan.

8 George Alagiah, *A Passage to Africa*, 200–1.

9 Yasmin Alibhai-Brown, 'Museveni in Neasden', *Prospect Magazine*, December 20, 1997, https://www.prospectmagazine.co.uk/magazine/museveniinneasden.

10 Mahadev Desai, 'Tide of Fortune: A Family Tale by Manubhai Madhvani'; Rashna Batliwala Singh, 'Uganda Asians', *Transition* 126, Bla(c)kness in Australia (2018), 132–44.

11 Dolar Vasani, 'Amin kicked the Asians out of Uganda 50 years ago – I spoke to some who left, remained, or returned', *Daily Maverick*, 30 June 2022, https://www.dailymaverick.co.za/article/2022-06-30-uganda-50-years-after-amins-asian-expulsion-voices-past-and-present/.

12 Farhana Dawood, 'Ugandan Asians dominate economy after exile', *BBC News*, May 15, 2016, https://www.bbc.co.uk/news/world-africa-36132151.

13 Rashna Batliwala Singh, 'Uganda Asians', 143.

14 'About Ruparelia Foundation', *Ruparelia Foundation*, https://www.rupareliafoundation.org/about-us/.

15 Yoweri Museveni, 'The expulsion of Ugandan Asians was a shameful chapter. But now we should focus on closer relations', *Telegraph*, August 6, 2022, https://www.telegraph.co.uk/news/2022/08/06/expulsion-ugandan-asians-shameful-chapter-now-should-focus-closer/.

16 'Vali Jamal: Uganda Asians, Uganda Asians book, and the incidental Ismaili angle', Ismailimail, June 22, 2017, https://ismailimail.blog/2017/06/22/vali-jamal-uganda-asians-uganda-asians-book-and-the-incidental-ismaili-angle/. Vali Jamal's forthcoming book is called *Ugandan Asians: Then and Now, Here and There, We Contributed, We Contribute.*

17 Rashna Batliwala Singh, 'Uganda Asians', 132.

18 Mahmood Mamdani, 'The Asian Question'; Al-Mahdi Ssenkabirwa, 'Museveni Applauds Indian Community, Backs Bayindi Tribe Quest', *Daily Monitor*, December 16, 2021, https://

www.monitor.co.ug/uganda/news/national/museveni-applauds-indian-community-backs-bayindi-tribe-quest-3655168; 'Fifty years after expulsion, Asians are thriving again in Uganda', *Economist*.

19 Anneeth Kaur Hundle, '1970s Uganda', 459–60.

20 Alex von Tunzelmann, 'The Last King of Scotland: Getting Away Scot-free with Genocide', *Guardian*, June 11, 2009, https://www.theguardian.com/film/2009/jun/10/last-king-of-scotland-history.

21 'Forest Whitaker Wins Best Actor | 79th Oscars (2007)', *Oscars*, April 25, 2008, https://www.youtube.com/watch?v=4-fGCHGTaGE.

22 'U-report: Amplifying Voices For Young People', What We Do, *Unicef Uganda*, https://www.unicef.org/uganda/what-we-do/u-report.

23 Yunusu Abbey, 'An audience with Big Daddy', Idi Amin interview in *Uganda's Sunday Vision* weekly newspaper, reproduced in *Guardian*, February 17, 1999, https://www.theguardian.com/world/1999/feb/17/uganda.

24 Kim Wall, 'Ghost Stories: Idi Amin's Torture Chambers', *Harper's Magazine*, December 27, 2016, https://harpers.org/2016/12/ghost-stories/.

25 Richard Reid speaking in 'Ugandan Asians: The Reckoning', *BBC Radio 4*, September 14, 2022, https://www.bbc.co.uk/sounds/play/m001bykk.

26 'Beyond the Headlines featuring Andrew Rice and Duncan Muhumuza Laki', *International Peace Institute*, October 2009, https://www.ipinst.org/wp-content/uploads/2009/10/pdfs_transcript_andrewrice_oct2009.pdf. Andrew Rice, *The Teeth May Smile*, 15.

27 'Archive Materials', *Derek R Peterson*, https://derekrpeterson.com/archive-materials/. Andrew Rice, *The Teeth May Smile*, 13.

28 Alicia C. Decker, *In Idi Amin's Shadow*, 131–3.

29 'Truth Commission: Uganda 86', *United States Institute for Peace*, May 16, 1986, https://www.usip.org/publications/1986/05/truth-commission-uganda-86; Andrew Rice, *The Teeth May Smile*, 11–13. 'Archive Materials', *Derek R Peterson*, https://derekrpeterson.com/archive-materials/.

30 'Beyond the Headlines'.

31 Andrew Rice, *The Teeth May Smile*, 21–38; 'Beyond the Headlines'.

32 Edward Siedle, *A Tree Has Fallen In Africa,* 215, 218, 243, 245.

33 Anneeth Kaur Hundle, '1970s Uganda', 467–8.

34 Donatella Lorch, 'Kampala Journal; Cast Out Once, Asians Return: Uganda Is Home', *The New York Times,* March 22, 1993, https://www.nytimes.com/1993/03/22/world/kampala-journal-cast-out-once-asians-return-uganda-is-home.html.

35 Anneeth Kaur Hundle, 'Exceptions to the expulsion', 166.

36 Anneeth Kaur Hundle, 'Exceptions to the expulsion', 170–1.

37 Anneeth Kaur Hundle, 'Exceptions to the expulsion', 166, 178.

38 Palash R. Ghosh, 'Uganda: The Legacy of Idi Amin's Expulsion of Asians in 1972', *IB Times,* March 13, 2012, https://www.ibtimes.com/uganda-legacy-idi-amins-expulsion-asians-1972-214289.

39 Anneeth Kaur Hundle, 'Exceptions to the expulsion', 169, 171.

40 Dolar Vasani, 'Amin kicked the Asians out of Uganda 50 years ago – I spoke to some who left, remained, or returned', *Daily Maverick,* June 30, 2022, https://www.dailymaverick.co.za/article/2022-06-30-uganda-50-years-after-amins-asian-expulsion-voices-past-and-present/.

41 Anneeth Kaur Hundle, 'Exceptions to the expulsion', 175.

42 Anneeth Kaur Hundle, '1970s Uganda', 466.

43 Jack Losh, 'When Nature Conservation Goes Wrong', *Foreign Policy,* April 2, 2021, https://foreignpolicy.com/2021/04/02/uganda-conservation-poaching-crisis-poverty-national-park/.

44 Nicholas Best, 'The day Princess Elizabeth became Queen', *Guardian,* January 8, 2012, https://www.theguardian.com/uk/2012/jan/08/queen-elizabeth-treetops-kenya.

45 Florence Kuteesa, Emmanuel Tumusiime-Mutebile, Alan Whitworth, Tim Williamson (ed.), 'Uganda's Economic Reforms: Insider Accounts', (Oxford, OUP, 2009), 363.

46 Yoweri Museveni, 'The expulsion of Ugandan Asians was a shameful chapter.'

47 'Museveni allows Indians to be citizens, get permanent residence status and multiple re-entry visas', *Ben – LIVE,* November 4, 2022, https://www.youtube.com/watch?v=8ztD9hJ53eE.

48 Anneeth Kaur Hundle, '1970s Uganda', 464–5.

Chapter Ten – Good Immigrants and Glass Ceilings

1 Klaus Neumann, *Across the Seas*, 2.
2 '50 years on from the arrival of the Ugandan Asians', *Economist*.
3 Yasmin Alibhai-Brown, 'Flight of the Ugandan Asians', *Saga Magazine*, September 7, 2022, https://www.saga.co.uk/magazine/entertainment/real-lives/flight-of-ugandan-asians; 'Ugandan Asians are part of Britain's secret weapon for success', *Spectator*, December 6, 2012, https://www.spectator.co.uk/article/ugandan-asians-are-part-of-britain-s-secret-weapon-for-success/; 'They fled with nothing but built a new empire', *Guardian*, August 11 2002, https://www.theguardian.com/uk/2002/aug/11/race.world.
4 J. Portes, S. Burgess, S. and J. Anders, 'The long-term outcomes of refugees: tracking the progress of the East African Asians', *Journal of Refugee Studies*, 2020, https://doi.org/10.1093/jrs/feaa078; Shailesh Vara, 'Ugandan Asians, Volume 554: debated on Thursday 6 December 2012,' *Hansard*, December 6, 2012,
5 https://hansard.parliament.uk/commons/2012-12-06/debates/12120640000001/UgandanAsians.
6 Rina Valeny, *'From Pariah to Paragon?': The Social Mobility of Ugandan Asian Refugees in Britain*, PhD Thesis, (Swansea: University of Wales, 1998), 87–8. The emphasis on presenting Ugandan Asians as middle class, and different from the Indian and Pakistani migrant labourers who had already come to Britain, helped shift public opinion. By September, 58 per cent of people polled would accept small numbers of Ugandan Asians into their locality.
7 Thomas Brown, 'Ugandan Asians: 50 years since their expulsion from Uganda', *House of Lords Library*, August 31, 2022, https://lordslibrary.parliament.uk/ugandan-asians-50-years-since-their-expulsion-from-uganda/.
8 Anthony Grant, 'Industrial Policy And Employment, Volume 967: debated on Monday 21 May 1979', *Hansard,* https://hansard.parliament.uk/Commons/1979-05-21/debates/340892fc-8c56-4aed-a5c2-bcce88c6be6d/IndustrialPolicyAndEmployment.
9 Norman Tebbit, 'I was wrong about Asian immigration, but don't expect Philip Hammond to say he was also wrong about the consequences of a Brexit vote', *Daily Telegraph*, September 16, 2019,

https://www.telegraph.co.uk/politics/2019/09/16/philip-hammond-should-learn-come-clean-proven-wrong/.

10 Julia Llewellyn Smith, 'Small wonder Britain is my God: I fled Idi Amin's slaughter to be here', *Sunday Times*, August 4, 2019, https://www.thetimes.co.uk/article/small-wonder-britain-is-my-god-i-fled-idi-amins-slaughter-to-be-here-gq8rs555t.

11 Derek Humphry and Michael Ward, *Passports and Politics*, 149, 153.

12 L. Beaman, 'Social Networks and Dynamics of Labour Market Outcomes: Evidence from Refugees Resettled in the U.S.', *The Review of Economic Studies* 79, no.1 (2012): 128–61. Economists have found that social networks within refugee communities are correlated with better employment outcomes.

13 Hardeep Matharu, 'The Identity Trap: no one narrative can encompass the different dimensions of diversity', *Byline Times*, November 18, 2022, https://bylinetimes.com/2022/11/18/the-identity-trap-no-one-narrative-can-encompass-the-different-dimensions-of-diversity/.

14 'Ma'amalade sandwich Your Majesty?', *The Royal Family*, June 6, 2022, https://www.youtube.com/watch?v=7UfiCa244XE.

15 Jessica Cullen, 'The Queen and Paddington Bear: the fascinating history behind the monarch's connection to the beloved bear', *Stylist*, https://www.stylist.co.uk/entertainment/queen-elizabeth-ii-paddington-bear-connection/707799; 'Floral tributes in the Royal Parks', *The Royal Parks*, September 9, 2022, https://web.archive.org/web/20220909124108/https://www.royalparks.org.uk/ceremonial/floral-tributes-in-the-royal-parks; Colin Yeo, 'An immigration lawyer reviews Paddington', *Free Movement*, December 1, 2014, https://freemovement.org.uk/an-immigration-lawyer-reviews-paddington/.

16 Daniel Renshaw, 'What Makes a 'Good' Migrant?', *History Today* 67, no.11 (November 2017), https://www.historytoday.com/archive/history-matters/what-makes-good-migrant.

17 Maya Goodfellow, *Hostile Environment*, 54.

18 Maya Goodfellow, *Hostile Environment*, 55, 64.

19 William Allen and Scott Blinder, *Migration in the News: Portrayals of Immigrants, Migrants, Asylum Seekers and Refugees in National British Newspapers, 2010 to 2012*, (Oxford: Migration Observatory, 2013), 3, in Maya Goodfellow, *Hostile Environment*, 31.

20 James Kirkup and Robert Winnett, 'Theresa May interview: "We're going to give illegal migrants a really hostile reception"', *Daily Telegraph*, May 25, 2012, https://www.telegraph.co.uk/news/0/theresa-may-interview-going-give-illegal-migrants-really-hostile/.

21 Maya Goodfellow, *Hostile Environment*, 3–4; 'The Hostile Environment explained', the Joint Council for the Welfare of Immigrants, https://www.jcwi.org.uk/the-hostile-environment-explained.

22 Nadine El-Enany, *(B)ordering Britain: Law, Race and Empire*, 17.

23 Maya Goodfellow, *Hostile Environment*, 37.

24 Daniel Renshaw, 'What Makes a 'Good' Migrant?'.

25 Caroline Mortimer, 'Philip Hammond's demonising of 'marauding' migrants is shameful, says Amnesty International', *Independent*, August 10, 2015, https://www.independent.co.uk/news/uk/politics/philip-hammond-s-demonising-of-marauding-migrants-comments-is-shameful-10447901.html.

26 Victoria Richards, '"Invasion, swarm": Words matter – when they're being used like this, they're being used as a weapon', *Independent*, November 1, 2022, https://www.independent.co.uk/voices/suella-braverman-invasion-migrants-firebombing-b2214905.html.

27 Home Office (@ukhomeoffice), 'Many Hong Kongers have said living in Britain is like coming home', Twitter, January 31, 2023, https://twitter.com/ukhomeoffice/status/1620478885086515206.

28 Heather Stewart, '"Here to stay": Colchester's Hongkongers on making new lives in the UK', *Guardian*, November 20, 2022, https://www.theguardian.com/uk-news/2022/nov/20/how-colchester-hongkongers-are-making-new-life-in-the-uk. The Hong Kong migration is also far greater than the highest number of citizens who arrived in the UK in a single year from the EU8 accession countries, including Poland and Hungary, which was 112,000 in 2007.

29 Heather Stewart, '"Here to stay"'. 'Hong Kong BN(O) visa: UK government to honour historic commitment', *Gov.uk*, 9 January 20, 2021, https://www.gov.uk/government/news/hong-kong-bno-visa-uk-government-to-honour-historic-commitment; 'UK PM Johnson 'immensely proud' as visa offer for Hong Kong citizens launches', *Reuters*, January 29, 2021, https://www.reuters.com/article/us-hongkong-security-britain-passports-idUSKBN29Y00R.

30 Dominic Casciani, 'UK net migration hits all-time record at 504,000', *BBC News*, November 24, 2022, https://www.bbc.co.uk/news/uk-63743259.

31 'Ex-chancellor Rishi Sunak launches Tory leadership campaign – video', *Guardian*, July 8, 2022, https://www.theguardian.com/politics/video/2022/jul/08/rishi-sunak-launches-tory-leadership-campaign-video.

32 Kishan Devani (@Kishan_Devani), 'Being the Son of Ugandan Refugees …' Twitter, February 12, 2021, https://twitter.com/Kishan_Devani/status/1360258911937454085.

33 Musa Okwonga, 'The Dangers of Priti Patel's Racial Gatekeeping', *Byline Times*, October 3, 2019, https://bylinetimes.com/2019/10/03/the-dangers-of-priti-patels-racial-gatekeeping/.

34 'Priti Patel says she will end free movement of people – video', *Guardian*, October 1, 2019, https://www.theguardian.com/politics/video/2019/oct/01/priti-patel-says-she-will-end-free-movement-of-people-video.

35 Taj Ali, 'The government is using its 'diverse' cabinet to deflect from racial inequality', *The Runnymede Trust blog*, January 29, 2021, https://www.runnymedetrust.org/blog/the-government-is-using-its-diverse-cabinet-to-deflect-from-racial-inequality.

36 Yasmin Alibhai-Brown in conversation with Hardeep Matharu and Peter Jukes, '"The Revolving Door of Unelected PMs Continues": Friday Night with Byline Times', *Byline TV*, streamed October 28, 2022, https://www.youtube.com/watch?v=k3RdfscUbDs&t=484s.

37 Neha Shah, 'How did British Indians'. Amar Diwakar, 'Brown Skin, Tory Masks', *TRT World*, June 26, 2020, https://www.trtworld.com/magazine/brown-skin-tory-masks-37638.

38 Hardeep Matharu, 'The Identity Trap'.

39 Shrai Popat, 'My family's anti-blackness and Boris Johnson's cabinet', *The Juggernaut*, February 26, 2020, https://www.thejuggernaut.com/anti-blackness-boris-johnson-cabinet https://www.npeu.ox.ac.uk/mbrrace-uk/reports.

40 'Review launched into police "race discrimination"', *BBC News*, July 10, 2020, https://www.bbc.co.uk/news/uk-53359269; Gareth Iacobucci, 'Most black people in UK face discrimination from

healthcare staff, survey finds', *BMJ*, September 27, 2022, https://www.bmj.com/content/378/bmj.o2337.

41 Patrick Butler, 'Britain "not close to being a racially just society", finds two-year research project', *Guardian*, April 9, 2023, https://www.theguardian.com/world/2023/apr/09/britain-not-close-to-being-a-racially-just-society-finds-two-year-research-project.

Chapter Eleven – Where Are You (Really) From?

1 Vanessa Kisuule, 'Hollow', *Poetry International*, https://www.poetryinternational.com/en/poets-poems/poems/poem/103-30428_HOLLOW.

2 Kofo Ajala, 'The Seven Saints of St Pauls: Memorials and Black Joy in Bristol', *Bristol Museums*, https://www.bristolmuseums.org.uk/stories/the-seven-saints-of-st-pauls-memorials-and-black-joy-in-bristol/.

3 Madge Dresser, 'The Bristol Bus Boycott: A Watershed Moment for Black Britain', *Bristol Museums*, https://www.bristolmuseums.org.uk/stories/bristol-bus-boycott/.

4 Afua Hirsch, *Brit(ish), On Race, Identity and Belonging*, (London: Vintage, 2018), 37.

5 Terry Townsend, *Bristol & Clifton Slave Trade Trails*, (Wellington: PiXz Books, 2016), 21–2.

6 Terry Townsend, *Bristol & Clifton*, 31, 83–4.

7 Terry Townsend, *Bristol & Clifton*, 119.

8 Terry Townsend, *Bristol & Clifton*, 87.

9 Michael Savage, 'Bristol University to Confront Its Links with the Slave Trade', *Observer*, May 5, 2019, https://www.theguardian.com/education/2019/may/05/bristol-university-slave-trade-history.

10 'How Have British Universities Grappled with Links to the Slave Trade?' *Reuters*, April 30, 2019, https://www.reuters.com/article/us-britain-slavery-universities-factbox-idUSKCN1S61TX.

11 Freya Shaw, 'Sign of the Times', *Epigram*, November 9, 2022, https://epigram.org.uk/2022/11/09/sign-of-the-times/; 'Past Matters: the University of Bristol and Transatlantic Slavery', University of Bristol, https://web.archive.org/web/20180728070229/https://www.bristol.ac.uk/university/history/past-matters/.

12 Ian Sanjay Patel, *We're Here Because You Were There*, 19.

13 Sathnam Sanghera in *Empire State of Mind*, Episode 1, Channel 4, https://www.channel4.com/programmes/empire-state-of-mind

14 Sathnam Sanghera, *Empireland: How Imperialism Has Shaped Modern Britain*, (London: Viking, 2021), 199.

15 Yasmin Alibhai-Brown, 'The Revolving Door of Unelected PMs Continues'.

16 Hardeep Matharu, 'The Story of Brexit is the Story of Empire: Why Did Asian Immigrants Vote to Leave the EU?', *Byline Times*, April 8, 2019, https://bylinetimes.com/2019/04/08/the-story-of-brexit-is-the-story-of-empire-why-did-so-many-asian-immigrants-vote-for-brexit/.

17 '1998 Qantas TVC-Australia Home II', *Kelvin Li*, September 14, 2006, https://www.youtube.com/watch?v=hbGuqmaDgLA; 'I Still Call Australia Home', *Qantas*, https://www.qantas.com/au/en/promotions/i-still-call-australia-home.html.

18 Afua Hirsch, *Brit(ish)*, 32–3.

19 Shezan Muhammedi speaking at 'Beyond Resettlement: Exploring the History of the Ugandan Asian Community in Exile', Carleton University, November 14–16, 2022; Soo-Jung Kim, '"Gifts from Amin" that keep on giving: Q&A with author Shezan Muhammedi', *UNHCR Canada*, https://www.unhcr.ca/news-stories/special-features/50uganda/gifts-from-amin-that-keep-on-giving-qa-with-author-shezan-muhammedi/.

20 Anita Sethi, 'Dear Prince Charles, do you think my brown skin makes me unBritish?', *Guardian*, April 19, 2018, https://www.theguardian.com/world/commentisfree/2018/apr/19/prince-charles-brown-skin-british-people-head-of-commonwealth.

21 Sunil Shah, 'Uganda Stories', *Sunil Shah*, https://www.sunilshah.info/uganda-stories.

22 Riz Ahmed, 'Typecast as a terrorist', *Guardian*, September 15, 2016, https://www.theguardian.com/world/2016/sep/15/riz-ahmed-typecast-as-a-terrorist; Adam Elliott-Cooper, 'When did we come to Britain? You must be mistaken, Britain came to us', *Verso Books Blog*, October 20, 2015, https://www.versobooks.com/blogs/2294-when-did-we-come-to-britain-you-must-be-mistaken-britain-came-to-us.

23 David Olusoga, 'Wake up, Britain. Should the empire really be a

source of pride?', *Guardian*, January 23, 2016, https://www. theguardian.com/commentisfree/2016/jan/23/britain-empire-pride -poll.

24 Tony Kushner, *The Battle of Britishness: Migrant Journeys, 1685 to the Present*, (London: Palgrave Macmillan, 2012), 67 in Akala, *Natives: Race and Class in the Ruins of Empire*, (London: Two Roads, 2019).

25 Sathnam Sanghera, *Empireland*, 6–7.

26 Abdul Mohamud, Robin Whitburn, 'Britain's involvement with New World slavery and the transatlantic slave trade', *British Library*, June 21, 2018, https://www.bl.uk/restoration-18th-century-literature/arti-cles/britains-involvement-with-new-world-slavery-and-the-transat-lantic-slave-trade; Laura Clancy, 'Five ways the monarchy has bene-fited from colonialism and slavery', *The Conversation*, March 24, 2022, https://theconversation.com/five-ways-the-monarchy-has-benefited-from-colonialism-and-slavery-179911.

27 David Pegg and Rob Evans, 'Buckingham Palace banned ethnic minorities from office roles, papers reveal', *Guardian*, June 2, 2021, https://www.theguardian.com/uk-news/2021/jun/02/buck-ingham-palace-banned-ethnic-minorities-from-office-roles-papers-reveal.

28 Trevor Burnard, 'As a historian of slavery, I know just how much the royal family has to answer for in Jamaica', *Guardian*, 25 March 2022, https://www.theguardian.com/commentisfree/2022/mar/25/slavery-royal-family-jamaica-ducke-duchess-cambridge-caribbean-slave-trade.

29 Kevin Rawlinson, 'George the Poet: I Rejected MBE 'Over "Pure Evil" of British Empire', *Guardian*, November 25, 2019, https://www.theguardian.com/politics/2019/nov/25/george-the-poet-rejected-mbe-pure-evil-british-empire.

30 'Knighthoods, CBEs, OBEs and MBEs: 11 People Who Have Said No Over the Years', *Sky News*, January 1, 2022, https://news.sky.com/story/knighthoods-cbes-obes-and-mbes-11-people-who-have-said-no-over-the-years-11593840.

31 Sathnam Sanghera, *Empire State of Mind*, Sandpaper Films, 2021, Episode 1, *Channel 4*, https://www.channel4.com/programmes/empire-state-of-mind/on-demand/72029-001.

32 Debika Ray, 'Manchester Museum's new South Asia Gallery focuses on personal stories', *FT*, February 20, 2023, https://www.ft.com/content/b405a4b4-9841-4427-9052-a8987ebfb07e.

33 S. Tomlinson, 'Enoch Powell, empires, immigrants and education', *Race, Ethnicity and Education* 21, no.1 (2018): 1–14, 11; Warwick Mansell, 'Michael Gove redrafts new history curriculum after outcry', *Guardian*, June 21, 2013, https://www.theguardian.com/education/2013/jun/21/michael-gove-history-curriculum.

34 'Report: Teaching Migration, Belonging, and Empire in Secondary Schools', *TIDE-Runnymede*, 2019, 2, https://assets.website-files.com/61488f992b58e687f1108c7c/61bcc9eca927205637e401b8_TIDERunnymedeTeachingMigrationReport.pdf.

35 Amelia Gentleman, 'Windrush: Home Office has failed to transform its culture, report says', *Guardian*, March 31, 2022, https://www.theguardian.com/uk-news/2022/mar/31/windrush-home-office-has-failed-to-transform-its-culture-report-says.

36 'Speech by Prime Minister Mark Rutte about the role of the Netherlands in the history of slavery', *Government of Netherlands*, 19 December 2022, https://www.government.nl/documents/speeches/2022/12/19/speech-by-prime-minister-mark-rutte-about-the-role-of-the-netherlands-in-the-history-of-slavery.

37 Caroline Elkins, 'Britain has said sorry to the Mau Mau. The rest of the empire is still waiting', *Guardian*, June 7, 2013, https://www.theguardian.com/commentisfree/2013/jun/06/britain-maumau-empire-waiting; 'UK to compensate Kenya's Mau Mau torture victims', *Guardian*, June 6, 2013, https://www.theguardian.com/world/2013/jun/06/uk-compensate-kenya-mau-mau-torture.

38 Ian Cobain, 'Revealed: the bonfire of papers at the end of Empire', *Guardian*, November 29, 2013, https://www.theguardian.com/uk-news/2013/nov/29/revealed-bonfire-papers-empire; Akala, *Natives*, 145.

39 Salman Rushdie, *The Satanic Verses*, 343.

40 Will Dahlgreen, 'The British Empire is "something to be proud of"', *YouGov*, July 26, 2014, https://yougov.co.uk/news/2014/07/26/britain-proud-its-empire/.

41 Matthew Smith, 'How unique are British attitudes to empire?', *YouGov*, March 11, 2020, https://yougov.co.uk/topics/international

/articles-reports/2020/03/11/how-unique-are-british-attitudes
-empire.

42 David Olusoga, 'Wake up, Britain. Should the empire really be a
source of pride?'

43 Sathnam Sanghera, *Empireland*, 73.

44 Ian Sanjay Patel, *We're Here Because You Were There*, 73.

Chapter Twelve – Fifty Years

1 Mohsin Hamid, *Exit West*, (London: Riverhead Books, 2017), 209.

2 Radhika Sanghani, 'As I crossed the border, I cried. This year I went
to Uganda 50 years after my parents were expelled', *i* newspaper,
December 26, 2022, https://inews.co.uk/inews-lifestyle/went-
uganda-this-year-50-years-after-parents-expelled-2042840.

3 Reha Kansara, 'The Documentary: Finding home in Uganda', *BBC
World Service*, September 20, 2022, https://www.bbc.co.uk/sounds/
play/w3ct4dt0.

4 Meera Dattani, 'How tracing my Ugandan-Asian heritage has
helped me connect with my roots', *Conde Nast Traveller*, November
30, 2022, https://www.cntraveller.com/article/how-tracing-my-
ugandan-asian-heritage-has-helped-me-connect-with-my-roots/.

5 Thomas Brown, 'Ugandan Asians'.

6 Colin Yeo, *Welcome to Britain: Fixing Our Broken Immigration
System*, (London: Biteback, 2020), 30.

7 Boris Johnson, 'Africa is a mess'. On slavery, Johnson wrote:
'Consider Uganda, pearl of Africa, as an example of the British
record. Are we guilty of slavery? Pshaw. It was one of the first duties
of Frederick Lugard, who colonised Buganda in the 1890s, to take
on and defeat the Arab slavers.'

8 Thomas Brown, 'Ugandan Asians'.

9 Musa Okwonga, 'The Ungrateful Country', in Nikesh Shukla ed.,
The Good Immigrant, (London: Unbound, 2016), 224, 231.

10 Edward Heath, *The Course of My Life: My Autobiography*,
(London: Hodder and Stoughton, 1998), 457.

11 Colin Yeo, *Welcome to Britain*, 32; Robert Winder, *Bloody
Foreigners*, 384.

12 Ian Sanjay Patel, *We're Here Because You Were There*, 278.

13 Fiyaz Mughal, 'Ugandan Journeys: Fiyaz Mughal', Series 1, Part 11 of 11, British Ugandan Asians at 50, https://www.bua50.org/project/fiyaz-mughal-obe/; 'From East to West: The History of Ugandan Asians', *Ugandan Asians,* https://www.ugandanasians.com/.

14 Karim H. Karim at 'Beyond Resettlement'.

15 'Zadie Smith Interview on Writers & Company CBC Radio', *King Philosophy*, December 17, 2017, https://www.youtube.com/watch?v=L1OSTD6wA4A in Ian Sanjay Patel, *We're Here Because You Were There*, 20.